TM

References for the Rest of Us! ®

BESTSELLING BOOK SERIES

Are you intimidated and confused by computers? Do you find that traditional manuals are overloaded with technical details you'll never use? Do your friends and family always call you to fix simple problems on their PCs? Then the *...For Dummies*® computer book series from IDG Books Worldwide is for you.

...For Dummies books are written for those frustrated computer users who know they aren't really dumb but find that PC hardware, software, and indeed the unique vocabulary of computing make them feel helpless. *...For Dummies* books use a lighthearted approach, a down-to-earth style, and even cartoons and humorous icons to dispel computer novices' fears and build their confidence. Lighthearted but not lightweight, these books are a perfect survival guide for anyone forced to use a computer.

> *"I like my copy so much I told friends; now they bought copies."*
>
> — Irene C., Orwell, Ohio

> *"Quick, concise, nontechnical, and humorous."*
>
> — Jay A., Elburn, Illinois

> *"Thanks, I needed this book. Now I can sleep at night."*
>
> — Robin F., British Columbia, Canada

Already, millions of satisfied readers agree. They have made *...For Dummies* books the #1 introductory level computer book series and have written asking for more. So, if you're looking for the most fun and easy way to learn about computers, look to *...For Dummies* books to give you a helping hand.

IDG BOOKS WORLDWIDE ®

LEGO®

MINDSTORMS™

FOR

DUMMIES®

LEGO® MINDSTORMS™ FOR DUMMIES®

by Michael Meadhra and Peter J. Stouffer

IDG BOOKS WORLDWIDE

IDG Books Worldwide, Inc.
An International Data Group Company

Foster City, CA ◆ Chicago, IL ◆ Indianapolis, IN ◆ New York, NY

LEGO® MINDSTORMS™ For Dummies®

Published by
IDG Books Worldwide, Inc.
An International Data Group Company
919 E. Hillsdale Blvd.
Suite 400
Foster City, CA 94404
www.idgbooks.com (IDG Books Worldwide Web Site)
www.dummies.com (Dummies Press Web Site)

Library of Congress Control Number: 00-103655

ISBN: 0-7645-0767-2

Printed in the United States of America

10 9 8 7 6 5 4 3 2

1O/SQ/RS/QQ/IN

Distributed in the United States by IDG Books Worldwide, Inc.

Distributed by CDG Books Canada Inc. for Canada; by Transworld Publishers Limited in the United Kingdom; by IDG Norge Books for Norway; by IDG Sweden Books for Sweden; by IDG Books Australia Publishing Corporation Pty. Ltd. for Australia and New Zealand; by TransQuest Publishers Pte Ltd. for Singapore, Malaysia, Thailand, Indonesia, and Hong Kong; by Gotop Information Inc. for Taiwan; by ICG Muse, Inc. for Japan; by Intersoft for South Africa; by Eyrolles for France; by International Thomson Publishing for Germany, Austria and Switzerland; by Distribuidora Cuspide for Argentina; by LR International for Brazil; by Galileo Libros for Chile; by Ediciones ZETA S.C.R. Ltda. for Peru; by WS Computer Publishing Corporation, Inc., for the Philippines; by Contemporanea de Ediciones for Venezuela; by Express Computer Distributors for the Caribbean and West Indies; by Micronesia Media Distributor, Inc. for Micronesia; by Chips Computadoras S.A. de C.V. for Mexico; by Editorial Norma de Panama S.A. for Panama; by American Bookshops for Finland.

For general information on IDG Books Worldwide's books in the U.S., please call our Consumer Customer Service department at 800-762-2974. For reseller information, including discounts and premium sales, please call our Reseller Customer Service department at 800-434-3422.

For information on where to purchase IDG Books Worldwide's books outside the U.S., please contact our International Sales department at 317-572-3993 or fax 317-572-4002.

For consumer information on foreign language translations, please contact our Customer Service department at 800-434-3422, fax 317-572-4002, or e-mail rights@idgbooks.com.

For information on licensing foreign or domestic rights, please phone 650-653-7098.

For sales inquiries and special prices for bulk quantities, please contact our Order Services department at 800-434-3422 or write to the address above.

For information on using IDG Books Worldwide's books in the classroom or for ordering examination copies, please contact our Educational Sales department at 800-434-2086 or fax 317-572-4005.

For press review copies, author interviews, or other publicity information, please contact our Public Relations department at 650-653-7000 or fax 650-653-7500.

For authorization to photocopy items for corporate, personal, or educational use, please contact Copyright Clearance Center, 222 Rosewood Drive, Danvers, MA 01923, or fax 978-750-4470.

® is a registered trademark under exclusive license to IDG Books Worldwide, Inc., from International Data Group, Inc.

IDG BOOKS
WORLDWIDE

About the Authors

Michael Meadhra is an author and consultant who has written or contributed to more than 30 computer book titles and innumerable software newsletter articles. Other titles from IDG Books Worldwide, Inc., include *SmartSuite 97 For Windows For Dummies, SmartSuite Millennium Edition For Dummies, Banking Online For Dummies, StarOffice For Linux For Dummies, Windows 2000 Professional Bible,* and *KDE For Linux For Dummies*. He sits on the committee that oversees technology use in his local school when he isn't refereeing confrontations between his robot creations and the four-legged members of his household.

Peter J. Stouffer has been building LEGO products since he received a kit in his stocking 25 years ago. He continues to receive them today, but Santa has trouble fitting them into his stocking now. His most ambitious project before MINDSTORMS was the TECHNIC car with a 4-speed transmission, 4-wheel drive, and 4-wheel steering. When he wasn't building LEGOs, Pete managed to earn a B.S. in Electrical Engineering from GMI and today, he applies that knowledge in a consumer-electronics company. He specializes in embedded systems with microprocessors programmed in assembly language but has extensive experience in many computer languages. Pete lives in a 150-year-old farmhouse (a different type of hobby) with his wife, Linda, and three children, Jessica, Andrew, and Jack.

ABOUT IDG BOOKS WORLDWIDE

Welcome to the world of IDG Books Worldwide.

IDG Books Worldwide, Inc., is a subsidiary of International Data Group, the world's largest publisher of computer-related information and the leading global provider of information services on information technology. IDG was founded more than 30 years ago by Patrick J. McGovern and now employs more than 9,000 people worldwide. IDG publishes more than 290 computer publications in over 75 countries. More than 90 million people read one or more IDG publications each month.

Launched in 1990, IDG Books Worldwide is today the #1 publisher of best-selling computer books in the United States. We are proud to have received eight awards from the Computer Press Association in recognition of editorial excellence and three from Computer Currents' First Annual Readers' Choice Awards. Our best-selling ...*For Dummies®* series has more than 50 million copies in print with translations in 31 languages. IDG Books Worldwide, through a joint venture with IDG's Hi-Tech Beijing, became the first U.S. publisher to publish a computer book in the People's Republic of China. In record time, IDG Books Worldwide has become the first choice for millions of readers around the world who want to learn how to better manage their businesses.

Our mission is simple: Every one of our books is designed to bring extra value and skill-building instructions to the reader. Our books are written by experts who understand and care about our readers. The knowledge base of our editorial staff comes from years of experience in publishing, education, and journalism — experience we use to produce books to carry us into the new millennium. In short, we care about books, so we attract the best people. We devote special attention to details such as audience, interior design, use of icons, and illustrations. And because we use an efficient process of authoring, editing, and desktop publishing our books electronically, we can spend more time ensuring superior content and less time on the technicalities of making books.

You can count on our commitment to deliver high-quality books at competitive prices on topics you want to read about. At IDG Books Worldwide, we continue in the IDG tradition of delivering quality for more than 30 years. You'll find no better book on a subject than one from IDG Books Worldwide.

John Kilcullen
Chairman and CEO
IDG Books Worldwide, Inc.

Eighth Annual Computer Press Awards ➤1992

WINNER

Ninth Annual Computer Press Awards ➤1993

WINNER

Tenth Annual Computer Press Awards ➤1994

WINNER

Eleventh Annual Computer Press Awards ➤1995

Authors' Acknowledgments

While the authors and a publishing company get their names on the cover of a book, a book isn't the result of the efforts of the authors and some cold corporate publishing entity — it's a team effort by a lot of talented people. Please take a moment to look at the publisher's acknowledgments page to see a list of the great people who all made important contributions to this book. All those folks deserve recognition for their roles, but the authors wish to give special recognition to some of the IDG staff we've worked with directly over the course of this project.

David Mayhew was the original acquisition editor who had the vision to see the potential for this book and get it started. Laura Moss and then Steve Hayes managed to keep the book going after David moved on to new responsibilities. No book of this type could become a reality without the efforts of a dedicated project editor, and Tere Drenth did a great job in that role. Bob Guaraldi, the technical editor, helped ensure that all the instructions work as advertised.

Bob Correll and Arthur Griffith both made important contributions during the early stages of the book's development even though other commitments prevented them from becoming full fledged coauthors. Sorry you missed out guys, this has been a fun book to write.

Thanks also to the folks at Switzer Communications, the U.S. contacts for the LEGO Group, who provided much needed support for the book.

Authors' Acknowledgments, continued

Michael Meadhra:

I want to thank Amber Druen and the staff of Kinetic Corporation for their invaluable assistance with the photography for the robot construction chapters. My wife, Peggy, and my daughter, Erin, also deserve special mention for their many hours of work as my in-house robot construction and testing staff. Thanks also to my agent, David Fugate of Waterside Productions, for his help in getting the contract for this book.

Peter Stouffer:

My thanks go to my wife, Linda Stouffer, for her patience and support while I was writing this book. Thanks also to our kids, Jessica, Andrew, and Jack, for technical support and quick feedback on what's really cool. Richard and Anne Stouffer, my parents, deserve recognition instilling in me a sense of curiosity and lifelong learning. Thanks to Santa for never forgetting to give me a LEGO set in my stocking for the last 20 years. Thanks, also, to Tere Drenth for her efforts to provide me with the opportunity to write this book and for support during the process. Finally, thanks to Chuck Stouffer for his assistance with the photography process.

Publisher's Acknowledgments

We're proud of this book; please register your comments through our IDG Books Worldwide Online Registration Form located at http://my2cents.dummies.com.

Some of the people who helped bring this book to market include the following:

Acquisitions, Editorial, and Media Development

Project Editor: Tere Drenth

Senior Acquisitions Editor: Steven Hayes

Proof Editor: Teresa Artman

Technical Editors: Team @llmarin, LLc including Robert Guaraldi, Benjamin Peck, Ben Guaraldi, Catherine Lambe, Virginia Guaraldi, Montse and Stephanie Lambe

Permissions Editors: Carmen Krikorian, Laura Moss

Associate Media Development Specialist: Megan Decraene

Editorial Manager: Constance Carlisle

Media Development Manager: Laura Carpenter

Production

Project Coordinator: Dale White

Layout and Graphics: LeAndra Johnson, Julie Trippetti, Jeremey Unger, Erin Zeltner

Photography: Amber Druen (Kinetic Corporation), Charles D. Stouffer

Proofreaders: Corey Bowen, Susan Moritz, Marianne Santy, York Production Services, Inc.

Indexer: York Production Services, Inc.

Special Help

Amanda M. Foxworth, David H. Mayhew, Laura Moss

General and Administrative

IDG Books Worldwide, Inc.: John Kilcullen, CEO; Bill Barry, President and COO; John Ball, Executive VP, Operations & Administration; John Harris, CFO

IDG Books Technology Publishing Group: Richard Swadley, Senior Vice President and Publisher; Mary Bednarek, Vice President and Publisher; Walter R. Bruce III, Vice President and Publisher; Joseph Wikert, Vice President and Publisher; Mary C. Corder, Editorial Director; Andy Cummings, Publishing Director, General User Group; Barry Pruett, Publishing Director

IDG Books Manufacturing: Ivor Parker, Vice President, Manufacturing

IDG Books Marketing: John Helmus, Assistant Vice President, Director of Marketing

IDG Books Online Management: Brenda McLaughlin, Executive Vice President, Chief Internet Officer; Gary Millrood, Executive Vice President of Business Development, Sales and Marketing

IDG Books Packaging: Marc J. Mikulich, Vice President, Brand Strategy and Research

IDG Books Production for Branded Press: Debbie Stailey, Production Director

IDG Books Sales: Roland Elgey, Senior Vice President, Sales and Marketing; Michael Violano, Vice President, International Sales and Sub Rights

◆

The publisher would like to give special thanks to Patrick J. McGovern, without whom this book would not have been possible.

◆

Contents at a Glance

Cartoons at a Glance

By Rich Tennant

page 7

page 41

page 175

page 241

page 305

Fax: 978-546-7747
E-mail: richtennant@the5thwave.com
World Wide Web: www.the5thwave.com

Table of Contents

Part III: Giving Your Bots Life through Programming *175*

Chapter 6: Scouting Out the Micro Scout 177

Chapter 7: Programming the Scout 181

Chapter 8: Beginning Programming with the Robotics Invention System 1.5 197

Introduction

W elcome to *LEGO MINDSTORMS For Dummies.* As the title suggests, this is a book about LEGO MINDSTORMS, the line of robotic building sets from the makers of the famous LEGO building blocks. But this isn't a book for dumb people. Far from it! It's a book for smart people who are new to the strange realm of robotics and using LEGO MINDSTORMS sets. Even smart people may momentarily feel like dummies when confronted with the hundreds of pieces in a LEGO MINDSTORMS robotics set and with the task of programming a robot for the first time.

This book doesn't get bogged down in robotics theory, and it doesn't give you plans for building a robot that will do your homework and housework (while walking the dog). What it does do is provide an introduction to using the LEGO MINDSTORMS robotics sets — building and programming selected sample robots — and some suggestions for starting your own explorations into robotics.

About This Book

This book is a tool that you can pick up and use to find out how to do something. It's not a novel or a tutorial that you must start reading at page one and proceed through the chapters in sequence. (Believe me, you aren't going to spoil the ending if you skip ahead and read part of Chapter 12 before you read Chapter 5.)

You can use the Index or Table of Contents to look up a topic that interests you and then turn to that part of the book and start reading. Read a chapter, a section, or a few pages to discover how to do something useful. You can follow the instructions in the book to build a complete robot or just refer to the book when you get stumped while working on your own.

Oh sure, you can read this book straight through if you really want to, but that isn't necessary. You aren't going to miss anything critical by skipping a chapter, especially if the chapter focuses on a particular LEGO MINDSTORMS set that you don't own or don't have access to. If one task requires knowledge of something that's covered in another part of the book, cross references in the text tell you where you can find the supporting material, if you aren't already familiar with it.

Foolish Assumptions

While writing this book, we made some assumptions about you, the reader. We tried to minimize those assumptions because some of them would, inevitably, be wrong. But a few basic assumptions were necessary. Here's a summary of the assumptions that we made:

- **You own (or plan to purchase) at least one of the LEGO MINDSTORMS robotics sets.** Of course, while we cover all the major starter sets in this book, we don't assume that you plan to buy every LEGO MINDSTORMS product on the market. No matter which set you start out with, you'll find information about it in this book.

- **You have access to a personal computer running Windows 95/98/ME, and you're familiar with the basic operation of that computer.** You'll need a Windows-based computer in order to develop RCX programs for robots from the Robotics Invention System. You'll also need a computer to run the Droid Developer Kit CD, but that's optional. A computer isn't required with the Robotics Discovery Set. If you need help with the basic computer operations, we suggest visiting the Dummies Web site (`www.dummies.com`) for a list of books to meet your every need!

- **You want to use your LEGO MINDSTORMS sets to build robots.** You didn't buy your LEGO MINDSTORMS set to leave it setting on a shelf somewhere, did you? We assume that you want to liberate those pieces from the box and assemble them into a working robot. Maybe you want to build one of the robots pictured on the box. Maybe you eventually want to invent your own robots. Either way, this book should be a good starting point.

How This Book Is Organized

We tried to organize the information in this book in an accessible hierarchy. The book is divided into parts that correspond to the major robot-building tasks. Each part is divided into chapters, and the chapters are divided into sections and subsections.

Part I: Taking Off the Shrink-Wrap

If you're the "begin at the beginning" sort of reader, start with the chapters in Part I. They provide an introduction to LEGO MINDSTORMS. Chapter 1 introduces the LEGO MINDSTORMS product line and the individual robot building sets. Chapter 2 covers the LEGO MINDSTORMS components and the terminology used in this book and in the *Constructopedia* books that come with your LEGO MINDSTORMS sets.

Part II: Power Up the Lab, Igor — It's Time to Build Bots

The chapters in this part provide the narrative instructions for constructing robots that are missing from the *Constructopedia* diagrams. This includes step-by-step building instructions interspersed with building tips and tricks. Individual chapters cover building robots from specific LEGO MINDSTORMS sets, including the Droid Developer Kit, the Robotics Discovery Set, and the Robotics Invention System.

Part III: Giving Your Bots Life through Programming

LEGO MINDSTORMS robots aren't just static models — they move around and respond to changes in their environments. The chapters in Part III show you how to control robot behavior with programming, whether you're just selecting a predefined program on the Micro Scout microprocessor, doing some basic programming on the Scout microprocessor, or developing and downloading programs for the RCX microprocessor.

Part IV: Special Projects to Make You a Robot Scientist

When you're ready to move on beyond the sample robots you can build with each LEGO MINDSTORMS set, the chapters in this chapter will give you some additional building and programming projects. You may even get ideas for robots that you can build and program on your own. Go for it! Your only limitation is your imagination and resourcefulness.

Part V: The Part of Tens

The Part of Tens is a tradition in *...For Dummies* books. The chapters in this section are a mixed bag. There's a collection of what we hope you think are amusing anecdotes and a brief guide to LEGO MINDSTORMS sites on the Internet.

Appendixes

Tucked away at the back of the book is some reference information that you may find useful and interesting. There's a parts reference to help you identify the various pieces that come in the MINDSTORMS robot building sets and a programming reference for the RCX programming environment. This is also where you can find information on how to install and use the stuff on the CD that's stuck to the back cover of this book.

Icons Used in This Book

One cool thing about a ...*For Dummies* book is the assortment of icons that appear in the page margins beside selected paragraphs, sidebars, and lists. The icons mark paragraphs that deserve special attention, either because the paragraph covers something important or because it includes information that you can skip. Here's a list of the icons used in this book and what they mean:

This icon flags the tips, tricks, and shortcuts that can make working with LEGO MINDSTORMS easier and more convenient.

This icon marks the general principles and background information to keep in mind as you build and program LEGO MINDSTORMS robots.

This icon alerts you to potential traps and trouble spots. You get to benefit from our mistakes so that you don't have to go through the painful experience of discovering why we stuck a warning in the text.

This icon serves as a geek alert, marking technical details and background information that may be interesting but aren't necessary for mere mortals to bother with.

This icon highlights the programs that you'll find on the CD that comes with this book.

Where to Go from Here

Now that the preliminary stuff is out of the way, you're ready to get started. You can begin by browsing through the book until something catches your eye. Or you can scan the Table of Contents for an interesting topic and begin reading the related chapter. Or you can look up a specific topic in the index and turn to the page where it's discussed and begin reading there. The approach that you choose depends on your personal style and what you want to accomplish right now. Just pick one and do it. The sooner you begin reading, the sooner you'll have a working LEGO MINDSTORMS robot doing your bidding.

Part I
Taking Off the Shrink-Wrap

The 5th Wave   By Rich Tennant

Ned Beally, of Beally Construction Co., helps his children with a LEGO® MINDSTORMS™ robotics project.

@RICHTENNANT

"Oh, big surprise — another announcement of cost overruns and a delayed completion date."

In this part . . .

This part gives you an introduction to the LEGO MINDSTORMS family and takes the mystery out of those hundreds and hundreds of pieces. We include information about the MINDSTORMS product line — including kits, sets, systems, and add-ons — and give you a rundown of the parts and pieces that come with each MINDSTORMS product.

Chapter 1

Opening the Box and Getting Started

··

··

*I*magine opening a box that contains everything you need to create your own robotic inventions. From the plastic components in this box, you can build colorful robots and then program your creations to move and react to their environment according to your instructions.

It's not a dream. Using LEGO MINDSTORMS kits, you can design, build, and program robots without lifting a screwdriver or writing a line of computer program code. You don't have to be a robotics expert, a mechanical engineer, or a computer programmer. (Of course, if you have some of these talents, you can put them to good use, but advanced degrees and specialized knowledge aren't required.) LEGO MINDSTORMS robotics kits open the world of robotics to everyone from enthusiastic kids (as young as 9 years old) to serious adult hobbyists.

The robots you can create with LEGO MINDSTORMS kits are limited only by your imagination. You can build simple animated toys or design and construct custom projects, build predesigned robots (such as the robots inspired by the popular *Star Wars* movies), or create your own robotic inventions. Your robots can use light and touch sensors to interact with their environment — and with you.

Sound like fun? You bet it does! This chapter helps you get started selecting and using your LEGO MINDSTORMS kits.

What Are LEGO MINDSTORMS Sets?

Nearly everyone is familiar with LEGO building blocks: the interlocking plastic blocks that kids use to build everything from castles to fantastic creatures. The versatile blocks can be combined in so many ways that they challenge children (and numerous adult hobbyists) to exercise their imaginations. Using the unique connector system, you can assemble and disassemble the interlocking pieces without tools or glue. And by adding a few specialized pieces such as wheels and gears to the basic blocks, you can create model vehicles, machines, buildings, and other structures out of LEGO blocks.

The LEGO MINDSTORMS robotics sets take that same concept one step further. Each set contains an assortment of interlocking bricks and other specialized pieces (see Figure 1-1) that you can use to build model robots. In addition, each kit comes with motors, gears, and pulleys that you can use to make your creation move.

Seymour Papert and the MIT connection

The LEGO MINDSTORMS product line is named after a book called *Mindstorms: Children, Computers, and Powerful Ideas* by Seymour Papert, a mathematician and professor at the Massachusetts Institute of Technology (MIT). Papert's book is considered a seminal work on using technology to help children learn. Papert is the cofounder of the Artificial Intelligence Laboratory at MIT and founding faculty member of the MIT Media Lab.

Papert created the Logo programming language, which introduced many children to mathmatical concepts by using a simple computer program to control a kid-friendly turtle to draw shapes on the computer screen. Papert's labs were also the birthplace of some of the first children's toys that incorporated built-in computation.

The LEGO Group has been involved with MIT since 1984, working on ways to link the Logo programming language to LEGO bricks. The LEGO RCX microprocessor brick, the heart of the LEGO MINDSTORMS Robotics Invention System, is based on the MIT Programmable Brick that was developed at the MIT Media Lab as a result of more than a decade of theoretical research and technical development. Some of the early MIT Programmable Bricks were incorporated into Logo Turtles that were a physical manifestation of the onscreen turtles. Later, MIT Programmable Bricks were used to build mechanical creatures used to facilitate the study of machine behaviors. Other versions of the MIT Programmable Brick formed the basis of educational project kits intended for classroom use. Then, in 1998, the LEGO Company created the LEGO MINDSTORMS product line to bring this technology out of the lab and classroom and deliver it to the general public.

If you're interested in finding out more about some of the theories and technology that lead up to the LEGO MINDSTORMS products, check out the books and articles by Seymour Papert, Valentino Braitenberg, Fred Martin, and Mitchel Resnick.

Figure 1-1:
Each
LEGO MIND-
STORMS
set contains
hundreds of
interlocking
pieces, plus
gears,
sensors,
motors, and
a micro-
processor.

While most of the LEGO MINDSTORMS pieces are smaller in size than the standard LEGO building blocks and you have many more specialized pieces at your disposal, the pegs (sometimes called *studs*) connecting the interlocking pieces work the same. The size and assortment of pieces in the LEGO MIND-STORMS robotics sets enable users to build working robots of a manageable size. (You could probably build a robot out of regular-size LEGO blocks, but the resulting robot would be several feet tall and too heavy to move with battery-powered motors.)

But that's not all. The heart of the LEGO MINDSTORMS system is a micro-processor that you can program to control the motors according to your instructions or in response to input from sensors. The result is a robot, such as the one shown in Figure 1-2, that moves and reacts to changes in its environment.

Figure 1-2:
You can use the LEGO MIND- STORMS kit pieces to build robots such as this one.

The microprocessor accepts input from sensors that can detect light, touch, temperature, or axle rotation. The microprocessor also controls one or more motors that you can configure to move an assortment of wheels, gears, and pulleys to propel the robot or take another action such as move a lever arm. The motors, the sensors, and the microprocessor brick itself are all fitted with the pegs and holes that enable them to connect to the other interlocking pieces of the LEGO MINDSTORMS system. Figure 1-3 shows the RCX micro- processor brick from the LEGO MINDSTORMS Robotics Invention Set (covered in the following section).

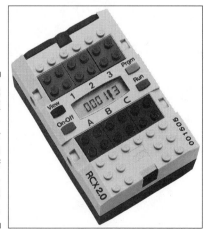

Figure 1-3:
The RCX micro- processor is the brains of the MIND- STORMS robot.

You control the robot's actions by programming the microprocessor to make the motors go forward or back — often in response to input from the sensors. For example, if you program the robot to go forward toward the light, the robot will follow a flashlight beam around a dimly lit room. Conversely, if you program the robot to go in reverse when it detects light, the robot will promptly back itself into the darkest corner of the room. If you equip your robot with a bumper connected to a touch sensor, you can make the robot stop and change direction if it runs into an obstacle. By cleverly combining the various sensors and motors with a series of programming instructions, you can make your MINDSTORMS robots perform complex tasks.

Depending on the LEGO MINDSTORMS kit you have, you can program the microprocessor by pressing buttons on the microprocessor brick, by using an infrared Remote Control, or by developing a program on your computer and downloading the instructions to the microprocessor brick in the robot.

Using the LEGO MINDSTORMS robotics kits, you can create anything from a simple animated toy to a sophisticated robot capable of carrying out complex instructions. As a result, LEGO MINDSTORMS kits appeal to everyone from inquisitive children to serious adult hobbyists. MINDSTORMS robots can be a means of expression and experimentation for a tech-savvy youth or a fun, hands-on activity for someone who normally steers clear of technology.

Introducing the *LEGO MINDSTORMS* Family

The LEGO MINDSTORMS product line is an integrated family of products. The pieces from one MINDSTORMS set are interchangeable with pieces from any of the other MINDSTORMS sets. As you add more pieces to your collection, you can build larger and more complicated robots.

The only significant exception to the interchangeability of pieces within the LEGO MINDSTORMS product line is that the motor and sensor components designed for the Robotics Invention System won't work with the simpler microprocessor unit from the Droid Developer Kit. That microprocessor brick, the Micro Scout, has its own built-in Light Sensor and motor but no place to plug in external sensors or motors.

In addition to using pieces from other LEGO MINDSTORMS sets when you build a robot, you can also use many of the pieces from the LEGO TECHNIC series.

Each LEGO MINDSTORMS set includes one or more *Constructopedia* books that give you step-by-step instructions for constructing predesigned robot projects. Most of the MINDSTORMS kits also include a CD-ROM containing more robot building tips and ideas.

Droid Developer Kit

The robots from Lucasfilm's popular *Star Wars* movies are the inspiration for the LEGO MINDSTORMS Droid Developer Kit — a great starter kit that's recommended for ages 9 and up. There is no computer required because all the programming is built into the Micro Scout microprocessor (see Chapter 6) that comes with the kit. The Micro Scout includes a built-in Light Sensor and a built-in motor and allows you to select one of seven pre-programmed behaviors for your robot.

The Droid Developer Kit contains more than 650 pieces, including the pieces needed to build the R2-D2 droid shown in Figure 1-4. The *Constructopedia* that comes with the kit shows you how to build three *Star Wars* inspired robots: the L-3GO Trainer Droid, the R2-D2 Astromech Droid, and the Jedi Knight Droid. This kit also contains an optional CD-ROM. It retails for about $100.

Figure 1-4:
You can build R2-D2 with components from the Droid Developer Kit.

Dark Side Developer Kit — coming soon

Coming soon from LEGO, the Dark Side Developer Kit will contain more than 500 pieces in addition to the Micro Scout microprocessor. The three *Constructopedia* books contain instructions for building robots of three distinct difficulty levels, including the four-legged AT-AT (All Terrain Armored Transport).

Robotics Discovery Set

The LEGO MINDSTORMS Robotics Discovery Set (shown in Figure 1-5) is recommended for ages 9 and up. Its Scout microprocessor (discussed in Chapter 7) is somewhat more sophisticated than the Micro Scout found in the Droid Developer Kit. The Scout includes a built-in Light Sensor and enables you to create more than 3,000 different behaviors by programming the micro-processor with the touch of a button — no computer required. The Robotics Discovery Set contains a little less than 400 pieces, including two Touch Sensors and two motors. The *Constructopedia* books included in the set show you how to build the Bug robot to explore your house, the basketball playing Hoop-o-bot robot, and an intruder alarm to protect your room. The suggested retail price for the Robotics Discovery Set is roughly $150.

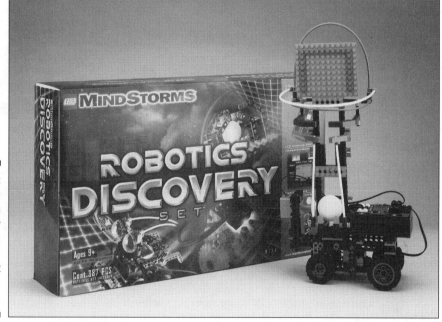

Figure 1-5:
The
Robotics
Discovery
Set includes
the mid-
range Scout
micro-
processor.

A booster kit for the Robotics Discovery Set enables you to program the Scout from a computer and enhance the sensor capabilities. The separate add-on kit is scheduled to be available by the time this book reaches bookstores' shelves.

Robotics Invention System

The flagship of the LEGO MINDSTORMS product line is the Robotics Invention System, which is shown in Figure 1-6. It's built around the RCX microprocessor brick (see Chapters 8 and 9), which is the most powerful robot controller in the MINDSTORMS family. After you build a robot using the 700-plus pieces in the Robotics Invention System, you use your computer to create a program to control the robot and download the program from your computer to the RCX microprocessor using a special Infrared Transmitter. The CD-ROM that comes with the set contains all the software you need to develop programs for the RCX microprocessor brick. The RCX-powered robot can gather information about its environment from sensors, process that information according to your programmed instructions, and signal output motors to turn on or off to perform desired actions.

Figure 1-6:
The Robotics Invention System is the MIND-STORMS set for advanced users.

The power of the RCX programming system requires that you use a computer to develop and download your programs to your robot. Therefore, the Robotics Invention System is recommended for ages 12 and up. It's also worth noting that most of the LEGO MINDSTORMS expansion sets (covered in the following section) are designed to work with the Robotics Invention System, not with the sets that use the Micro Scout or Scout microprocessor bricks. The Robotics Invention System retails for approximately $200.

Expansion sets and add-on components

The LEGO MINDSTORMS product line includes several expansion sets: boxed sets of extra pieces along with *Constructopedia* books that show how to build advanced robots using components from the Robotics Invention System and the expansion sets. Each set retails for around $50. You can also purchase individual components such as extra sensors, a Remote Control, and a camera that enable you to add capabilities to MINDSTORMS robots.

✔ **Extreme Creatures Expansion Set:** This expansion set contains about 140 pieces, including fiber optic strands, plus a *Constructopedia* book and a CD-ROM. The Extreme Creatures Expansion Set, added to the Robotics Invention System components, enables you to build robotic creatures that exhibit animal-like behavior such as stalking prey, biting, stinging, pinching, and fleeing from danger (see Figure 1-7).

Figure 1-7:
Create robotic animals with the Extreme Creatures Expansion Set.

✔ **RoboSports Expansion Set:** The LEGO MINDSTORMS RoboSports Expansion Set enables you to build game-playing robots such as the one shown in Figure 1-8. Using the 90-piece set and the Robotics Invention System, you can build robots that grab balls, slap pucks, shoot hoops, and dodge obstacles. The set includes a CD-ROM, *Constructopedia,* balls, pucks, and a playing field sheet, all for the suggested retail price of $50.

Figure 1-8:
Play ball
with robots
you create
with the
help of the
RoboSports
Expansion
Set.

✔ **Exploration Mars Expansion Set:** The goal is to create a robotic rover
vehicle capable of navigating the rough terrain of the red planet (or your
backyard). The LEGO MINDSTORMS Exploration Mars Expansion Set
provides more than 150 pieces, along with the instructions you need to
build such a robot (see Figure 1-9). The set also includes a CD-ROM
loaded with interactive Mars mission details and a rover control panel
program. Like the other expansion sets, Exploration Mars requires the
Robotics Invention System and costs about $50.

Figure 1-9:
The
Exploration
Mars
expansion
set lets you
build robotic
exploration
vehicles.

✔ **Ultimate Accessory Set:** Unlike the other expansion sets, the LEGO MINDSTORMS Ultimate Accessory Set isn't based on a theme or geared toward building a specific kind of robot. Instead, it's a collection of sensors and useful pieces that you can use to add capabilities to your own robot designs. The Ultimate Accessory Set retails for about $50 and contains the following:

- An assortment of LEGO MINDSTORMS pieces, mostly arm and joint components

- A Touch Sensor

- A Rotation Sensor to count revolutions of an axle, thus giving you better control over motors

- A LEGO Lamp to illuminate your robot's surroundings

- A LEGO infrared Remote Control to enable you to send instructions to your robot without having to download them from your computer

✔ **Accessory parts:** You can order the Remote Control, the Touch Sensor, the Light Sensor, the Rotation Sensor, and a Temperature Sensor (which, of course, detects changes in temperature) as individual items. They're available from LEGO Shop at Home at 800-453-4652 and on the Web at www.legoworldshop.com.

What's In the Box?

What do you see when you open a LEGO MINDSTORMS product box? Well, it's nothing resembling a robot, that's for sure. Instead, you find lots and lots of little pieces — literally hundreds of 'em. In fact, there are so many pieces in a LEGO MINDSTORMS kit, that it can be overwhelming when you first open the box. Many of the pieces, such as those shown in Figure 1-10, are quite small (note that many of the pieces are smaller than the coins in the picture).

Coming soon — Vision Command System

Soon you can give your robot eyes with the LEGO MINDSTORMS Vision Command System, a PC camera that's specially designed to be integrated into your MINDSTORMS robots. The camera mounts on your robot and sends images back to your computer via a long cable. You can program your robot to recognize and react to motion or light, or you can send your robot on remote-controlled exploration missions and watch its progress on your computer. The Visual Command System can double as a standard PC video camera when it isn't providing robot vision.

Figure 1-10:
A LEGO MIND-STORMS kit contains hundreds of pieces — most of them very small.

After you get over the initial shock of viewing the awesome assortment of pieces in a LEGO MINDSTORMS kit, you can begin to pick out some of the major components from the masses of small parts.

✔ **Microprocessor brick:** The largest single piece in each LEGO MIND-STORMS set is the microprocessor brick, which serves as the brains of your robot. The microprocessor looks different depending on whether it's the Micro Scout, Scout, or RCX model, but it's always recognizable as the only piece with a display screen and control buttons. (Refer to Figure 1-3.) The microprocessor brick also contains a battery compartment where you must insert the batteries that power your robot.

✔ **Sensors and motors:** If you're working with the Robotics Discovery Set or the Robotics Invention System, you'll find some separate sensor and motor components. The motors are larger than most other pieces and have a shaft sticking out of one end. They power the wheels, gears, and other movable parts. The sensors are what enable the robot to detect changes in its environment. They look like medium-sized blocks and have a button, electric eye, or other detection device on one end (or, in the case of the rotation sensor, on the side). It's relatively easy to distinguish the differences between the motors and the different sensors, and you can refer to drawings in the instructions if you need help identifying the specific parts.

✔ **Infrared Transmitter:** The Robotics Invention System includes a black box that's about as large as an RCX brick and contains a battery compartment on the back. This is the Infrared Transmitter that enables your computer to send instructions to the microprocessor in the robot. You can identify it by the telltale computer-cable socket on the back.

- **CD-ROM disk:** If you're working with the Robotics Invention System, the CD-ROM disk contains the RCX software that you use to program your robotic creations. Even the MINDSTORMS sets that don't require a computer usually include a CD-ROM disk containing multimedia files and other information about each set and the robots you can build with it.

- *Constructopedia* **books:** The instruction books are usually packed in the bottom of the box, under the clear plastic divider. Be sure to retrieve them from their hiding place before you start opening the pouches of smaller parts. That way, you can reduce the chances of spilling lots of tiny pieces as you dig for these much-needed references.

In addition to the big components, each LEGO MINDSTORMS set includes huge quantities of small pieces, such as

- Pulleys, gears, wheels, and tires

- Large decorative pieces

- Axles and connectors

- Building blocks, arms, and special components

Initially, most of the small parts are packed in clear plastic bags that keep them from getting lost or scattered during shipping. Of course, you must remove them from their packaging before you can start building robots. Even though the box contains a plastic insert that helps organize the parts into several compartments, it's a good idea to store the smaller pieces in resealable plastic sandwich bags.

Always work with your LEGO MINDSTORMS sets on a large, level work surface where small parts don't get lost easily. We discovered that carpeting and upholstered furniture have a disturbing tendency to gobble up any small parts that you happen to drop. As a result, we strongly recommend against trying to build MINDSTORMS robots in your lap as you sit in a favorite easy chair. It may look comfortable, but the frustration of trying to find the inevitable dropped piece isn't worth it.

Following Instructions from the Constructopedia

It's hard to imagine how all those small parts in a LEGO MINDSTORMS set fit together to create a working robot. That's why every LEGO MINDSTORMS kit includes one or more *Constructopedia* books to show you how to assemble a few sample robots from the pieces provided in the kit (see Figure 1-11). The sample projects in each *Constructopedia* get you started on your robot-building adventure. Then, after you build a few bots and begin to develop a sense of how the pieces fit together, you can begin designing your own robot creations (see Part IV for more information).

Figure 1-11:
A *Construc-topedia* with a partially assembled robot.

For the most part, the *Constructopedia* diagrams are clear and easy to follow. However, there is minimal text instruction to go along with the drawings. As a result, you sometimes must study one drawing and carefully compare it to the preceding step in order to find where you need to add a piece to the assembly.

In order to overcome this limitation of the *Constructopedia* books in the MINDSTORMS sets, we wrote the chapters in Part II of this book to provide the narrative instructions that are missing from the *Constructopedias*. We also try to include plenty of construction tips, shortcuts, and warnings to help you make your robot construction projects successful. If you use the *Constructopedia* and the corresponding section of this book in tandem, you have complete and clear instructions for building your robot project at your disposal.

Building a MINDSTORMS robot by following the *Constructopedia* instructions and programming it to perform simple behaviors is just the beginning of your adventures in robotics. The *Constructopedia* books just contain sample projects to help you get familiar with the LEGO MINDSTORMS components and programming tools. The great thing about the MINDSTORMS pieces is that they can be assembled, disassembled, and reassembled in different configurations with virtually no limit. The chapters in Part IV provide a few more sample robot projects that may give you some ideas. But don't stop there; the possibilities are endless! With a little imagination and ingenuity, you can soon be creating and programming your own MINDSTORMS robots that look and act very different from anything described in any of the MINDSTORMS kits or in this book.

Chapter 2

Getting to Know the MINDSTORMS Components

● ●

In This Chapter

▶ Getting acquainted with the MINDSTORMS parts and pieces

▶ Installing LEGO MINDSTORMS software

▶ Installing the LEGO MINDSTORMS RCX programming software

● ●

"Programs — get your programs. You can't identify the players without a program."

*T*hat's the familiar cry of the program vendors at the ballpark. From up in the stands, the players look so small that you can't identify their faces. To fully appreciate the game, you need to use the program as a key to help you identify the players by their jersey numbers. Only the most devoted fans can keep all of the players straight without the help of background information in the program.

This chapter serves a similar purpose in helping you identify the components (the players) in your LEGO MINDSTORMS kit and install and use the bundled software. Just as you can watch a ball game without a program, you can build MINDSTORMS robots without reading this chapter. But investing some time in getting acquainted with the MINDSTORMS components will almost certainly pay dividends by making your robot-building experience more efficient and enjoyable.

Identifying the Parts and Pieces

Each LEGO MINDSTORMS kit is composed of hundreds of individual pieces. In fact, the sheer number of pieces that confront you when you first open the box can be overwhelming. It's hard to imagine how you can ever assemble all those pieces into a working robot.

Don't let the quantity of components in a LEGO MINDSTORMS kit intimidate you, though. What may seem like an incomprehensible mess of disparate pieces at first glance begins to make more sense upon closer examination. Some of the pieces in a MINDSTORMS kit are simple building blocks, while other pieces perform specialized functions. Some of the pieces (such as axles, wheels, gears, and pulleys) enable you to build a machine that moves, while other pieces provide specialized structural components for robot arms and bodies. Some pieces are purely decorative. And a select few pieces comprise the robot's brain and the motors and sensors that enable your robot to interact with its environment.

If you're a veteran LEGO model builder, you'll undoubtedly recognize some pieces in your MINDSTORMS kit and be able to guess how to use some of the other pieces. If you're new to working with Lego models, you may need to build a sample robot or two before you begin to see the many different ways that each component can be combined with others to create an endless variety of MINDSTORMS robots.

Whether you plan to carefully re-create an exact replica of a robot pictured on the cover of your LEGO MINDSTORMS kit box or design and build your own robot from scratch, the first step is to familiarize yourself with the various components in your Lego MINDSTORMS kit. As you handle and identify the pieces, you can begin to get ideas for ways to use the components in your robots. At the very least, you can sort the pieces so that it will be easier to find the component you need to complete a step in the *Constructopedia* instructions.

Assigning names to objects helps you identify those objects and helps us refer to them in instructions and discussions. The hundreds of pieces in the LEGO MINDSTORMS kits make it impractical to assign labels to every piece, but we still need some way to identify specific pieces in this book and in your own thoughts. A few key MINDSTORMS pieces do have names. Other pieces, such as gears and wheels, are relatively easy to identify by their functions. Descriptions will have to serve to label the others.

If you take a few minutes to sort through the MINDSTORMS pieces, you can easily group them into a few general categories such as the microprocessor, sensors, motors, blocks, gears, wheels and tires, axles, and so on. Then you can further subdivide each category by size and other attributes of each piece to arrive at effective descriptions.

Microprocessor

The microprocessor brick is the brain of your MINDSTORMS robot. It's the one component that's guaranteed to be at the core of every robot project you build. It contains the small onboard computer that enables your robot to process input and execute instructions, motor and sensor connections, a small status display screen, control buttons for selecting operating modes, and batteries to power your creation.

It's easy to recognize the microprocessor: It's generally the largest single piece in the MINDSTORMS kit, and it's the only one with both a small display screen and a compartment for batteries.

Actually, the LEGO MINDSTORMS family has three different microprocessor bricks: the Micro Scout, Scout, and RCX (all shown in Figure 2-1). Each of the three microprocessor bricks have different capabilities, which dictate the programming capabilities of the robots you create with them. Here's the low-down on the LEGO MINDSTORMS microprocessor bricks:

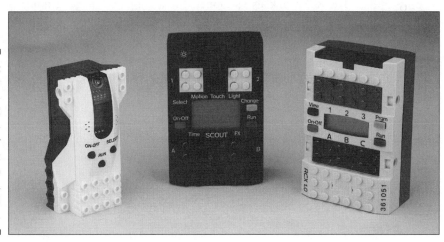

Figure 2-1:
The LEGO MIND-STORMS micro-processor bricks: Micro Scout, Scout, and RCX.

✔ **Micro Scout:** As the simplest of the three microprocessor bricks, the Micro Scout features a built-in Light Sensor and a built-in motor, but it doesn't support external sensors or motors. Having the Light Sensor and motor built into the microprocessor brick keeps the construction of Micro Scout-based robots simpler than other MINDSTORMS robots. Programming the Micro Scout is simple: You just select one of seven pre-programmed behaviors. The Micro Scout is the basis for the Droid Developer Kit.

✔ **Scout:** The Scout is significantly more sophisticated than the Micro Scout microprocessor. Like the Micro Scout, the Scout includes a built-in Light Sensor, but unlike the Micro Scout, it supports external touch sensors and external motors, thus enabling you to create more sophisticated robots. The Scout offers many more programming options than the Micro Scout, with up to 3,000 program behaviors that you create by selecting program steps from the Scout's display. The Scout doesn't require a separate computer to create and download programs to your robot, but an upcoming, optional, add-on booster kit enables you to add that capability to the Scout. The Scout is found in the Robotics Discovery Set.

✔ **RCX:** The most powerful and sophisticated microprocessor brick in the LEGO MINDSTORMS family is the RCX. The RCX supports all the available external sensors and motors in the LEGO MINDSTORMS line, thus giving you the maximum flexibility in the design of your robots. The sensors connect to special ports on the body of the RCX brick using snap-on plates that attach just like any other LEGO building block (see the "Blocks, plates, and beams" section later in this chapter). There's no need for any tools to attach wires or special electrical connectors.

The RCX brick also supports the most powerful programming options of any of the LEGO MINDSTORMS microprocessor bricks. You create the programs on your personal computer using a special RCX programming language and a Windows-based programming environment, and then download the finished program to the RCX brick via an infrared transmitter. The RCX includes a built-in infrared receiver so it can receive instructions from your computer without a hard-wired link. The RCX microprocessor brick is the heart and brain of the Robotics Invention System.

The CD that comes with this book also gives you several programs that you can copy and put to use right away.

Sensors

Sensors enable your robots to see and feel things in their environment, which is important because you can program your robots to react in response to input from the sensors. This enables you to build a robot that can follow a light around the room and back up when it detects an obstacle in its path. The Micro Scout and Scout both include light sensors built into the microprocessor brick. A separate Light Sensor (shown in Figure 2-2) is available for use with the RCX microprocessor. The Touch Sensor (also shown in Figure 2-2) works with the Scout or RCX microprocessor bricks. Other sensors are available separately or in some of the add-on expansion kits. Having sensors that are separate components gives you more flexibility in how you incorporate the sensors into your robot design.

Figure 2-2:
The touch
and light
sensors are
standard
components
of the
Robotics
Invention
System.

Sensors look like blocks with some sort of detection device, such as a small button or an electric eye, embedded in the side or in one end. You attach the sensors to the microprocessor brick with a *connecting wire* (two small plates connected by a length of wire). One plate connects to the sensor and the other connects to pegs on the microprocessor brick. Note that the connector snaps onto the microprocessor brick just like any other LEGO building block: You don't need screws or electrical terminals to make the connection. Separating the sensor from the microprocessor with a wire gives you the flexibility to position the sensor in different places, such as on a robotic arm, instead of having to have the sensor anchored directly to the front of the microprocessor brick. Note that some of the following sensors are available only in Expansion Sets designed to augment the Robotics Invention System.

✔ **Touch Sensor:** This is the most common of the separate MINDSTORMS sensors. The Touch Sensor sends a signal to the microprocessor when its button is depressed. If you position a Touch Sensor where it will be tripped if the robot arm bumps into something, you can program your robot to avoid obstacles in its path. The Touch Sensor is included in the Robotics Discovery Set and the Robotics Invention System as well as in some Expansion Sets.

✔ **Light Sensor:** The Light Sensor contains an *electric eye* that can detect changes in light levels. You can use it to make your robot set off an alarm when the lights come on in a room or, by placing the light sensor so that it points down, make your robot follow a line on the floor. The Micro Scout and Scout microprocessors both include built-in Light Sensors. A separate Light Sensor has a permanently attached connecting wire and is available as part of the Robotics Invention System and some Expansion Sets.

✔ **Temperature Sensor:** Just as the Light Sensor can detect changes in light intensity, the Temperature Sensor can detect changes in temperature. You can use the Temperature Sensor to build a robot that will alert you if it gets too hot or cold. The Temperature Sensor isn't included as a standard component in any of the Lego MINDSTORMS kits, but you can order the Temperature Sensor as a separate accessory for about $30. The Temperature Sensor is a yellow block with a metal-tipped probe sticking out of one end.

✔ **Rotation Sensor:** The Rotation Sensor block contains a small hub in the side of the block into which you can insert an axle. The Rotation Sensor counts revolutions of the axle, thus giving you a feedback mechanism that you can use to exercise precise control over a motor. The Rotation Sensor is part of the Ultimate Accessory Set and is also available separately.

✔ **Connecting wires:** Connecting wires are two small plates with embedded electrical contacts joined by a wire. You use the connecting wires to connect Touch Sensors or motors to the microprocessor brick.

The Micro Scout microprocessor brick (found in the Droid Developer Kit) has a motor and a Light Sensor built into the microprocessor brick. It doesn't support separate sensors or motors.

You use motors to make your robots move. Usually, the motor is connected to a series of gears or pulleys that transfer the motor's motion to where it's needed. The motor can turn wheels to propel your robot across the floor, or the motor can move an arm or flap wings. So, while the sensors provide input for your robot, the motors give your robot an output option. In other words, the motors enable your robots to take an action based on sensor input and the instructions in the robot's program.

✔ **Motors:** At first glance, MINDSTORMS motors look a lot like sensors — they're blocks with something embedded in one end. The difference is that a motor (shown in Figure 2-3) has an axle protruding from one end of the block instead of the button or eye that you typically find on a sensor.

✔ **LEGO Lamp:** The LEGO Lamp also looks like a sensor, but it isn't really a sensing device at all. Instead, it's an output device — a small lightbulb that you can add to your robot to provide general illumination or to serve as a visual alarm. If you position a LEGO Lamp to provide constant input for a Light Sensor, you can easily program your robot to detect any interruption in the light source caused by an object passing between the lamp and the Light Sensor. Like the Rotation Sensor, the LEGO Lamp is available separately or as part of the Ultimate Accessory Set.

Figure 2-3:
Motors give
your robots
mobility.

Blocks, plates, and beams

For many people, the most familiar components in a Lego MINDSTORMS kit are the blocks and plates such as the ones shown in Figure 2-4. They are simply smaller-scaled versions of the full-sized LEGO building blocks and feature the unique peg system for interlocking the blocks that's common to nearly all LEGO products. The blocks in the LEGO MINDSTORMS sets come in a variety of sizes and are mostly interchangeable with those in the LEGO TECHNIC series.

Figure 2-4:
The
standard
interlocking
building
blocks can
be
combined in
many
different
ways.

✔ The size of a block is determined by the number of pegs on its top side. The *Constructopedia* that comes with each kit describes block sizes by giving the number of rows of pegs and the number of pegs in each row; for example, a 2x6 brick has two rows of six pegs each.

Many MINDSTORMS blocks have holes in the sides as well as the pegs on top. The holes enable the blocks to accept axles and connector pins, thus giving you more construction options than standard solid blocks do. The trade-off is that the blocks with holes don't have the smooth finished appearance of a wall of solid blocks. For lack of a better term, we call these *perforated brick*. Hey, it's better than calling them "holey blocks."

✔ *Plates* are one-third the height of regular blocks.

✔ *Top plates* have no pegs.

✔ Another very common construction component in a LEGO MINDSTORMS set has a row of holes running the length of the piece, but unlike a block, the piece has no pegs on the top. (See Figure 2-5.) We haven't found an official name for these pieces, so we call them *beams*.

The holes in beams are sized and spaced to match the pegs on top of a block or plate, but you typically connect beams with axles and connector pins. Beams come in a variety of lengths and shapes including angled pieces. Some are the same width as a block with one row of pegs; others are half that width. Beams often include one or more X-shaped holes to lock onto an axle instead of allowing the axle to turn as it can in a round hole.

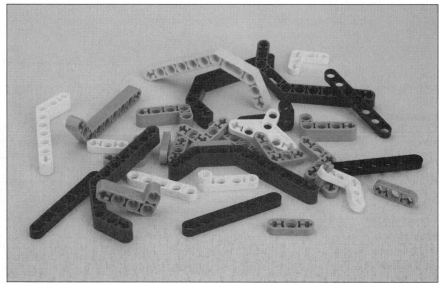

Figure 2-5:
You use axles and connector pins to connect pieces with holes in the side.

TIP

Because most of the blocks from LEGO TECHNIC sets are interchangeable with blocks from the MINDSTORMS sets, you can use blocks and other structural components from TECHNIC sets to build your MINDSTORMS robots. Buying TECHNIC model sets is a fun (and relatively inexpensive) way to expand your robot-building options.

Gears

You probably won't have any trouble identifying the gears among the other MINDSTORMS components. (Figure 2-6 shows an assortment of gears.) The teeth around the circumference of a wheel-like piece are a dead giveaway that the piece is a gear. All the gears in a MINDSTORMS kit are designed to mesh with the other gears. Some gears are beveled on the edges so you can mesh them at an angle to change axis of rotation. You can mix and match different gear sizes to achieve gear ratios that speed up or slow down the output speed of a MINDSTORMS motor. Here are some other tips:

- ✔ Straight gears come in a variety of sizes.

- ✔ The *Constructopedia* identifies gears by the number of teeth. (Counting teeth can be tedious, but you don't have to be exact. It's not hard to tell whether a gear has 12 teeth or 24 teeth.)

- ✔ A *worm gear* is a screw thread sized to engage the teeth of a regular gear wheel. It's typically used in a steering mechanism.

Figure 2-6:
Gears,
gears, and
more gears.

Wheels and tires

Wheels and tires are another category of MINDSTORMS components that you can easily identify. There are just a few wheels in each kit, but you can expect to find an assortment of sizes instead of just one set of four wheels. As Figure 2-7 shows, some wheels are relatively large in diameter and narrow (proportioned like bicycle wheels), while others have a smaller diameter and are fatter (more like the proportions of automobile wheels).

The tires have the donut shape you expect of a tire, and most tires are made of soft black plastic, although some of the smaller tires are gray. The tires are designed to mount on the rim of the correspondingly sized wheel — it's probably no surprise that mounting the tires on the wheels is a do-it-yourself operation. Some kits also include treads (or caterpillar tracks) that you can mount on wheels in place of tires.

While you're sorting through your MINDSTORMS pieces, go ahead and mount the tires on the corresponding wheels and store them as complete wheel/tire assemblies. Doing so saves time later because you almost always use the wheel and tire together, and you need to mount the tire on the wheel before adding the wheel to your robot, anyway. If you do need to remove a tire from a wheel (such as when you need to use a larger or smaller tire), it's quick and easy to do.

Figure 2-7:
Wheels and
tires give
your robots
mobility.

Pulleys and belts

What looks like a wheel but has a rim that is too thin to mount a tire? The answer is a *pulley*. You can use a pair of pulleys connected with a belt to transfer output of a motor in much the same way you use gears. But pulleys and belts offer an advantage in certain circumstances because the belt will slip on the pulley if the part meets too much resistance. So you can use a pulley and belt system to power a grasping claw that may cause a gear train to jump gears or stall the motor if the claw closed around a large object. MINDSTORMS sets include pulleys of different sizes (as shown in Figure 2-8) and belts to go with them.

The belts are really just high-quality rubber bands, and in a pinch, you can replace a broken or worn belt with a suitably sized rubber band from an office supply store.

Axles

All the wheels, gears, and pulleys need shafts to connect them and to provide an axis around which to turn. The MINDSTORMS axles do just that. But the axles don't have the smooth, cylindrical shape you may expect. Instead, axles have an X-shaped cross-section that facilitates attaching gears and wheels so that they don't spin free on the axle. The axles are sized to rotate freely within the holes in beams and other LEGO pieces.

Figure 2-8:
Pulleys and belts have some advantages over gears.

Axles come in a variety of different lengths, as shown in Figure 2-9. The *Constructopedia* that comes with each kit identifies the various axle lengths by comparing them to the pegs on a brick. So, a size 4 axle is as long as a 1x4 brick, and a size 5 axle is as long as a 5-peg brick or a beam with five holes.

Keep a long brick handy to use as a ruler to measure axles and measure each axle carefully before using it. It's sometimes hard to tell the difference between similarly sized axles without measuring, and the axle length can be critical in some steps as you assemble robots according to the instructions in the *Constructopedia*.

In addition to the axles themselves, each MINDSTORMS set includes a supply of spacers or end caps that you can slide onto an axle to hold it in place. This prevents the axle from slipping through the hole in a brick or beam.

Connector pegs

Each MINDSTORMS kit includes a large supply of pieces that snap into the holes in a beam, perforated block, elbow (covered in the following section), or other piece. We call them *connector pegs* because they connect larger pieces together and they're sized to match the diameter of the pegs on the regular blocks. Figure 2-10 shows an assortment of connector pegs.

Figure 2-9:
Axles and
spacers.

Figure 2-10:
Connector
pegs come
in a variety
of sizes and
end configu-
rations.

Connector pegs come in several sizes ranging from small to smaller. They also have a variety of end configurations that enable the connector pegs to perform different duties. Some connector pegs grip the hole into which they are inserted; others rotate freely in the hole. Some connector pegs have the X-shaped cross-section of an axle; others mate perfectly with the pegs on the top of regular blocks.

Elbows and tees

Yet another category of MINDSTORMS pieces look like miniature pipe fittings and brackets (see Figure 2-11); they are called *elbows* and *tees.* The pieces come in various angles and end combinations. Some have smooth holes like those in beams, while others have X-shaped holes to grip axles. Some cross at 90-degree angles; some intersect at odd angles. Some attach to the ends of axles and connector pegs; some can slide to the middle of an axle. The possible combinations with various axles and connector pegs are almost endless.

Figure 2-11:
Elbows
and tees
resemble
miniature
pipe fittings
and
brackets.

Various specialty pieces

After you sort through the components of a MINDSTORMS kit and set aside those pieces that fit into easily identifiable categories, what remains is a pile of assorted specialty pieces. Many of the specialty pieces are one or two of a kind. Although there are only a few of each specialty piece in a MINDSTORMS set, collectively, the specialty pieces make a sizable portion of the components in your MINDSTORMS set. The specialty pieces include the following:

- ✔ Modified blocks and beams that are like regular blocks except for an angled side or other special feature.
- ✔ Flexible shafts, which are axles made of soft flexible plastic instead of rigid material.
- ✔ Flexible tubing.
- ✔ Decorative pieces such as the distinctive head pieces for the R2-D2 Astromech droid in the Droid Developer Kit.
- ✔ Specialized construction pieces that create ball and socket joints, robot arms, and the like. There are a whole bunch of these in each MIND-STORMS set.

Organizing Your Pieces

A LEGO MINDSTORMS set is composed of hundreds of small pieces that may be easy to lose. Plus, the sheer number of pieces makes it difficult to find the particular component you need among the masses of other pieces. The LEGO MINDSTORMS box includes a divider insert with compartments that you can use to help sort the various pieces, and while that gives you a start at organizing the MINDSTORMS pieces, it's a less-than-ideal solution. The smaller pieces are easily mixed up and spilled if you tip the box, even with the lid in place.

Here are some tips that may help:

- ✔ Sort the pieces so that similar pieces are grouped together. For example, you may choose to store axles along with the spacers that go on axles because you tend to use those pieces together.

- ✔ If you're not prepared to invest in special cases for storing your MIND-STORMS components, try using resealable sandwich bags to keep your pieces from getting scattered. Sandwich bags of parts sorted into the divider insert in the LEGO MINDSTORMS box make an effective and inexpensive storage system.

- ✔ If you have the luxury of a dedicated workspace and want to invest in some special storage containers, you can store your MINDSTORMS pieces in open, wide-mouth containers that provide easy access to their contents. On the other hand, if you need to move your collection of MINDSTORMS pieces around and store them out of the way, store them in closed containers to keep them from spilling.

- ✔ Use plastic part bins and drawers to organize the parts. One popular storage option is the kind of parts case that includes about 16 clear plastic drawers in a case that measures about 18 inches square by 6 inches deep.

One enterprising individual that we know purchased a map cabinet consisting of several large shallow drawers. (Architects and engineers use the cabinets to store drawings laying flat in the drawers.) He added pencil trays and other dividers to the drawers to create an elaborate storage system for his large collection of LEGO blocks and components.

Part II

Power Up the Lab, Igor — It's Time to Build Bots

The 5th Wave   By Rich Tennant

"So, you want to tell me what you're building in your bedroom?"

In this part . . .

This part is about building robots, including step-by-step building instructions, plus building tips and tricks. With the chapters in this part, you can build robots from the Droid Developer Kit, the Robotics Discovery Set, and the Robotics Invention System.

Chapter 3

Starting with *Star Wars* Droids

In This Chapter

▶ Building everyone's favorite droid: R2-D2

▶ Become a Jedi Master droid builder with the Droid Developer Kit CD

*T*he LEGO MINDSTORMS Droid Developer Kit is based on robot designs resembling the droids from the popular *Star Wars* movies. The Lego MINDSTORMS Droid Developer Kit (along with its upcoming sister-product, the Dark Side Developer Kit) is built around the Micro Scout microprocessor brick, which is the easiest LEGO MINDSTORMS microprocessor to program. You simply select one of seven preprogrammed behaviors (see Chapter 6), and your robot does its thing, moving about and responding to light. This makes the LEGO MINDSTORMS Droid Developer Kit a recommended beginner-level robotics set.

This chapter augments the Droid Developer Kit's *Constructopedia* with robot-building instructions and some tips and insights into robot-building techniques. The instructions in this chapter, along with the illustrations in the Droid Developer Kit *Constructopedia,* show you how to build the R2-D2 Astromech Droid.

The *Constructopedia* also includes instructions for building two other robots — the L-3GO Trainer Droid and the Jedi Knight Droid. However, there aren't enough pages in this book for detailed coverage of all the sample robots in the LEGO MINDSTORMS kits, so we concentrate on the most popular project in the Droid Developer Kit: R2-D2.

You don't need a personal computer to build and program robots with the Droid Developer Kit, but if you have a Windows 95/98/Me (*Me* stands for millennium edition) computer available, you can use it to run the game-like robot-building tutorial on the Droid Developer Kit CD. The CD contains animated instructions for building the L-3GO Trainer Droid and R2-D2. The CD doesn't contain instructions for building the Jedi Knight Droid, although it does include three similar robot-building projects that aren't in the Droid Developer Kit's *Constructopedia.*

Building the R2-D2 Astromech Droid

The *Star Wars* movies include a lot of different droids and robots of various descriptions, but R2-D2 and C3PO are the droids that arguably qualify as stars of the movies. R2-D2's antics make the mechanized creature especially endearing.

You can build your own LEGO MINDSTORMS version of R2-D2 with the Droid Developer Kit. Figure 3-1 shows the completed robot, as does the photo on page 38 of the Droid Developer Kit *Constructopedia*. (Mark this page for easy reference to that photo as you build the robot.) Instructions for building the R2-D2 robot begin on page 39 of the *Constructopedia*.

Figure 3-1:
The LEGO MIND-STORMS version of the R2-D2 Astromech Droid.

When you're ready to begin construction, follow these steps and also the correspondingly numbered steps in the Droid Developer Kit *Constructopedia*. (Step 1 begins at the top of page 38.) Use the steps on these pages as general building instructions and tips. Refer to the *Constructopedia* drawings to identify the pieces you need for each step and to see how the assembled pieces should look. The *Constructopedia* drawings show the parts and subassemblies from various different angles that are convenient for viewing and illustration. The subassemblies are often *not* shown in the same orientation they will be in as part of the finished robot. Some instructions need to relate to the orientation of the part (front, back, left, right, and so on), and that can get confusing with the views of the part changing all the time. So, for the sake of consistency, instructions in this book are based on the orientation of the part in the finished robot. Any instructions that include terms such as left, right, top, and bottom, relate to that orientation, which may or may not match the orientation of a specific *Constructopedia* drawing.

In the *Constructopedia,* the drawings of MINDSTORMS pieces in the box beside each step number indicate what pieces you need for that step. A number with an x beside a piece indicates how many of that piece you will need. So, 2x means that you need two identical pieces to complete the step. A number in a circle beside an axle indicates the length of the axle. For example, a 4 beside an axle means that the axle is the same length as a block with four pegs on its top. Just be sure you're using the correct pieces for each step — axles, connector pegs, tee fittings, and other pieces come in slightly different sizes and configurations that are very easy to get confused. (See Chapter 2 for more on these pieces.)

If you've lost your copy of the *Constructopedia* book, don't despair. You can order a replacement copy of the *Constructopedia* from LEGO Consumer Affairs by calling 800-422-5346. There is a service charge for replacing lost LEGO MINDSTORMS set pieces such as the *Constructopedia.*

Building the main drive foot module

You begin building the R2-D2 Astromech Droid from the ground up, starting with the main drive foot. The drive foot, shown in Figure 3-2, attaches to the motor in the bottom end of the Micro Scout and is designed to swivel in a limited arch so that R2-D2 can turn and change direction. This is R2-D2's middle or front foot. With a few exceptions, the *Constructopedia* drawings show the drive foot module as viewed from the top-right-front corner.

Step 1

Construction of the R2-D2 Droid begins with the main drive foot.

 1. **Start with a 1x6 perforated block.**

Figure 3-2:
The R2-D2
main drive
foot.

Step 2

In this step, you add a pair of gears and axles to the block, as shown in the *Constructopedia*.

1. **Insert a size 5 axle into a 24-tooth gear. Make two of the axle/gear units.**

2. **Insert the axles into holes in the perforated block.**

   Insert the axles from the left side of the block. One axle goes into the end hole (which will become the bottom of the module) farthest from you, and another axle goes into the second hole from the top. The two gears should mesh. The gears should be on the left side of the block and the axles should protrude from the right side of the block.

Step 3

In this step, you add a wheel and tire to one axle and a couple of spacer rings to the other axle, as shown in the *Constructopedia*.

1. **Mount a solid tire onto a small solid wheel.**

2. **Add the wheel/tire unit to the axle in the end hole.**

   The wheel goes on the axle so that the flat side is toward the block.

3. **Add a thick spacer ring and a thin spacer ring to the other axle.**

Step 4

In this step, you add a spacer ring to one axle and a gear to the other, as shown in the *Constructopedia*.

1. **Add a thick spacer ring to the axle with the wheel.**

2. **Add a small half-beveled gear to the other axle.**

   The toothed side of the gear goes next to the spacer ring.

Step 5

In this step, you add a 1x6 perforated block to the other side of the assembly, as shown in the *Constructopedia*.

1. **Slip a 1x6 perforated block onto the protruding ends of the axles.**

   The block isn't locked into place yet — it just sits on the tips of the two axles.

Step 6

In this step, you assemble the following unit and add it to the assembly, as shown in the *Constructopedia*.

1. **Start with two small corner plates positioned to form a U.**

2. **Add a 1x2 perforated block spanning the joint between the corner plates.**

3. **Add a small half-beveled gear to the end of a size 4 axle and insert the axle into the hole in the perforated block.**

   Place the gear on the axle so that the teeth are at the tip of the axle. Insert the axle into the block from the side where the corner plates stick out.

4. **Attach the unit to the module.**

   The exposed pegs of the corner plates attach to the backs of the 1x6 blocks that form the sides of the module. The 1x2 block sits between the top ends of the 1x6 blocks. When you attach the unit to the assembly, it locks the two side blocks together and the small beveled gears mesh. As a result, turning the protruding axle transfers motion through the gears to turn the wheel.

Step 7

In this step, you reinforce the top corners of the module, as shown in the *Constructopedia*.

1. **Add two small corner plates to the upper corners of the module.**

   The plates lock the side blocks to the 1x2 block between them.

Step 8

In this step, you add a 1x4 plate and two peg extender buttons to the back of the assembly, as shown in the *Constructopedia*. (Note that the *Constructopedia* drawing shows the assembly with its back side up. It's been rotated 180 degrees around the axle protruding from the top.)

1. **Add a 1x4 plate across the upper edge of the module and attach it to the back side.**

   You must turn the assembly over and add these pieces to the back of the assembly. Examine the *Constructopedia* drawing carefully for proper positioning of the pieces.

2. **Add a peg extender button immediately below each end of the 1x4 plate.**

Step 9

In this step, you add a couple of mounting brackets to the back of the module, as shown in the *Constructopedia*.

1. **Add two 2x2 single-hole bracket plates to the back side of the module.**

   The pieces you need for this step are black 2x2 plates with round sockets attached to the under side. The dark blacks and grays of the *Constructopedia* drawing make it hard to see the shape of the piece. You can get a better look at them in the end view of the piece in the drawing for Step 10.

Attach the pieces so that the holes in the plates are positioned at the top edge of the module.

Step 10

In this step, you add two small, 1-hole blocks onto small 1-peg plates, as shown in the *Constructopedia,* and add them to the top of the assembly. (Note that the *Constructopedia* drawing shows the assembly rotated back to its original front-side-up orientation.)

1. **Stack a 1x1 perforated block on a 1x2 single-hole plate. Make two.**

   The plates you use in this step are 2 pegs long but have only a single peg centered on the top surface. The blocks have one peg and one hole. Note that you turn the assembly over to work on the top again. Stack the blocks on the plates so that the side of the block with the hole in it aligns with the long side of the plate.

2. **Add the plate/block units to the top of the module.**

   Arrange the plates to sit atop the small corner plates so that the holes in the blocks mirror the holes in the 2x2 single-hole brackets on the back side of the module.

Step 11

In this step, you attach a lazy Susan piece to the module with four connector pegs, as shown in the *Constructopedia*.

1. **Insert the short ends of four short connector pegs into the corner holes of the lazy Susan piece.**

   Refer to the *Constructopedia* drawing to identify the lazy Susan piece. There's only one like it. It's composed of two halves that are permanently attached so that they can rotate freely. Insert the short ends of the pegs into the corner holes of the lazy Susan. Insert all of the pegs from the same side.

2. **Attach the lazy Susan piece to the top end of the module.**

   The pegs go into holes in the blocks you added in Step 10 and into holes in the 2x2 single-hole bracket plates on the back side of the module. Note that the axle protruding from the assembly passes through the center hole in the lazy Susan piece.

Step 12

In this step, you add two thin, 5-hole beams to the assembly, as shown in the *Constructopedia*.

1. **Insert a pair of regular connector pegs through the end holes of a 5-hole beam and into the right corner holes of the top half of the lazy Susan.**

2. **Repeat the process to add a beam to the left side of the lazy Susan.**

Figure 3-3 shows the drive wheel portion of the main drive foot module.

Figure 3-3:
The drive
wheel
subassembly.

Building the foot subassembly

Set the wheel assembly aside for a moment while you construct the foot to surround the wheel. The steps for this subassembly, shown in Figure 3-4, begin on page 42 of the *Constructopedia* and show the foot subassembly as viewed from the left-rear corner. The foot subassembly creates the wedge-shaped "toe" and "heel" that, when added to the drive wheel subassembly, gives R2-D2's front foot its distinctive appearance. The foot subassembly consists of the toe and heel wedges and a side bracket that holds the wedges together and attaches them to the drive wheel.

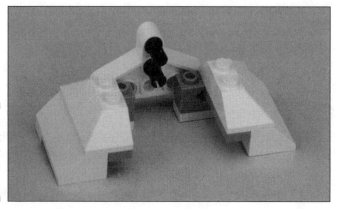

Figure 3-4:
The foot subassembly surrounds the wheel.

Step 1

Start the subassembly with a special T-beam piece, as shown in the *Constructopedia*.

1. **Insert size 2 axles in the lower corner holes of a pair of stacked T-beams.**

Don't confuse the T-beams with regular tee connectors. The T-beam is a triangular-shaped, half-thickness beam piece with five holes on its long side and two more holes arranged to intersect the middle hole in a "T." In this step, you use two T-beams stacked together to create a piece that's the thickness of a thick beam or a perforated block. Position the long side of the beams against your worktable as the base, with the triangular point sticking up. Insert the axles so that they lock the beams together and stick out of the left side of the beams.

Step 2

In this step, you add two regular connector pegs to the assembly, as shown in the *Constructopedia*.

1. **Insert a regular connector peg into the top hole of the T-beams.**

    Insert the peg from the left side of the beams.

2. **Insert another regular connector peg into the hole just beneath the top.**

Step 3

In this step, you attach a small block (with an X-shaped hole) to the end pegs of a 1x4 plate. Make two of these parts and attach them to the assembly, as shown in the *Constructopedia*.

1. **Stack a 1x2 X-hole perforated block onto the end pegs of a 1x4 plate. Make two.**

2. **Attach the block and plate units to the module.**

    The X-shaped holes in the blocks go onto the axle ends sticking out of the outer corner holes in the T-beams. The plates stick out to the front and of the T-beams.

Step 4

In this step, you add two 1x4 wedge blocks to the assembly, as shown in the *Constructopedia.*

1. **Snap the end of a 1x4 wedge block onto the 1x4 plates you just added to the front of the assembly.**

    The high side of the wedge goes against the block, and the tapered edge is forward. The wedge block sticks out of the opposite side of the plate from the T-beams.

2. **Repeat on the back side.**

Step 5

In this step, you join two 1x1 corner wedge blocks with a 1x3 plate across the bottom, as shown in the *Constructopedia,* and then add them to the assembly.

1. **Attach a 1x3 plate to the bottom of a 1x1 corner wedge block.**

    Align the plate with a vertical side of the wedge so that the wedge tapers to the left and away from the plate. One peg of the plate must be exposed to receive the other wedge block.

2. **Attach a second wedge block to the plate.**

    The wedge blocks combine to create a double corner. Look at the *Constructopedia* drawing for the next two steps to see how the finished assembly should look.

3. **Add the pair of wedge blocks to the front of the foot subassembly.**

    The tapered portions of the wedge blocks sit atop the long wedge at the front of the foot assembly.

Step 6

Repeat Step 5 on the back side of the assembly. This completes the foot subassembly.

Resuming building of the drive wheel module

After completing the foot subassembly, you're ready to resume building the robot by adding the foot subassembly to right side of the wheel and gear assembly (opposite the gears). On page 43 in the *Constructopedia*, the step numbering picks up again with Step 13, which shows the subassemblies as viewed from the upper-right corner.

Step 13

In this step, you add the foot subassembly to the drive wheel module, as shown in the *Constructopedia*.

1. **Attach the foot subassembly to the wheel and gear assembly.**

   Two connector pegs from the foot go into two open holes in the perforated block that forms the right side of the wheel assembly.

Step 14

Turn the drive foot assembly around so that you're looking at the bottom and left side and then check it against the *Constructopedia* drawing for proper fit. There's nothing to add in this step. (We're not sure why there's a numbered step in the *Constructopedia*.) It's really just another view of the assembly that you can use to check your progress.

Preparing the Micro Scout

Set the drive foot assembly aside while you prepare the Micro Scout microprocessor brick with the modifications shown in Figure 3-5. The subassembly steps start on page 44 of the *Constructopedia* with a view from the upper-right corner of the Micro Scout.

Step 1

In this step, you stack a 1x4 block on top of two plates and attach the unit to the Micro Scout, as shown in the *Constructopedia*.

1. **Stack two 1x2 plates and a 4-peg perforated block.**

   The plates fit under half of the longer block.

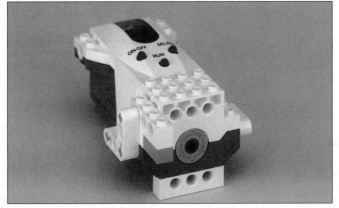

Figure 3-5:
Preparing
the Micro
Scout to
receive the
drive foot
module.

2. **Add the resulting part to the lower-right side of the Micro Scout, as shown in the *Constructopedia*.**

   The open portion of the block sits onto the two pegs on the side of the Micro Scout so that the rest of the block and the attached plates stick out below the bottom of the Micro Scout. This block and plate addition acts as a stop to limit steering motion in the drive wheel assembly.

Step 2

In this step, you reinforce the part you just added with a couple of beams, as shown in the *Constructopedia*.

1. **Insert three connector pegs into two stacked, 5-hole corner beams.**

   The pegs go into the end holes and the corner hole.

2. **Add the corner beams to the Micro Scout.**

   Two pegs go into holes in the lower-right side of the Micro Scout. The other peg goes into the upper end hole of the 1x4 block you added in Step 1.

Step 3

Add a block and a pair of stacked beams to the Micro Scout, as shown in the *Constructopedia*.

1. **Insert two axle-end connector pegs into the end holes of two stacked, 3-hole beams.**

2. **Snap the stacked beams onto the lower-left side of the Micro Scout.**

   The pegs in the beams fit into holes in the side of the Micro Scout.

3. Add a 1x4 perforated block to the back of the Micro Scout.

The block attaches to the back of the Micro Scout, flush with the bottom edge. Note that the Micro Scout has been turned around in the *Constructopedia* drawing for this step.

This completes the subassembly.

Continuing to build the main drive foot module

Return to the main construction sequence for Step 15, which appears on page 45 of the *Constructopedia*. The *Constructopedia* drawing views the Micro Scout and the drive foot assembly from the lower-left corner.

Step 15

In this step, you add the main drive foot module to the Micro Scout subassembly, as shown in the *Constructopedia*.

1. Attach the drive foot module to the bottom end of the Micro Scout.

The four connector pegs on top of the drive foot module go into holes on the end of the Micro Scout. The front pegs go into the end of the Micro Scout itself. The rear pegs go into holes in the 1x4 block attached to the back of the Micro Scout. Figure 3-6 shows the drive foot module attached to the Micro Scout.

What isn't obvious in the *Constructopedia* drawing is that the axle protruding from the top of the foot goes into the motor socket on the end of the Micro Scout. Of course, that's an important point if R2-D2 is going to move around.

Figure 3-6:
The Micro Scout with the main drive foot attached.

Building the robot's chassis

Set the Micro Scout with its attached wheel aside while you build the next module — a chassis (or framework) for the robot. The instructions for the chassis module, shown in Figure 3-7, start on page 46 of the *Constructopedia*. The *Constructopedia* drawings view the chassis from the upper-right corner.

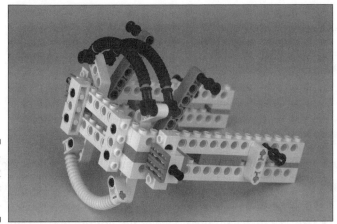

Figure 3-7:
The R2-D2
chassis
module.

Step 1

In this step, you lay out a pair of long blocks to serve as rear side-rails, as shown in the *Constructopedia*.

1. **Start with two 16-peg perforated blocks.**

   Position the blocks side by side, about eight pegs apart.

2. **Insert a regular connector peg into each block.**

   The peg goes into the next-to-the-top hole, inserted from the outboard side of the block.

Step 2

In this step, you set a cross block between the long side blocks, as shown in the *Constructopedia*.

1. **Position a 1x8 perforated block crossways between the top ends of the longer blocks.**

   The new block isn't attached to anything yet. It just sits there.

Step 3

In this step, you add plates to the module, as shown in the *Constructopedia*.

1. **Add two small corner plates on the top corners of the module to join the blocks.**

2. **Add a 2x10 plate spanning across the two side blocks.**

   The plate sits on pegs seven and eight (counting down from the top end) on both side blocks.

3. **Add four 1x2 plates to the module.**

   One plate goes on each side block just below the 2x10 plate. Another plate goes on the lower end of each side block.

Step 4

In this step, you add more plates to the module, as shown in the *Constructopedia*.

1. **Stack two more small corner plates on the top corners of the module.**

2. **Stack two more 1x2 plates on the 1x2 plates at the lower ends of the side blocks.**

3. **Stack two 1x4 plates on the plates in the middle of each side block.**

   The 1x4 plate sits on the 1x2 plate and the end pegs of the 2x10 plate.

Step 5

In this step, you add another layer of blocks (side- and top-rails) to the module, as shown in the *Constructopedia*.

1. **Add two 16-peg perforated blocks.**

2. **Add one 8-peg perforated block.**

Step 6

In this step, you lock the front and back side-rails together with short beams, as shown in the *Constructopedia*.

1. **Stack two 3-hole thin beams and connect them with two axle-end connector pegs in the end holes.**

   Make two identical parts.

2. **Attach the parts to the side-rails.**

   The pegs from the beam part go into the fifth hole from the bottom of the side-rails. The beam attaches from the outside and spans from front side-rail to back side-rail. Do the same on both sides.

3. **Insert a regular connector peg into each front side-rail in the second hole from the top end of the block.**

Step 7

In this step, you add a pair of angled beams to the module, as shown in the *Constructopedia.* The beams support some of the decorative pieces of R2-D2's body.

1. **Insert two long connector pegs into the long side of a 9-hole angled beam.**

   Insert the short ends of the long connector pegs into the beams. The long ends of the connector pegs should stick through the chassis blocks when the parts are installed. The pegs go into the third and fifth holes from the end of the long side.

2. **Make a second part that is the mirror image of the first.**

3. **Attach the beams to the chassis.**

   The beams go in the top corners of the module — they install from the inside of the module. The pegs stick through the front and back top-rails. The angled short sides of the beams point forward and out.

Step 8

In this step, you add two pair of stacked straight beams to the module, as shown in the *Constructopedia.* These beams support the top of the Micro Scout.

1. **Stack two thin 6-hole beams and insert a connector peg through the end hole.**

   Make two.

2. **Attach the beams to the inside of the front side-rail on each side of the module.**

   The connector peg from each new part attaches to a front side-rail in the first available hole down from the top corner. The beams stick forward from the front side-rail.

Step 9

In this step, you add axles and connector pegs to the angled beams and reinforce the chassis with a couple of blocks locking the top and bottom-rails together, as shown in the *Constructopedia.*

1. **Insert two size 3 axles into the holes in the ends of the two angled beams you added in Step 7.**

   2. **Insert two connector pegs into the holes on the lower ends of those same beams.**

     Insert the pegs from the top.

   3. **Add two 1x4 perforated blocks to the top end of the module.**

     The perforated blocks attach to the exposed ends of the long connector pegs that you used to attach the angled beams to the chassis.

Step 10

In this step, you add tee fittings to the axles and connector pegs on the angled beams, as shown in the *Constructopedia*.

   1. **Add two mid-axle tee fittings to the pegs on the lower part of the two beams you added in Step 7.**

   2. **Add four end-axle tee fittings to the axles in the other ends of those beams.**

     Position the tees so that the axle ends are pointed forward, perpendicular to the short arm of the beam.

Step 11

In this step, you construct two parts and add them to each side of the chassis assembly, as shown in the *Constructopedia*.

   1. **Snap a 1x4 perforated block onto a 2x2 plate. Make two.**

     Center the block on one side of the plate.

   2. **Add a 1x2 perforated block to the assembly and insert a long connector peg into the hole.**

     Snap the block onto the other two pegs of the 2x2 plate so that the center holes of the blocks align. Do the same for both parts.

   3. **Top each subassembly with two 1x2 grill-top plates.**

   4. **Attach the parts just created to the chassis module.**

     The parts attach to the pegs near the top of the side-rails. The grill plates point up toward the top of the chassis.

Step 12

In this step, you insert four double-head connector pegs into the assembly, as shown in the *Constructopedia*.

   1. **Insert one peg in each front side-rail just below the beam that ties the front and back side-rails together.**

2. **Insert one peg in the end of each pair of the beams added in Step 8.**

   Insert the long end of each connector peg into the hole, but don't push them all the way in. Leave each peg flush with the inner surface of the piece you put it into.

Step 13

In this step, you add arches made of flexible tubing to the top of the module, as shown in the *Constructopedia*.

1. **Insert axle-end connector pegs into both ends of each of three flexible tubes.**

   Use two blue tubes and one white tube.

2. **Bend each tube into an arch and insert the pegs into tees on the module.**

   The blue tubes go on the front of the module connecting to the tees on the angled beam. The white tube goes on the back of the module, connecting to the tees on the other end of the same beams.

Step 14

In this step, you build the front body sides using the following steps and then attach the resulting part to the chassis module, as shown in the *Constructopedia*.

1. **Insert connector pegs into holes in the two large, wing-shaped pieces.**

   Position the wings so that they lay face down on your work surface with the short sides adjacent to each other. (That puts the back surface of the wings, with the holes that accept connector pegs, facing up.) Insert a long connector peg in the outermost holes of each wing. Insert an axle-end connector peg in the second hole from the inner side of each wing. The axle end of the pegs points toward the top of the wings.

2. **Join two number 6 elbow fittings with a size 3 axle and then attach them to the wing pieces using two double-head connector pegs.**

   The connector pegs go up through the innermost holes in the wings and then through the holes in the elbows. The open ends of the elbows point up.

3. **Add four mid-axle tee fittings to the connector pegs on the outer ends of the subassembly. Insert connector pegs into each tee.**

   The connector pegs point up.

4. **Attach the subassembly to the chassis module.**

Set the wing subassembly beside and to the left of the chassis assembly with the wing tips oriented to point up. (In this case, "up" is defined by the top of the chassis.) Use the pair of pegs at the corner of the wing assembly next to the chassis and insert them into holes at the bottom end of the left front side-rail of the chassis assembly. You attach one side only and leave the wing pieces extended to the side until after Step 15.

Step 15

In this step, you add the Micro Scout and its attached foot to the chassis assembly, as shown in the *Constructopedia*.

1. **Align the double-head connector pegs that are in the ends of the pivoting beams that stick forward from the chassis with the holes in the side of the Micro Scout on either side of the display.**

Make the connection by pressing the long connector pegs in.

2. **Align the double-head connector pegs near the lower end of the front side-rails of the chassis with holes in beams on the sides of the Micro Scout and press those pegs in.**

Note that the Micro Scout sits at an angle in the chassis. When you finish the robot, it's actually the Micro Scout that will stand vertical while the slanted chassis gives R2-D2's body its characteristic backward lean.

Step 16

In this step, you move the front body panels into position in front of the Micro Scout, as shown in the *Constructopedia*.

1. **Swing the wing pieces over the top of the assembly and secure the right side by inserting the connector pegs in the pivoting tees into the right-front chassis side-rail.**

Step 17

The *Constructopedia* drawing shows the robot at this stage of construction as viewed from the top-right corner. There's no action required at the step, it's just an opportunity to check your progress against the *Constructopedia* diagrams. Figure 3-8 shows another view of the developing robot.

Building the right leg module

Set the main body of the robot aside while you build the R2-D2 robot's left and right legs. The instructions for building the right leg module, shown in Figure 3-9, begin on page 56 of the Droid Developer Kit *Constructopedia* and show the view from the right-rear. Construction starts with the foot and works up from there.

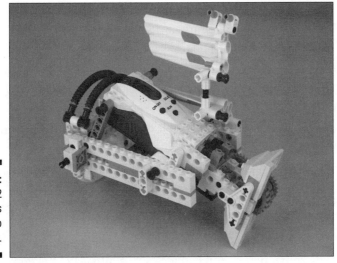

Step 1

Begin with a couple of side pieces and a plate across the end, as shown in the
Constructopedia.

1. **Snap a 2x4 plate across the front ends of two 1x10 plates.**

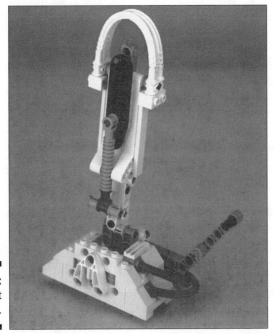

Step 2

In this step, you add a couple of wedge blocks to the module, as shown in the *Constructopedia*.

1. **Add a 1x4 wedge block across the end opposite the 2x4 plate.**

   This becomes the back of the module. The sloped part of the wedge faces out.

2. **Add a 1x1 wedge block to the right-front corner of the module.**

   The sloped part of the wedge faces out.

Step 3

In this step, you add a small block and another wedge to the front end of the module, as shown in the *Constructopedia*. The resulting assembly should start to take on the distinctive appearance of one of R2-D2's feet.

1. **Insert a short, button-end connector peg into a 1x1 perforated block.**

2. **Add the block to the plate at the front of the module adjacent to the 1x1 wedge.**

   The short end of the peg should stick out away from the center of the assembly (in between the wedge portions of the two wedge blocks flanking it.)

3. **Add a 1x2 wedge to the plate on the other side of the 1x1 block.**

   The pegs on top of the block and two wedges on the front end of the module should line up.

Step 4

In this step, you build the following wheel subassembly and add it to the foot assembly, as shown in the *Constructopedia*.

1. **Insert two short connector pegs into a 1x6 perforated block.**

   Stick the pegs in the holes on either side of the middle hole of the block. The pegs should stick out of the right side of the block.

2. **Add two pair of stacked peg extender buttons to the top of the block.**

   The buttons go on the second peg from each end.

3. **Add a thick spacer ring and a wheel/tire combination to a size 4 axle and insert the axle into the center hole of the block.**

   The spacer ring goes into the concave part of the wheel. The flat side of the wheel goes against the block with just enough axle sticking through the wheel to go into the hole in the block. Of course, the wheel has to be on the opposite side of the block from the connector pegs.

4. **Add another 1x6 perforated block to the other side of the wheel subassembly.**

5. **Attach the wheel subassembly to the module.**

   The 1x6 blocks snap onto the side plates of the module. The connector pegs should stick out of the right side of the module.

Step 5

In this step, you begin building up the module with a 1x4 wedge and a 1x4 plate, as shown in the *Constructopedia*.

1. **Add a 1x4 plate across the front of the module just behind the wedges.**

2. **Add a 1x4 wedge block to the back end of the module.**

Step 6

In this step, you add another plate to the front of a module, as shown in the *Constructopedia*.

1. **Add a 2x3 plate atop the plates and wedges at the front of the module.**

   Leave two pegs on the right side of the module open. Note how the plate overlaps the blocks beneath it to lock them into place.

Step 7

In this step, you add another small block to the top of the module, as shown in the *Constructopedia*.

1. **Insert a short button-end connector peg into a 1x1 perforated block.**

2. **Mount the block on the right-rear corner of the 2x3 plate at the front of the module.**

   The end of the connector peg sticks out toward the front of the module.

Step 8

In this step, you add a couple of small wedge blocks to the front of the module, as shown in the *Constructopedia*.

1. **Add a 1x2 wedge block to the left of the 1x1 block.**

   The sloped side of the wedge faces out.

2. **Add a 1x1 wedge block to the right of the 1x1 perforated block.**

Step 9

In this step, you add another block to the right side of the module, as shown in the *Constructopedia*.

1. **Insert a short connector peg into the center hole of a 1x4 perforated block.**

2. **Set the block atop the stacked buttons on the right side of module.**

   The short end of the connector peg sticks out.

Step 10

In this step, you dress up the foot assembly with some flexible axles and a triangular side brace, as shown in the *Constructopedia*.

1. **Add the special triangular side brace piece to the right side of the assembly.**

   The holes in the side brace should fit onto the exposed ends of the connector pegs in the right side of the module.

2. **Add a grill-top 1x2 plate to the top of the module at the front.**

   Center the plate on the pegs.

3. **Place two size 11 flexible shafts into the connector pegs on the front end of the module.**

Figure 3-10 shows the foot subassembly at this stage of construction.

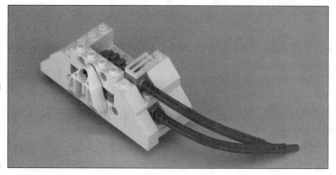

Figure 3-10:
The R2D2
rear foot
subassembly.

Building the lower leg subassembly

Set the foot assembly aside temporarily while you work on the subassembly that connects the foot to the R2-D2 body. Instructions for the lower leg and connector shaft subassembly begin on page 59 of the *Constructopedia*. The initial *Constructopedia* drawings show the connector shaft from the right side, but rotated 90 degrees counterclockwise from its final orientation so that the front of the assembly faces up. Then, beginning in Step 6, the subassembly appears in its proper orientation.

Step 1

Start the lower leg subassembly with a 1x4 perforated block and a couple of connector pegs, as shown in the *Constructopedia*.

1. **Insert regular connector pegs into the end holes of a 1x4 perforated block.**

   Insert the pegs into the right side of the block.

Step 2

In this step, you add four peg extender buttons, as shown in the *Constructopedia*.

1. **Stack two peg extender buttons on each of the end pegs of the block.**

Step 3

In this step, you add another 1x4 perforated block and a couple of long connector pegs to the subassembly, as shown in the *Constructopedia*.

1. **Insert two long connector pegs through the end holes in another 1x4 perforated block.**

   Insert the pegs into the right side of the block.

2. **Add the block to the front (temporarily, the top) of the assembly.**

Step 4

In this step, you add a pair of offset end-axle tees to the subassembly, as shown in the *Constructopedia*.

1. **Slip two offset end-axle tee fittings onto the left end of the lower-front connector peg.**

   The tee fittings used in this step are unusual — the round portion of the tee is only half the usual width. Note how the two tee fittings fit together onto a peg that would hold only one normal tee.

If you're working with the assembly that's orientated to match the *Constructopedia* drawing for this step, the lower-front connector peg is temporarily located at the upper-right corner of the assembly.

Step 5

In this step, you add a beam to the back side of the subassembly, as shown in the *Constructopedia*.

1. **Insert an axle-end connector peg into the end hole of the long side of a 9-hole angled beam.**

   With the angled portion of the beam pointing up, insert the connector pegs from the right side of the beam.

2. **Insert a regular connector peg into the third hole from the end of the long side of the angled beam.**

3. **Add the beam to the assembly.**

   Attach the angled beam to the left side of the subassembly. The beam sticks out to the front of the assembly with the angled end pointing up (which means that the beam sticks up with the angled end pointing left in the *Constructopedia* drawing). The connector pegs in the beam go into the back side of the 1x4 blocks.

Step 6

In this step, you insert two more connector pegs into the beam, as shown in the *Constructopedia*. Note that the assembly has been rotated 90 degrees clockwise in the *Constructopedia* drawing for this step so that it appears in its proper orientation. As always, check your work against the drawing to make sure you get the correct connector pegs inserted into the proper holes.

1. **Insert an axle-end connector peg and a regular connector peg into the left side of the angled beam.**

   The axle-end connector peg goes into the end hole of the short arm of the beam. The regular connector peg goes into the second hole.

Step 7

In this step, you extend the short arm of the beam by adding a pair of stacked 6-hole beams, as shown in the *Constructopedia*.

1. **Stack two thin 6-hole beams and attach them to the assembly.**

   The stacked beams overlap the angled beam by two holes. The stacked thin beams fit onto the connector pegs you inserted in Step 6.

Step 8

In this step, you construct a connecting bracket made of an axle, three tees, and a connector peg and add it to the assembly, and you add a connector peg to the end of the stacked 6-hole beams, as shown in the *Constructopedia*.

1. **Push a mid-axle tee connector to the middle of a size 3 axle.**

2. **Add another mid-axle tee connector to each end of the axle and stick a regular connector peg into the top tee.**

   The outer tees point down, opposite the middle tee, which points up. Insert the connector peg from the right side of the connecting bracket.

3. **Attach the connecting bracket part to the subassembly.**

    Attach the lower tees of the connecting bracket part to the top pegs in the 1x4 blocks.

4. **Insert a connector peg into the end hole of the beams you added in the previous step.**

    Insert the peg from the right side of the beams.

Continuing to build the right leg module

At this point, the _Constructopedia_ returns to the step numbering for the main right leg assembly instructions. That's why the numbering on page 60 of the _Constructopedia_ jumps from 8 to 11. Figure 3-11 shows the lower leg and connector shaft subassembly attached to the foot subassembly.

Figure 3-11:
The lower leg subassembly.

Step 11

In this step, you attach the connector shaft subassembly to the foot assembly, as shown in the _Constructopedia_.

1. **Plug the lower leg subassembly into the left side of the foot module.**

    The lower two connector pegs on the lower leg subassembly should plug into the holes in the perforated block that forms the left side of the foot assembly. You can't see this in the _Constructopedia_ drawing, but there's really no place else for the pegs to go.

Step 12

In this step, you plug the free ends of the flexible shafts from the foot into the tees on the lower leg subassembly.

1. **Bend the two flexible shafts from the foot around and plug the free ends into the tee connectors on the newly added part.**

   The *Constructopedia* drawing for this step shows the module rotated so that you can better see the left side of the foot assembly. Still, it's hard to tell which shaft goes into which connector. The upper shaft plugs into the tee connector closer to the wheel, and the lower shaft plugs into the other tee connector.

Building the upper leg subassembly

You need to set the foot assembly aside while you work on the upper portion of R2-D2's right leg. The instructions for the right leg subassembly, shown in Figure 3-12, begin on page 61 of the *Constructopedia.* The Constructopedia drawing shows the leg lying on its left side and viewed from the lower-front corner.

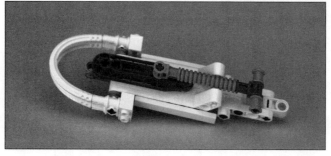

Figure 3-12:
The upper leg subassembly.

Step 1

In this step, you insert three long connector pegs into a thick angle beam, as shown in the *Constructopedia.*

1. **Insert the short ends of three long connector pegs into a 9-hole angled beam.**

   The short arm of the beam goes down toward the foot and points out to the right in the finished robot. In the *Constructopedia* drawing, the short arm of the beam points to the left and up. The pegs go into the corner hole and the two adjacent holes in the long arm of the beam. Insert the pegs from the front.

Step 2

In this step, you insert two short connector pegs into the beam, as shown in the *Constructopedia.*

1. **Insert two short connector pegs into the back side of the angled beam.**

   The pegs go into the next two available holes from the bottom.

Step 3

In this step, you add an axle and a thin beam to the assembly, as shown in the *Constructopedia*.

1. **Insert a size 6 axle into the top end of the beam.**

2. **Add a 5-hole beam to the assembly.**

   The top end of the beam slips over the bottom two long connector pegs in the angled beam.

Step 4

In this step, you add a long tee and a connector peg to the assembly, as shown in the *Constructopedia*.

1. **Insert a connector peg into the bottom end hole of the beam you added in Step 3.**

2. **Add a long mid-axle tee to the axle at the top of the emerging upper leg assembly.**

   The tee goes on the front side of the beam with the tee aligned parallel to the long arm of the angled beam and extending up.

Step 5

In this step, you add another 5-hole beam to the assembly, as shown in the *Constructopedia*.

1. **Stack a thin, 5-hole beam onto the one that's already on the assembly.**

Step 6

In this step, you build the following part and add it to the assembly, as shown in the *Constructopedia*.

1. **Insert a short size 2 axle into a mid-axle tee.**

2. **Add a dual-thickness beam and axle to the assembly.**

   Insert a size 3 axle into the thick end of a 4-hole dual-thickness beam. Insert the axle from the flat side of the beam. Attach the tee connector you just built to the other end of the beam. The tee goes on the opposite side of the beam from the protruding thick end so that the axle going through the tee and the axle in the thick end of the beam both stick out in the same direction.

3. **Add the part to the bottom end of the upper leg assembly.**

   It overlaps the stacked thin beams by two holes and attaches to the back side of the assembly.

Step 7

In this step, you add another dual-thickness beam and a tee/axle to the assembly, as shown in the *Constructopedia*.

1. **Add another 4-hole, dual-thickness beam to the assembly.**

   The beam goes onto the front side of the assembly, mirroring its counterpart on the back side of the assembly.

2. **Insert a cap-end axle through a mid axle tee.**

3. **Slip the tee over the only available long connector peg on the front of the assembly.**

   The axle points out to the right in the finished leg assembly, which means it points up in the *Constructopedia* drawing.

Step 8

In this step, you add another angle beam to the assembly, as shown in the *Constructopedia*.

1. **Add another 9-hole angle beam to the front of the assembly.**

   The beam mirrors its counterpart, which is already part of the assembly.

2. **Insert two short, button-end connector pegs into holes in the front beam.**

   The pegs go into the fourth and fifth holes from the corner — the first two available holes.

Step 9

In this step, you add a couple of top plates and a pair of spacer rings to the assembly, as shown in the *Constructopedia*.

1. **Add a 1x6 top plate to each side (front and back) of the assembly.**

   Make sure you get the top plate in the correct position on the assembly — leave one open hole in the side beams. The top plates don't attach very firmly, but that's okay because they aren't structural components; they're just decorative finish.

2. **Add a thin spacer ring on each side of the long axle and push them down next to the beams.**

Step 10

In this step, you add a small block and a double connector peg to each side of the assembly, as shown in the *Constructopedia*.

1. **Insert a double peg piece into the two holes of a 1x2 2-hole perforated block.**

   Make two. The step uses an unusual double connector peg piece and also small perforated blocks that have two holes in a 1x2-block.

2. **Attach one to each side of the assembly.**

   The parts attach to the assembly by slipping the X-shaped hole in the double peg pieces over the ends of the long axle.

Step 11

In this step, you add a heavy arm piece and a pair of flexible shafts to the assembly, as shown in the *Constructopedia*.

1. **Add a special heavy arm piece to the assembly.**

   The arm piece slips onto the axle that's sticking out from the upper leg assembly. The pointed end of the arm goes down.

2. **Add two size 11 flexible shafts to the top of the leg assembly.**

   The ends of the flexible shafts plug into the open pegs on the double peg pieces added in Step 10. They arch around the top of the assembly. Be careful, the tension of the flexible shafts can pop those pieces off the assembly easily.

Step 12

In this step, you build the following part and add it to the leg assembly, as shown in the *Constructopedia*.

1. **Insert a size 6 axle into an end-axle tee fitting.**

2. **Add a shorter axle and a piece of flexible tubing to the part.**

   Insert a size 3 axle through the cross part of the tee fitting and slide a flexible corrugated sleeve down over the long axle. The tee becomes the bottom end of the part you are assembling.

3. **Add thick spacer rings to the ends of the short axle and add a tee fitting to the top end of the long axle.**

   The cross tee portion of the top tee should be perpendicular to the tee at the other end.

4. **Attach the newly constructed part to the subassembly.**

The tee at the upper end of the part slips onto the axle sticking out through the heavy arm piece. The end with the spacer rings alongside the tee extends down over the pointed end of the arm piece. That completes the construction of the upper leg subassembly.

Continuing to build the leg module

Here's an interesting coincidence: The step numbering for the upper leg subassembly ended at Step 12, and the main leg assembly instructions also stopped at Step 12 when you set the foot aside to begin building the upper leg. The right leg assembly instructions resume with Step 13 on page 64 of the *Constructopedia*. The view is from the right-rear corner.

Step 13

In this step, you finish the leg module by joining the upper leg subassembly to the foot and lower leg assembly, as shown in the *Constructopedia*.

1. **Attach the upper leg subassembly to the lower leg and foot.**

The tee at the lower end of the upper leg subassembly slips onto the connector peg on the lower leg subassembly that's on top of the module. Make sure that the decorative parts of the upper leg (the heavy arm piece and corrugated tubing) are on the same side of the finished leg as the triangular brace on the foot.

Building the left leg module

Set the right leg assembly aside while you construct the left leg. You need to complete both legs before adding them to the R2-D2 body. The instructions for building the left leg begin on page 65 of the *Constructopedia*. Because the left leg is a mirror image of the right, we don't repeat the leg building instructions here.

Be careful not to lose your place in the *Constructopedia* as you build robot components — especially things like right and left legs that are mirror images of each other. If you stop to take a break and come back to your robot construction project, you may start again on the wrong page and end up with two right legs instead of a right leg and a left leg.

Continuing the R2-D2 robot construction

After you build both leg assemblies, you're ready to attach the legs to the robot body and finish building your R2-D2 Astromech Droid. This part of the robot assembly instructions begin on page 74 of the *Constructopedia* with a view from the right-rear quadrant of the robot.

Step 18

In this step, you attach both foot and leg subassemblies to the R2-D2 robot body, as shown in the *Constructopedia*.

1. **Attach the beam from the lower leg assembly of one leg module to the R2-D2 chassis.**

   Attach the connector beam from each foot to the rear side-rail of the robot chassis on the corresponding side. The peg in the end of the connector shaft goes into the chassis rail from the inner side.

   Note that the connector peg at the end of the beam goes into the second hole from the bottom of each chassis rail, not into the bottom corner hole as you may expect. Leave the upper leg subassemblies unconnected and sitting out of the way, as shown in the *Constructopedia* illustration.

Step 19

In this step, you construct the rear body panels, as shown in the *Constructopedia*.

1. **Insert a long connector peg and a regular connector peg into each of the two wing pieces.**

   Be sure to identify the left and right wing pieces and get them properly oriented face down on your work surface with the shorter sides of the two wing pieces adjacent to each other. (That puts the back surface of the wings, with the holes that accept connector pegs, facing up.) Insert a long connector peg into the outermost holes in each wing piece. Insert an axle-end connector peg into the second hole from the inner edge of each piece.

2. **Join two number 6 elbow fittings with a size 3 axle and then attach them to the wing pieces using two double-head connector pegs.**

   The connector pegs go up through the innermost holes in the wings and then through the holes in the elbows. The open end of the elbows point up.

3. **Add four mid-axle tee fittings to the ends of the long connector pegs you inserted into the outer holes of the wing pieces and insert a connector peg into each of those tee fittings.**

   The pegs stick up.

Step 20

In this step, you attach the back body panels (wing pieces) to the robot chassis, as shown in the *Constructopedia*.

1. **Attach the back body panels (wing pieces) to the robot chassis.**

   The four connector pegs you added to the wing assembly at the end of the preceding step attach to the back-rail of the robot chassis, mirroring the body panels on the front of the robot.

Step 21

In this step, you finish the leg attachment process, as shown in the *Constructopedia*.

1. **Swing both upper leg assemblies up and attach them to the robot body.**

   The long tee connectors at the top of each leg attach to the connector peg on the top corner the chassis.

Figure 3-13 shows the R2-D2 robot with its legs attached.

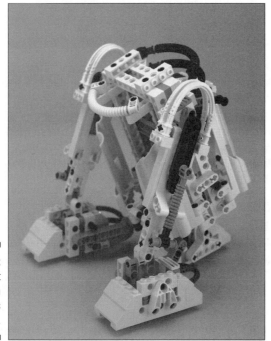

Figure 3-13:
The robot with both legs attached.

Building the head module

Now that R2-D2 can stand on its own, it can stand by and supervise while you complete its head module, as shown in Figure 3-14. The instructions for assembling the head start on page 78 of the *Constructopedia*.

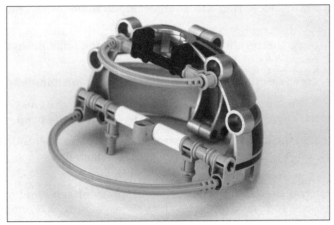

Figure 3-14:
The R2-D2
robot head
module.

Step 1

In this step, you add connector pegs to the head, as shown in the *Constructopedia.*

>   1. **Insert two connector pegs into the top and bottom holes of one half of the head.**

Step 2

In this step, you snap the two head sections together, as shown in the *Constructopedia.*

>   1. **Add the other half of the head to the assembly.**
>
>   Use the connector pegs to snap the pieces together.

Step 3

In this step, you insert four connector pegs into the back of the head, as shown in the *Constructopedia.*

>   1. **Insert a connector peg into each of the upper holes on the back of the head and a peg into each of the lower corners.**

Step 4

In this step, you assemble the lower head support piece according to the following steps and add it to the head, as shown in the *Constructopedia.*

>   1. **Insert a size 12 axle through a mid-axle tee fitting and add a smooth sleeve to the axle on either side of the tee.**
>   2. **Add an end-axle tee and a thick spacer ring to each side of the axle.**
>
>   The end-axle portion of the tees should be perpendicular to the center tee.

3. **Add a thin spacer ring and another mid-axle tee to each end of the axle.**

   The tees go perpendicular to the center tee and point down like the axle-end tees.

4. **Insert an axle-end connector peg into each of the middle tees.**

5. **Attach the support piece to the head by slipping the end tee fittings over the connector pegs on the lower corners of the head.**

   Note that the middle tee fitting faces back, not into the head.

Step 5

In this step, you assemble the upper head support piece according to the following steps and add it to the head, as shown in the *Constructopedia*.

1. **Insert a size 6 axle through two mid-axle tees.**

2. **Add two end-axle tee fittings to the ends of the axle.**

   The holes in all four fittings should be parallel.

3. **Attach the part to the head module.**

   The middle tees on the part snap onto the pegs near the top of the head.

Step 6

In this step, you add flexible shaft pieces to the rear of the head, as shown in the *Constructopedia*.

1. **Insert the ends of a size 12 flexible shaft into the open tee fittings on the upper head support.**

2. **Add a size 19 flexible shaft to the lower head support piece.**

Completing the robot construction

Finally, you return to the main robot construction procedure for one final step, which starts on page 81 of the *Constructopedia*.

Step 22

In this step, you attach the R2-D2 head to its body, as shown in the *Constructopedia*.

1. **Add the R2-D2 head module to the robot body.**

   The pegs on the lower head support go into holes in blocks on the top of the body chassis.

Congratulations! You finished building the LEGO MINDSTORMS version of R2-D2 Astromech Droid.

As you run R2-D2 through the various Micro Scout programs, pay attention to the way the main drive wheel pivots. The limit stop built into the steering mechanism allows the wheel to turn about 30 degrees in one direction and prevents it from turning in the other direction. The torque of the gear system turns the wheel assembly against the steering stop. As a result, the R2-D2 turning behavior isn't random at all. The robot always goes fairly straight when moving forward and always turns when moving in reverse.

R2-D2 needs a fair amount of floor space for its maneuvers. Don't attempt to run the Micro Scout programs with R2-D2 on a table unless you're prepared to watch your robot take a suicidal death plunge off the edge of the table.

Mastering Additional Challenges

If you have access to a Windows 95/98/Me computer with a CD-ROM drive and a sound card, you can run the Jedi Master droid builder workshop program from the Droid Developer Kit CD.

The program is a robot-building tutorial disguised as an interactive adventure game. The CD tutorial includes animated building instructions for the Jedi Trainer Droid and R2-D2 projects covered in the Droid Developer Kit *Constructopedia*.

In addition to these robot construction projects, the CD also includes instructions for building a couple of variations of R2-D2 and two other, more advanced robots. If you build all the projects in the Jedi Master workshop, you really will qualify for the title of Jedi Master droid builder.

Chapter 4

Discovering the Discovery Bots

· ·

In This Chapter

▶ Understanding how to connect motors and Touch Sensors to the Scout

▶ Getting bugged — by a Bug bot

▶ Building a robot that shoots hoops

· ·

*T*he LEGO MINDSTORMS Robotics Discovery Set is aptly named. It's an excellent way to discover the fun of exploring robotics.

Although the Robotics Discovery Set carries the same age-range recommendation (age 9 to adult) as the LEGO MINDSTORMS Droid Developer Kit, it's actually a slightly more advanced robotics kit. That's true despite the fact that there are fewer building pieces in the Robotics Discovery Set than in the other beginner-level members of the LEGO MINDSTORMS product line.

It's the Scout microprocessor brick that makes the difference. The Scout, along with its multiple sensors and motors, is capable of far more complex programming than the Micro Scout microprocessor that is the basis of the Droid Developer Kit.

Fewer building pieces packaged with a more powerful microprocessor brick puts the emphasis of the Robotics Discovery Set on programming robot behaviors instead of on building elaborate models. Chapter 7 has detailed information on programming the Scout microprocessor. Of course, the Scout microprocessor brick alone won't do anything very interesting. You must create a robot with wheels and arms and feelers and other appendages if you expect to see the Scout do anything more and than sit there and beep. That's where this chapter comes in — providing instructions for building two different robots.

This chapter augments the Robotics Discovery Set *Constructopedia* books with robot-building instructions and some tips and insights into robot-building techniques. The instructions in this chapter, along with the illustrations in the Robotics Discovery Set *Constructopedias,* show you how to build two robots:

- ✔ The Bug
- ✔ The Hoop-o-bot

In addition, the Robotics Discovery Set includes a third *Constructopedia* book with instruction drawings for an Intruder Alarm robot. However, there isn't enough space available in this book to give detailed instructions for all three sample robots, so we were forced to make a choice between them. We selected the Bug and Hoop-o-bot robots for inclusion in this book.

The drawings of MINDSTORMS pieces in the box beside each step number in the *Constructopedia* indicate what pieces you will need for that step. A number with an x beside a piece indicates how many of that piece you will need. So 2x means that you need two identical pieces to complete the step. A blue number beside an axle indicates the length of the axle. For example, a 4 beside an axle means that the axle is the same length as a block with four pegs on its top.

In this chapter, we identify blocks and plates by the number of LEGO pegs on the top of each piece, using numbers to indicate the number of rows of pegs and the number of pegs in each row. For example, a 2x8 plate has two rows of pegs with 8 pegs in each row for a total of 16 pegs. Examine the *Constructopedia* drawings carefully to make sure you're using the correct pieces for each step and that you install them in the proper position and orientation. Axles, connector pegs, tee fittings, and other pieces come in slightly different sizes and configurations that are easy to confuse with one another.

If you've lost your copy of the *Constructopedia* book, don't despair. You can order a replacement copy of the *Constructopedia* from LEGO Consumer Affairs by calling 800-422-5346. There is a service charge for replacing lost LEGO MINDSTORMS set pieces such as the *Constructopedia.*

Connecting Motors and Touch Sensors

Before you begin building robots based on the Scout microprocessor brick, it's a good idea to check out the Scout and the sensors and motors that enable it to do its thing. Unlike the Micro Scout found in the Droid Developer Kit, the Scout can work with multiple sensors and motors — and most of them are separate, externally mounted pieces that aren't built into the microprocessor brick. That makes the Scout quite a bit more versatile than the Micro Scout, but it also makes the Scout a little more complicated to use.

The first few pages of the first Robotics Discovery Set *Constructopedia (The Bug Book)* contain instructions for loading batteries into the Scout and checking out its motors and sensors. We recommend working through those instructions before starting your first robot-building project. The instructions are fairly clear and easy to follow, so we won't rehash them here — we just summarize the high points:

✔ The Scout takes six AA batteries. Pry off the back to gain access to the battery compartment.

✔ The two yellow squares of pegs just above the display on the front of the Scout are the Touch Sensor ports. They're labeled 1 and 2. (Refer to Figure 4-1.) The status light beside each port lights up to indicate when the sensor is triggered.

Touch Sensor port 1

Touch Sensor 1 status light

Touch Sensor 2 status light

Touch Sensor port 2

Figure 4-1: Sensors and motors connect to the Scout via electrical connections built into special sets of pegs called ports.

Motor port A

Motor port B

Motor port B status arrows

Motor port A status arrows

✔ The two black squares of pegs just below the display on the front of the Scout are the motor ports. They're labeled A and B. (Refer to Figure 4-1.) The arrows beside each port light up to show when the motor is running and in what direction.

✔ You use connecting wires (two special 2x2 plates joined by a length of wire) to connect motors and Touch Sensors to the Scout. The plates on the connecting wires snap onto the pegs on the motors, Touch Sensors, and the Scout just like any other LEGO building block. (See Figure 4-2.)

If you look closely, you can see small, gold-colored metallic contacts embedded in the pegs and holes of the connector wires, in the pegs on the tops of the motors and sensors, and in the pegs on the Scout's sensor and motor ports. These contacts automatically make the required electrical connections when the connector wire plates snap into place.

✔ The electrical connections on the motor are in the four pegs centered over the axle, not in the raised pegs over the rear of the motor or in the pegs on the outer edges of the unit.

✔ The electrical connections on the Touch Sensor are in the four pegs on the button end of the unit.

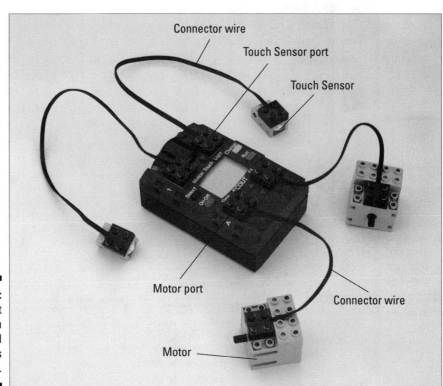

Figure 4-2:
The Scout with Touch Sensors and motors attached.

✔ The orientation of the connector wires on the motors and on the Scout's motor ports makes a difference in the direction the motor turns. Pay attention to whether the connector wire is trailing off to the front, back, left side, or right side of a motor. The same thing applies to the way the connector wires attach to the motor ports on the Scout. Reversing the orientation of the connector wire causes the motor to turn in the opposite direction.

✔ The orientation of the connector wire on the Touch Sensors and Touch Sensor ports doesn't make any difference.

✔ The Scout includes a built-in Light Sensor in the top end of the microprocessor brick (see Figure 4-3). It's permanently attached; you don't need to connect it. The status light on the face of the Scout indicates when the Light Sensor is triggered.

Light Sensor status indicator

Figure 4-3:
The Scout's
Light
Sensor.

Light Sensor

Don't try to insert a connector peg into the Light Sensor holes on the end of the Scout. The peg won't fit, and you may damage the sensor if you try to force a peg into the hole.

✔ See Chapter 7 for more information on how to operate the Scout's controls to select and run programs.

Building the Bug

The Robotics Discovery Set *Constructopedia* comes in three separate volumes. Volume 1, *The Bug Book,* is the recommended starting point for your robot-building adventure. It's even stamped with a "Start Here" label on the cover. So, by all means, begin with the Bug.

The Bug robot, shown in Figure 4-4, is a fairly simple contraption that's reasonably fast and easy to build, but still enables you to explore most of the basic program behaviors of the Scout microprocessor. Building and programming the Bug is a good way to get acquainted with LEGO MINDSTORMS robot-construction techniques and with the Scout's programs.

Figure 4-4:
The Bug.

The Bug robot consists of three modules attached to the Scout microprocessor brick.

✔ **Module 1 — the Bug drive:** The wheeled undercarriage of the Bug gives it the ability to move around.

✔ **Module 2 — the Bug feelers:** The feeler module uses Touch Sensors to enable the Bug to detect objects in its path.

✔ **Module 3 — the Bug eyes and wings:** These decorative additions don't do anything functional, but they're fun. They give the Bug a little personality instead of making it just a nondescript robot rover.

Building module 1 — the Bug drive

Construction of the Bug robot starts with the drive module, which consists of a simple chassis supporting two drive motors, gears, and wheels. The drive module, shown in Figure 4-5, forms the foundation for the Bug robot — the Scout and the other modules all build on the drive module base. The *Constructopedia* drawings show the drive module as viewed from the left-front corner.

Figure 4-5:
The Bug's drive module.

Step 1

Construction starts with a simple platform.

1. **Lay two 2x6 perforated plates out side by side.**

2. **Add two 2x8 perforated plates, one across each end of the base plates, as shown in the *Constructopedia*.**

   Indent the bottom plates one peg width from the ends of the longer top plates.

Step 2

In this step, you add two motors to the assembly, as shown in the *Constructopedia*.

1. **Add a small 8-tooth gear to the shaft of each motor.**

2. **Snap the motors onto the base assembly.**

   The motors mount back to back, parallel with the long plates. Note that the curved underside of the motors means that you can't mount them onto a solid flat surface (or a surface of uniform-height LEGO pegs). Instead, motors must be mounted by the edges, and the base must have a sort of trough to accommodate the motors.

Step 3

In this step, you construct the rear axle assembly and add it to the main drive assembly, as shown in the *Constructopedia*.

1. **Add two 1x2 plates to each end of a 2x8 perforated plate, as shown in the *Constructopedia*.**

   The long sides of the small plates go parallel to the long sides of the larger base plate.

2. **Stack a 2x2 plate on top of a 2x2 block and add them to the center of the base plate.**

3. **Add an axle to each end of the base plate.**

   Place a thick spacer ring onto the end of a size 8 axle and insert the axle through the holes in two 1x2 perforated blocks. Snap this assembly onto one end of the base plate with the long end of the axle sticking out. Repeat the process on the other end.

4. **Add two 2x4 perforated plates to cover the top of the assembly.**

5. **Add a 2x2 round block to the middle of each of the plates you added in the previous step.**

6. **Attach the rear axle subassembly to the motor assembly.**

The axle subassembly attaches to the assembly containing the drive motors by snapping onto one of the rows of pegs alongside the motors. (The base of the axle assembly hangs over the edge on the drive assembly by one row of pegs.) The drive assembly is symmetrical at this point, so the axles can go on either side of the motors. Whichever side you attach the axle assembly to becomes the rear of the drive assembly.

Step 4

In this step, you construct the front axle assembly and add it to the main drive assembly, as shown in the *Constructopedia*.

1. **Add two 1x2 plates to each end of a 2x8 perforated plate, as shown in the *Constructopedia*.**

The long sides of the small plates go parallel to the long sides of the larger base plate.

2. **Add a 1x2 block and a 2x3 reverse wedge block to the center of the base plate and top them with a 2x2 plate.**

Refer to the *Constructopedia* for the proper wedge block (2x3 top and 1x2 bottom) and how to position it on the assembly. The narrow base of the wedge and the 1x2 block occupy the four center pegs of the base plate with the wedge sticking out to the front of the assembly.

3. **Add an axle to each end of the base plate.**

Stick a thick spacer ring onto the end of a size 8 axle and insert the axle through the holes in two 1x2 blocks. Snap this assembly onto one end of the base plate with the long end of the axle sticking out. Repeat the process on the other end.

4. **Add two 2x4 perforated plates to cover the top of the assembly and a 2x2 top plate to the exposed pegs on the wedge block.**

5. **Insert two double-head long connector pegs into the holes of a 1x2 block and add it to the front edge of the top plates.**

The 1x2 block (with two holes) sits on the upper plates above the wedge block. The protruding ends of the long double-head connector pegs stick out over the wedge.

6. **Attach the front axle subassembly to the motor assembly.**

Snap the front axle subassembly onto the other row of pegs alongside the motors — the front edge of the drive assembly. Like the rear axle assembly, the front axle assembly hangs over the edge of the drive assembly base by one row of pegs.

Step 5

In this step, you add connector wires and a pair of blocks to the assembly, as shown in the *Constructopedia*.

1. **Snap one end of a long connector wire onto the contact pegs of a motor.**

   Do the same on the other motor. The orientation of the connector wires on the motors is important: The wires from the connector wires on both motors point back across the rear axle assembly.

2. **Add two 2x4 blocks to the front axle assembly — one on each side of the central block.**

   The 2x4 blocks extend out to the front of the assembly on either side of (and above) the wedge block.

Step 6

In this step, you add topping plates to the drive assembly, as shown in the *Constructopedia*.

1. **Add two 2x10 plates to the top of the drive assembly.**

   The plates run lengthwise on top of the drive assembly, sitting on the round blocks at the rear and extending over the motor and connector wire plates and on top of the blocks added in Step 5.

2. **Add two 1x8 top plates to the drive assembly.**

   The top plates go in between the 2x10 plates, flush at the rear and indented in the front, so that the connector pegs above the wedge block aren't covered.

Step 7

In this step, you add gears to the axles, as shown in the *Constructopedia*.

1. **Add a 40-tooth gear to each of the four axles.**

   Make sure that both gears on each side of the drive mesh with the small gear on the motor.

2. **Add a thick spacer ring to each of the rear axles.**

Step 8

In this step, you add wheels to the axles, as shown in the *Constructopedia*.

1. **Assemble a pair of medium rim wheels with medium 20x30 lug tires and a pair of small solid wheels with large solid tires.**

2. **Add the larger hub wheels to the rear axles.**

   The flat side of the wheel goes out.

3. **Add the smaller hub wheels to the front axles.**

   The concave side of the wheels goes out.

That competes the first module — the Bug drive. Set it aside for a moment as you begin building the next module.

Building module 2 — the Bug feelers

The Bug feeler module, shown in Figure 4-6, is built around a pair of Touch Sensors. A pair of bumpers triggers the Touch Sensors if the Bug encounters an obstacle in its path. Rubber bands provide tension to keep the bumpers clear of the Touch Sensors until the Bug runs into something. The feeler module is just a simple construction to house the Touch Sensors and bumpers and attach them to the front of the Bug's drive module. The *Constructopedia* drawings show the module as viewed from the left-front corner.

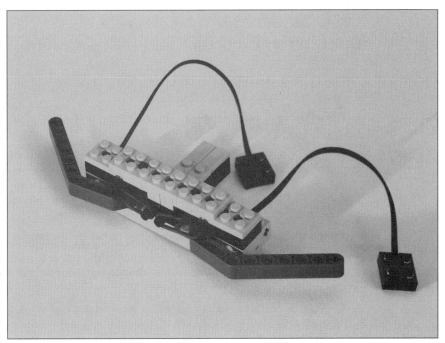

Figure 4-6:
The Bug's
feeler
module.

Step 9

Start by creating a base for the module.

1. **Add two 2x6 perforated plates end to end on top of a 2x8 perforated plate, as shown in the *Constructopedia*.**

   The result is a 2x12 base platform for the module.

Step 10

In this step, you add the Touch Sensors to the feeler module, as shown in the *Constructopedia*.

1. **Add a Touch Sensor to each end of the base plate.**

   The Touch Sensors are mounted on the outer ends of the base plates so that the button end is facing forward and is flush with the front edge of the base plate. Each sensor hangs over the back of the base plate one peg width.

Step 11

In this step, you add a central mounting arm to the feeler module and add connector wires to the sensors, as shown in the *Constructopedia*.

1. **Start with two 1x6 plates lying side-by-side.**

2. **Add a 2x4 block to the center and two 1x1 perforated blocks to each end.**

   The 1x1 blocks are positioned to create a pair of holes at each end of the mounting arm subassembly.

3. **Finish the arm with a layer of plates on top and connector pegs in the end.**

   Add two 1x4 plates to the top-front, running lengthwise. (Notice how the plates lock the 1x1 blocks to the larger 2x4 block in the center of the arm.) Add two 1x2 top plates to the top rear surface. (These plates lock the back 1x1 blocks to the central block.) Insert a pair of connector pegs into the blocks on the front end of the arm subassembly.

4. **Attach the mounting arm subassembly to the feeler module base.**

   The mounting arm attaches to the center of the feeler module base. The front end of the mounting arm is flush with the front side of the base pieces.

5. **Attach one end of a short connector wire to the top of each Touch Sensor.**

   Remember that the connector pegs on the sensor are the four pegs on the end over the button. That's where the plate from the connector wire must go.

Step 12

In this step, you assemble the bumpers (perhaps you'd rather call them whiskers or feelers) and attach them to the feeler module base, as shown in the *Constructopedia*.

1. **Insert a size 4 axle and a connector peg into holes in an 11-hole double angle beam.**

   Make two bumpers that are mirror images of each other. When making each, lay the beam on its side. The axle goes into the end hole in the shorter end of the beam. It should stick out on both sides of the beam — more on top. The connector peg goes into the hole in the corner of the beam closest to the axle, inserted from the top.

2. **Slip the end hole of a 3-hole beam onto the axle in each bumper.**

   The beam fits onto the axle from the top so that it sticks out parallel to the long end of the beam.

3. **Attach the bumpers to the feeler module base, as shown in the *Constructopedia*.**

   The axle protruding from the bottom of each arm goes into the hole in the base plate between the Touch Sensor and the central mounting arm. The long part of the beam sticks out around the front of the module.

Step 13

In this step, you add a pair of top plates to the feeler module, as shown in the *Constructopedia*.

1. **Add two 2x6 perforated plates to the top of the feeler module.**

   The plates fit parallel to the corresponding plates that form the base of the module. The axles from the bumpers should stick through holes in the plates.

Step 14

In this step, you top off the feeler module with another plate and make the bumpers spring-loaded by adding rubber bands to the module, as shown in the *Constructopedia*.

1. **Add a 2x8 perforated plate to the top of the feeler module.**

   The plate is centered on the top of the module, parallel to the corresponding plate on the base of the module. The axles from the bumpers should stick through holes in the plate.

2. **Add a short rubber band to each bumper.**

   The rubber band loops around the connector peg in the top of the bumper and around one of the pegs sticking out of the front of the feeler module.

Step 15

In this step, you mount the feeler module onto the front of the Bug's drive module, as shown in the *Constructopedia*.

1. **Attach the feeler module to the drive module.**

   The feeler module's mounting arm slides into the notch in the front of the drive module. The two connector pegs on the drive module should go into the holes in the back of the feeler module's mounting arm. The wedge piece below the notch in the front of the drive module helps support the weight of the feeler module. Be sure to keep the connector wires from the feeler module's Touch Sensors clear.

Step 16

In this step, you add the Scout microprocessor brick to the Bug and connect the wires from the Touch Sensors and motors, as shown in the *Constructopedia*.

1. **Snap the Scout microprocessor brick into place on top of the Bug's drive module.**

   The top of the Scout (the end with the Light Sensor) should point forward over the top of the feeler module with the base of the Scout aligned with the front edge of the drive module. The bottom end of the Scout hangs over the back of the drive module.

2. **Attach the connecting wires from the Touch Sensors in the feeler module to the Touch Sensor ports on the Scout.**

   Make sure you don't get the wires crossed. The wire from the Touch Sensor on one side of the feeler module must connect to the sensor port on the same side of the Scout. In other words, as you look down on the Bug from the top, the left Touch Sensor must be connected to sensor port 1 on the Scout.

3. **Attach the connecting wires from the motors in the drive module to the motor ports on the Scout.**

   Make sure you don't get the wires crossed. Connect the wire from the left side of the drive module to motor port A on the Scout. Connect the wire from the right side of the drive module (looking down on the Bug) to motor port B. Make sure you orient the connector plates on the motor ports so that the wires trail off the back of the Bug.

This completes the first two parts of the Bug robot assembly. Figure 4-7 shows the robot as it looks at this stage. Basically, it's a working robot; it just needs some decoration to give it personality.

Figure 4-7:
The functional parts of the Bug are in place.

Checkpoints

Before going any further with construction of your Bug robot, it's a good idea to check the operation of the feelers (Touch Sensors) and drive module (motors). The *Constructopedia* includes two checkpoints on page 23 to do just that.

1. **Check the feelers by tapping each of the feeler arms.**

   Make sure the Scout is turned on. When you tap a feeler arm, the indicator light beside the corresponding Touch Sensor port should blink on. If it doesn't, check the connector wires and make sure the feeler arm is pressing the button on the Touch Sensor when you tap the arm.

2. **Check the drive motors by selecting the Forward motion program and pressing the Run button.**

   See Chapter 7 for detailed instructions on how to select programs on the Scout. Be sure to catch the Bug before it gets away and press the Run button again to stop the program. If the Bug goes straight forward, the motors are hooked up properly. If the Bug goes backward or spins around in circles, you probably have a connector wire reversed on a motor or on one of the Scout's motor ports.

Building module 3 — the Bug eyes and wings

The final component of the Bug robot is the eyes and wings module shown in Figure 4-8. This is a non-functional part of the robot that serves only to make it look interesting. But the difference is significant. The eyes and wings transform a non-descript robotic rover into the Bug.

Unlike the other modules, which you build separately and then assemble into the robot, you build the Bug's eyes and wings directly onto the robot. The *Constructopedia* drawings show the robot as viewed from the left-front corner.

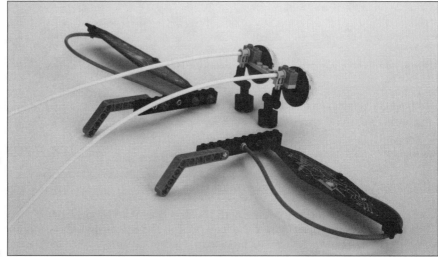

Figure 4-8:
The Bug
eyes and
wings
module.

Step 17

In this step, you insert connector pegs into the sides of the Scout, as shown in the *Constructopedia*.

1. **Insert six short connector pegs into the holes on the sides of the Scout.**

   Insert the short ends of three short connector pegs into each side of the Scout. Connector pegs should fill three of the four holes on each side of the Scout. Leave the bottom (back) hole on each side open.

Step 18

In this step, you add side-rails and hind legs to both sides of the Scout, as shown in the *Constructopedia*.

1. **Insert connector pegs and a hinge peg into a 1x10 perforated block.**

   Make two mirror-image pieces. To make each, insert a regular connector peg into the end hole of the 1x10 block. Insert an axle-end connector peg into the next hole so that the axle part sticks out. Skip two holes and insert a short button-end connector peg into the next hole. Finally, skip two more holes and insert a small hinge peg into the next-to-last hole in the block. All the pegs should stick out of the same side of the block.

2. **Add a 9-hole angle beam to each block.**

Attach the angle beam to the block by snapping the last two holes in the long side of the beam over the two paired connector pegs in the end of the block. The angle end of the beam should point down, away from the pegs on top of the block.

3. **Attach the side pieces to each side of the Scout.**

Push the side-rails onto the connector pegs in the sides of the Scout. The angle beams stick out behind the robot body and angle down like hind legs.

Step 19

In this step, you assemble the bug wings and add them to the robot, as shown in the *Constructopedia*.

1. **Add two 1-peg hinge plates to the underside of each bug wing piece.**

The hinge plates attach to the only pegs available on the underside of the wings. Assemble both wings.

2. **Snap a long flexible tubing piece into the hinge plates.**

Snap one end of the green tubing into the hinge at the wing's midpoint. Bend the tubing to go through the hinge at the tip of the wing. Leave the remaining tubing extending back from the wing tip. Repeat for the other wing.

3. **Add the wings to the robot.**

Snap the base of the left wing into the hinge peg on the left side of the robot. Stick the tip of the flexible tubing on the left wing into the connector peg in the middle of the side-rail on the left side of the Scout. Repeat the process to attach the right wing.

Step 20

In this step, you make a pair of eye stalks and add them to the top of the robot, as shown in the *Constructopedia*.

1. **Stick one end of a size 2 axle into a number 1 elbow and insert the other end into the hole in the center of a 2x2 round block.**

The elbow sticks up out of the middle of the round block forming a tee. Make two identical pieces.

2. **Join the elbow in the subassembly to another number 1 elbow using a connector peg. Do it to both pieces.**

   The X-shaped hole of the elbow sticks up.

3. **Add the eye stalks to the robot.**

   One eye stalk goes on top of each Touch Sensor connector plate. Snap the round block into place on the connector plate so that the elbows stick up and out to the side of the robot.

Step 21

In this step, you assemble the bug's eyes and add them to the robot, as shown in the *Constructopedia*.

1. **Add a large 12-peg disk to each end of a 1x8 plate.**

   The disks attach to the plate by the plate-like protrusion on the back of the disk, not by the pegs in the disk surface. Both disks should face the same way.

2. **Add two 1x2 X-hole blocks to the assembly and add bug eye domes to the disks.**

   The blocks attach to the 1x8 plate immediately above the disk attachments. The bug eye domes snap onto the fronts of the two disks.

3. **Add two pieces of long tubing and two axle-tip tees to the assembly.**

   Slip an axle-tip tee onto a piece of long yellow tubing near the end and then stick the end of the tube into the hole in the 1x2 block behind one eye. Repeat on the other side.

4. **Attach the eyes to the eye stalks on the top of the robot.**

   The axle tips of the tees go into the holes in the upturned elbows of the eye stalks you made in Step 20.

Congratulations, you've built the Bug. Now you can use your newly constructed robot to try out some of the many behaviors you can program into the Scout microprocessor. See Chapter 7 for more information on programming the Scout.

Evolving the Bug

The Bug, as described on these pages, is just a starting point for other robot experiments you can do on your own. One of the advantages of the Bug is that it provides a basic platform that you can easily adapt and change by simply changing a few pieces here and there.

For example, you can quickly replace the wings and eyes that give the robot its bug-like appearance with a happy face or a dog's head. Those are just two of the suggested alternatives you can find in the pages of the *Constructopedia*. With just a little thought and experimentation, you can probably come up with a dozen or so ideas of your own.

One interesting bug adaptation is a change in the gearing of the drive module that makes the bug go faster. You can find that on page 52 in the *Constructopedia*. Page 53 of the *Constructopedia* has building instructions for a set of feet that can replace the Bug's normal wheels. It's definitely worth the time to give your Bug legs and feet — you'll enjoy watching it clomp along.

Hanging with Hoop-o-bot

The third volume of the Robotics Discovery Set *Constructopedia* books is *The Hoop-o-bot Book*. It details how to build the robot named, you guessed it, Hoop-o-bot.

The Hoop-o-bot, shown in Figure 4-9, is designed to be an automated game player. The robot features a backboard and hoop that serves as a target into which you throw a small foam ball. After catching the ball, the robot can throw it across the room, presumably back to you. Depending on the combination of program modules you choose to run on the Scout microprocessor, you can instruct the robot to present a stationary target or to dash back and forth, thus creating a more challenging moving target.

The Hoop-o-bot uses two separate drive motors: one to power the ball thrower and one to move the whole robot back and forth. The Scout's built-in Light Sensor enables it to know when a ball is in position, ready to be tossed back to you by the ball thrower.

The Hoop-o-bot robot is composed of three modules, plus the Scout microprocessor brick:

- **Module 1 — the Hoop-o-bot drive:** This is the robot's main chassis, wheels, and drive motor. The drive module serves as the foundation for the Scout and the other modules as well as providing the wheeled transport mechanism for the Hoop-o-bot.

- **Module 2 — the Hoop-o-bot ball thrower:** The ball thrower module contains the second motor and the mechanics to throw a foam ball back to you.

- **Module 3 — the Hoop-o-bot hoop:** The hoop module has some decorative elements, but it serves the useful purpose of being the target for your ball tosses. The hoop module sits atop the ball thrower module so that balls going through the hoop are automatically channeled into the ball-thrower module.

Figure 4-9:
The Hoop-o-
bot.

Building module 1 — the Hoop-o-bot drive

Construction of the Hoop-o-bot robot starts with the drive module. The drive module, shown in Figure 4-10, is a four-wheeled base chassis that contains a motor and gear train to drive the wheels. It also provides a platform on which to mount the Scout and the other modules of the Hoop-o-bot. The *Constructopedia* drawings show the drive module as viewed from the left-front corner. The robot is designed for the player (you) to be on its left side. So the backboard, hoop, and ball thrower are all set up to face left.

Step 1
Begin by creating a side-rail, as shown in the *Constructopedia*.

Figure 4-10:
The Hoop-o-
bot drive
module.

1. **Add a 1x2 block to the bottom of each end of a 1x16 perforated block.**

   The result is a long block that sits up on two "feet." This piece is the lower-right side-rail of the drive module chassis.

2. **Insert two connector pegs, one short and one regular, into holes in the long block.**

   Looking down on the long block with the end that will be the front pointed away from you, insert the connector pegs into the right side of the block. Insert the short connector peg into the hole at the front end of the block. Insert the regular connector peg into the middle hole.

While you're getting pieces for Steps 1 and 2, get double quantities of everything. You need those same pieces to build the other side-rail in Step 4.

Step 2

In this step, you add a pair of 1x2 plates with side tabs, as shown in the *Constructopedia*.

1. **Add one plate to the top of the long block.**

   Looking down on the module, snap the plate onto the pegs immediately to the rear of the center peg. (Counting back from the front end of the block, that's pegs nine and ten.) The tab should extend out to the left side of the block, opposite the connector pegs.

2. **Add the second plate to the bottom of the long block, immediately below the matching plate on the top.**

Step 3

In this step, you add two axles and three gears to the module, as shown in the *Constructopedia.*

1. **Insert a size 10 axle into a 24-tooth clutch gear and then into the long perforated block.**

   Position the gear on the axle about three pegs from one end. The short end of the axle goes into the next-to-last hole of the block at the rear end (the opposite end from the short connector peg). The long end of the axle sticks out to the left — the opposite side of the block from the connector pegs.

2. **Add an 8-tooth gear and a 24-tooth gear to a size 6 axle and insert the axle into the perforated block.**

   The gears set one peg in from each end of the axle. The axle end with the small gear goes into the block in the first available hole in front of the other axle/gear combination. The small gear on the shorter axle and the larger gear on the longer axle should mesh. Note that there is nothing holding the axles in the block at this point in the assembly.

Step 4

In this step, you construct another side-rail and add it to the module, as shown in the *Constructopedia.* This becomes the lower-left side-rail.

1. **Add a 1x2 block to the bottom of each end of a 1x16 perforated block.**

2. **Insert two connector pegs, one short and one regular, into holes in the long block.**

   Looking down on the long block with the front end pointing away from you, insert the connector pegs into the left side of the block. Insert the short connector peg into the hole at the front end of the block. Insert the regular connector peg into the middle hole.

3. **Add two 1x2 plates with side tabs to the long block.**

   Looking down on the module, snap the plates onto the top and bottom of the block immediately to the rear of the center connector peg. (Counting back from the front end of the block, that's pegs nine and ten.) The tabs should extend out to the right side of the block, opposite the connector pegs.

4. **Add the side-rail to the module by sliding it onto the two exposed axles.**

The side-rail should mirror the one you built in Steps 1 and 2.

Step 5

In this step, you add two small plates, an axle, and four spacer rings to the module, as shown in the *Constructopedia*.

1. **Add a 1x2 plate, stacked on top of the plate on each side-rail.**

2. **Add a thick spacer ring to each end of the axle with the clutch gear.**

3. **Insert a size 10 axle into the other end of the side-rails and cap it with thick spacer rings on each end.**

The axle goes into the next-to-last hole at the front end of each side-rail. This is the front axle.

Step 6

In this step, you add a motor, hat gear, and two small blocks to the module, as shown in the *Constructopedia*.

1. **Add a 24-tooth hat gear to the shaft of a motor.**

The teeth of the gear face out away from the motor.

2. **Mount the motor onto the side-rails of the module.**

Position the motor between the two side-rails near the front axle (the one with no gears) and with the motor shaft facing the rear axles (the ones with gears). Slide the motor toward the rear axles so that the slots in the sides of the motor slip onto the tabs extending from the plates on the side-rails. The hat gear on the motor shaft should mesh with the 24-tooth gear on the closer axle.

Note how the motor is attached to the side-rails using the small plates with tabs to engage the slots in the sides of the motor. This is a different construction technique from the other sample robots in the Robotics Discovery Set — in those robots, the motors mount like blocks by snapping onto rows of pegs on the top of blocks or plates.

Also note how the use of the hat gear changes the direction of rotation from the motor by 90 degrees. The hat gear is an alternative to using the beveled gears to accomplish the same thing.

3. **Add a 1x2 solid block to the end of each side-rail.**

The blocks go on the rear ends of the side-rails.

Step 7

In this step, you add two 2x6 blocks and two 2x2 plates to the module, as shown in the *Constructopedia*.

1. **Add a 2x6 block to each end of the module.**

   The blocks span the two side-rails as cross pieces. The front one mounts directly to the side-rails; the other sits on the blocks on the rear ends of the side-rails.

2. **Add a 2x2 plate to each side of the motor.**

   The plates lock the motor to the plates on the side-rails.

Step 8

In this step, you add a connector wire, a 2x4 plate, and two 1x2 plates to the motor and add four 1x2 blocks to the chassis, as shown in the *Constructopedia*.

1. **Snap one end of a long connector wire onto the motor.**

   The plate on one end of the connector wire snaps onto the pegs on top of the motor just above the shaft. The wire trails out over the back end of the motor, away from the shaft. (That's the back of the motor, but the front of the drive module.) Note that there's a channel in the top of the motor to accept the wire.

2. **Add a 2x4 plate to the top surface of the motor.**

3. **Stack a 1x2 plate on each end of the plate you just added to the top of the motor.**

   The long sides of the plates go parallel to the side-rails.

4. **Add a 1x2 block to each corner of the front 2x6 cross piece block.**

   The long sides of the blocks go parallel to the long sides of the 2x6 block. Note that these blocks bring this end of the module up to the same level as the blocks on the gear end.

Step 9

In this step, you add four 1x2 plates and two 1x8 top plates to the module, as shown in the *Constructopedia*.

1. **Add a 1x2 plate to each corner of the module.**

   The long sides of the plates go parallel to the side-rails.

2. **Add two 1x8 top plates to the module between the motor and the end blocks.**

Each top plate goes from a plate on top of the motor to the blocks on the front end of the module.

Step 10

In this step, you add two upper side-rails and four connector pegs to the module, as shown in the *Constructopedia*.

1. **Add two 1x16 perforated blocks to the top of the module.**

   The blocks create upper side-rails, positioned above the lower side-rails.

2. **Insert a regular connector peg into the center hole of each of the long blocks.**

   The connector pegs stick out to the outside of the module.

3. **Insert a short connector peg into the end hole of the long blocks.**

   The connector pegs go into holes at the front end of the blocks, immediately above the matching pegs in the lower side-rails.

Step 11

In this step, you add two plates as cross pieces and add pairs of beams and blocks to lock the top and bottom side-rails together, as shown in the *Constructopedia*.

1. **Attach a thin 5-hole beam to the short connector pegs on one side of the front of the module.**

   The beam goes from the front end of the upper side-rail to the front end of the lower side-rail on the same side. Repeat on the other side.

2. **Attach a 1x6 perforated block to each side of the module.**

   The block attaches to the connector pegs in the middle of the top and bottom side-rails. The pegs on the blocks face the front of the module (the end with the axle that has no gears).

3. **Add two 2x6 perforated plates to the top of the module as cross pieces.**

   The plates span from one side of the module to the other. One plate installs at the rear end of the module (over the double axles with gears). The other plate installs in the middle of the module. Note that the connector wire from the motor should be lead out the rear of the module, under the newly added cross pieces.

Step 12

In this step, you add wheels and tires to the front and rear axles. You also add four round blocks to the top of the module and four double-head connector pegs to the top-rails, as shown in the *Constructopedia*.

1. **Assemble a pair of small solid wheels with large solid tires and add them to each end of the front axle.**

   The concave side of the wheel goes out.

2. **Assemble a pair of medium rim wheels with medium 20x30 lug tires and add them to each end of the rear axle.**

   The concave side of the wheel goes in.

3. **Add a 2x2 round block to each end of the two cross pieces on top of the module.**

4. **Add two double-head connector pegs to each top side-rail.**

   One peg goes into the second hole from the front; one goes into the third hole back from the first. Insert the pegs from the outside of the module until the first click, making them flush with the inside. Don't push them all the way in at this time.

Step 13

In this step, you mount the Scout microprocessor brick on top of the drive module and connect the connector wire from the motor, as shown in the *Constructopedia*.

1. **Snap the Scout onto the four round blocks you added in Step 12.**

   The top end of the Scout (the end with the Light Sensor) faces the front of the robot with the front edge of the Scout aligned with the round mounting blocks in the middle of the module. The other end of the Scout hangs out over the rear end of the drive module.

2. **Plug the connector wire from the motor into the Scout's drive port.**

   Snap the connector wire into place on motor port A. Make sure that the wire extends back toward the bottom of the Scout, not off to one side or up over the Scout's face.

This completes the first stage of the Hoop-o-bot's construction. The result, shown in Figure 4-11, is a motorized platform that's capable of moving back and forth in a straight line. The robot is a little imbalanced at this stage because of the way the Scout hangs over the rear end of the drive module, but the lopsided arrangement improves as you add the other modules to the Hoop-o-bot.

Checkpoint 1

This is a good place to pause construction for a moment and make sure that the motor is properly connected to the Scout. Be sure that the Scout is turned on and that it's on a smooth floor or other suitable surface.

Figure 4-11:
The Hoop-o-
bot drive
module with
the Scout
attached.

1. **Select the Forward motion program.**

   See Chapter 7 for instructions on selecting programs from the Scout's display.

2. **Press Run.**

   Catch that rascal before it gets away! Press Run again to stop the motor. If the robot moves forward, all is well. If it moves backward, you probably have a connector wire reversed on the motor or on the Scout's motor port.

After testing the drive module, set it aside for a few moments while you build the Hoop-o-bot's ball thrower module.

Building module 2 — the ball thrower

The Hoop-o-bot ball thrower module, shown in Figure 4-12, does exactly what its name implies — it throws balls. The module receives balls dropping through the hoop and kicks them back out — presumably tossing the ball back to you so you can catch it and try for another hoop.

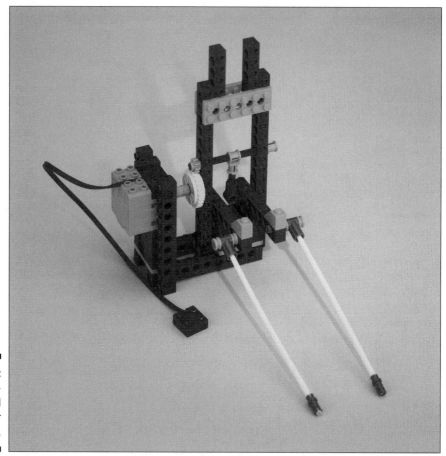

Figure 4-12:
The Hoop-o-
bot ball
thrower
module.

The ball thrower module uses the second motor from the Robotics Discovery Set to power the throwing arm, which is actually more like a mallet that knocks the ball out of its cradle than a catapult arm that slings the ball.

The module's design takes advantage of the clutch-like mechanism built into a 24-tooth clutch gear to allow the motor to continue to run after the throwing arm has reached the end of its travel. The gearing can be set to spin the throwing arm at high speed even though it uses only a small portion of the duration of the motor's run. When the throwing arm reaches its limit, the motor can continue to spin for a second or so. The clutch allows the axle to spin while the toothed part of the clutch gear remains stationary. As a result, there is no need for elaborate sensor arrangements (and programming) to detect when the throwing arm reaches its limit and then shut down the motor. It's a simple but effective design that makes use of a special feature of the clutch gear.

The *Constructopedia* drawings show the ball thrower module as viewed from the left-front corner — the same orientation as most other drawings of the Hoop-o-bot robot. Remember that the ball thrower is designed to kick the ball out to the left side of the robot.

Step 14

You begin building the ball thrower module by assembling two 1x10 perforated blocks, a 2x4 plate, and a pair of regular connector pegs, as shown in the *Constructopedia.*

1. **Arrange two 1x10 perforated blocks side by side.**

2. **Join the 1x10 perforated blocks by adding a 2x4 plate across one end.**

   Add the plate to the front ends of the blocks.

3. **Insert a regular connector peg into the end hole of each perforated block.**

   The connector peg goes into the block in the hole beneath the plate. The peg ends should stick out to the sides of the assembly.

Step 15

In this step, you assemble two parts composed of a plate, a small perforated block, and a connector peg, and add them to the module, as shown in the *Constructopedia.*

1. **Insert a regular connector peg into the hole of a 1x2 perforated block and attach the block to the underside of a 2x4 plate. Make two.**

   The block attaches to the underside of the 2x4 plate so that it's centered on one of the long sides of the plate with the connector peg sticking out.

2. **Attach one of the parts to the rear end of the module.**

   The 2x4 plate attaches to the ball thrower module across the rear ends of the base-rails. The block attached to the underside of the 2x4 plate sits between the two side-rails, with the connector peg sticking out to the rear of the module.

3. **Attach the other part to the module just forward of the first part.**

   The 2x4 plate attaches to the ball thrower module adjacent to the 2x4 plate of the other part. The block attached to the underside of the 2x4 plate sits between the two base-rails with the connector peg sticking out toward the front of the module (the end with the connector pegs).

When you look down on the module from the top, you should see four connector pegs sticking out. At the front end of the module, there should be a connector peg sticking out from each side. The third connector peg should stick out from the middle of the back end of the module and face away from the other connectors. The fourth connector peg should stick out into the space between the two base-rails and stick out forward, toward the front of the module.

Don't use the drawing labeled "2x" on page 16 of the *Constructopedia* for orientation of both assembled pieces. One will face one way and the other will face the opposite way. That drawing shows only how to assemble the connector peg into the 1x2 block and attach the block to the plate.

Step 16

In this step, you add a pair of 2x4 blocks and a pair of 1x4 blocks to the module, as shown in the *Constructopedia*.

1. **Add a pair of 2x4 blocks atop the two 2x4 plates at the rear of the module.**

   The long sides of the blocks should be parallel to the long sides of the side-rails.

2. **Add a pair of 1x4 perforated blocks to the top of the module.**

   The 1x4 blocks stack on top of the 2x4 blocks you just added. The long sides of the 1x4 blocks attach across the ends of the 2x4 blocks.

Step 17

In this step, you build the rear side of the ball cradle and add it to the module, as shown in the *Constructopedia*.

As you get out the pieces for this step, go ahead and get double quantities of everything. You use the same pieces to build the other side of the ball cradle in Step 18.

1. **Insert a cap-end axle and a regular connector peg into holes in a 1x8 perforated block.**

   Insert the cap-end axle into the left end hole of the block. Insert a connector peg into the next-to-last hole in the block so that the exposed ends of the connector peg and axle stick out on the same side of the block. Looking at the module from its left side (with the axle end of the block closest to you), the axle and connector peg should stick out on the right side of the block (toward the rear of the module).

2. **Push a thin spacer ring onto the axle.**

3. **Add a number 1 elbow and a thin spacer ring to the axle, and a 1x1 wedge block to the 1x8 perforated block.**

   The elbow slides onto the axle and is held in place by the thin spacer ring. The wedge block snaps onto the end of the 1x8 perforated block over the axle so that the angled part of the wedge block points back to the other end.

4. **Add the newly constructed part to the ball thrower module base.**

The rear side of the ball cradle attaches to the rear end of the ball thrower module. The 1x8 perforated block sits atop the 1x4 block at the end of the module. The right end of the longer block sits flush with the block beneath it, and the axle-end of the block sticks out to the left of the module.

Step 18

In this step, you build the front side of the ball cradle and add it to the module, as shown in the *Constructopedia*.

1. **Repeat the first three instructions of Step 17 to build a mirror image of the part.**

This time, the axle and connector peg should stick out to the left side of the new part, toward the front of the module.

2. **Add the newly constructed part to the ball thrower module base.**

The front side of the ball cradle attaches to the remaining 1x4 block on the top of the ball thrower module. The right end of the longer block sits flush with the block beneath it, and the axle-end of the block sticks out to the left of the module.

Step 19

In this step, you add a long perforated block and a couple of connector pegs to the ball thrower module, as shown in the *Constructopedia*.

1. **Attach a 1x16 perforated block vertically to the rear end of the module.**

Holes in the 1x16 block attach to two regular connector pegs sticking out the rear end of the module. The lower connector peg goes into the hole in the end of the block. The pegs on the block should face the left of the module (the same direction as the axle-ends of the ball cradle pieces).

2. **Insert two regular connector pegs into the top two holes of the long perforated block.**

The connector pegs should stick out toward the front of the module, over the ball cradle pieces, not out the rear of the module.

Step 20

In this step, you assemble the ball kicker arm on its axle and add the part to the module, as shown in the *Constructopedia*.

1. **Slide a mid-axle tee to the middle of a size 8 axle.**

2. **Stick a size 3 axle into a number 1 elbow and stick the other end of the axle into the tee fitting on the other axle.**

   The smooth hole in the number 1 elbow should be perpendicular to the longer axle.

3. **Insert one end of the long axle through a hole in the long vertical block and cap the axle with a thick spacer ring.**

   The axle goes into the fourth hole available above the ball cradle piece so that the kicker arm dangles between the two ball cradle pieces.

Step 21

In this step, you add another long perforated block to the module, along with a pair of connector pegs and a small gear, as shown in the *Constructopedia*. You also stack three 2x4 blocks on the front end of the module.

1. **Attach a 1x16 perforated block vertically to the front side of the ball cradle portion of the module.**

   Holes in the 1x16 block attach to two connector pegs sticking out into the space between the two base-rails. The lower connector peg goes into the hole in the end of the block. The pegs on the block should face the left side of the module (the same direction as the axle-ends of the ball cradle pieces). The result is two matching vertical posts on either side of the ball cradle pieces.

2. **Stick the axle holding the kicker arm through a hole in the newly added vertical block and cap the end of the axle with an 8-tooth gear.**

   The axle goes into the fourth hole available above the ball cradle piece so that it matches the other side.

3. **Insert two regular connector pegs into the top two holes of the long perforated block.**

   The connector pegs should stick out toward their mates in the other vertical block.

4. **Stack three 2x4 solid blocks on top of the plate at the front end of the module.**

Step 22

In this step, you extend the shaft of a motor using a short pipe section and a size 3 axle, then add a 24-tooth clutch gear to that axle and mount the motor on the ball thrower module, as shown in the *Constructopedia*.

1. **Slip one end of a short pipe over the shaft of a motor and insert a size 3 axle into the other end of the pipe.**

2. **Slide a 24-tooth clutch gear onto the axle.**

   Slide the gear all the way down to the end of the pipe.

3. **Mount the motor onto the ball thrower module.**

   Stick the exposed end of the axle into the front vertical block on the module. The axle goes into the second open hole above the ball cradle piece so that the 24-tooth clutch gear meshes with the 8-tooth gear on the end of the axle for the ball kicker arm. The motor itself mounts onto the top of the stacked 2x4 blocks at the left end of the module.

   Note how the back end of the motor hangs out over the front end of the module. The 2x4 blocks support the business end of the motor without interfering with the rounded lower-rear section of the motor. This is yet another way to mount a motor, but it isn't very strong unless you do something to lock the motor down. In this case, the remaining steps in this section include instructions for adding blocks and connector pegs to the top of the motor and then tying those blocks to the base-rails with a pair of vertical blocks, thus locking the motor and its supporting blocks down onto the base.

Step 23

In this step, you add a pair of small blocks and connector pegs to the top of the motor and extend the long vertical blocks with a pair of 1x6 blocks, as shown in the *Constructopedia*.

1. **Insert a regular connector peg into each of two 1x2 perforated blocks and add the blocks to the top of the motor.**

   The blocks go on the lower sets of pegs on the motor, on either side of the electrical connection pegs. The connector pegs stick out to the sides of the motor.

2. **Add a 1x6 perforated block to each of the long vertical blocks on the module.**

   The lower two holes in the 1x6 block go onto the connector pegs sticking out of the top two holes of the long vertical blocks.

Step 24

Finish up the ball thrower module by adding a pair of plates to the vertical blocks, adding vertical blocks to lock the motor in place, adding a connecting wire to the motor, and adding flexible tubing and connector pegs to the ball cradle, all as shown in the *Constructopedia*.

1. **Add two 2x6 plates to the vertical posts.**

   The plates attach to the posts horizontally on the left and right surfaces of the blocks. The lower side of each plate aligns with the lower ends of the upper 1x6 blocks.

2. **Add two 1x10 perforated blocks to the front end of the module on either side of the motor.**

   The 1x10 blocks install vertically with one end hole fitting onto the connector peg in the end of the base-rails and the other end hole fitting onto the connector peg in the block on top of the motor. Note how these blocks securely lock the motor and the stacked blocks beneath it onto the base of the ball thrower module.

3. **Attach one end of a long connector wire to the socket on top of the motor.**

   Make sure that the wire from the connector wire trails over the top of the motor, toward the front of the module.

4. **Insert one end of a short, yellow, flexible tube into the elbow on either side of the ball cradle and cap the other ends of those tubes with a pair of short connector pegs.**

Checkpoint 2

Before adding the ball thrower module to the Hoop-o-bot, it's a good idea to check the module to make sure that it is operating properly.

1. **Attach the other end of the connecting wire from the ball thrower module motor to motor port B on the Scout.**

   Make sure the wire from the connecting wire on the motor port trails down toward the bottom end of the Scout.

   Although the *Constructopedia* illustration shows the Scout connected only to the ball thrower module, you can leave the Scout mounted on the drive module during this test.

2. **Set a yellow foam ball in the ball cradle of the ball thrower module.**

3. **Turn the Scout on and select Loop B in the Motion area.**

   See Chapter 7 for information on how to select Scout programming options.

4. **Press Run.**

   The motor should rotate the kicker arm to kick the ball out of the cradle and across the room.

5. **Press Run again to stop the motor.**

   Don't forget to retrieve the ball from beneath the bookcase or wherever it landed.

Step 25

In this step, you attach the ball thrower module to the drive module, as shown in the *Constructopedia*.

1. **Position the ball thrower module on the Hoop-o-bot drive module.**

   The ball thrower module mounts in front of the Scout with the motor-end of the module farthest from the Scout. The base-rails of the ball thrower module nestle down between the upper side-rails of the drive module.

2. **Lock the ball thrower module in place by pushing in the two double-head connector pegs on each side of the drive module.**

3. **Make sure the connector wire from the motor on the ball thrower module is connected to port B on the Scout.**

   If you disconnected the connector wire from the Scout after completing the checkpoint, you need to reconnect it before proceeding. At the very least, check the connections after moving the ball thrower module around to mount it onto the drive module base.

With the ball thrower module mounted on the drive module, as shown in Figure 4-13, the Hoop-o-bot starts to shape up. The robot is no longer lopsided now that the ball thrower module at one end offsets the Scout hanging off of the other end. However, the Hoop-o-bot is incomplete without its hoop. So set the main robot aside for a moment while you begin building the hoop module.

Building module 3 — the hoop

Unlike the other sample robot in this chapter that had one module that served no function other than decoration, the Hoop-o-bot has no purely decorative module. The hoop module, shown in Figure 4-14, certainly has some decorative elements, and it lacks any sensors or motors that would make it an active part of the robot. But when the robot is designed to play a game that involves getting a ball through a hoop, that hoop can hardly be considered mere decoration. In this case, the hoop module is more than a simple hoop. It's a funnel-like series of hoops that channel the ball down into the ball thrower module.

Figure 4-13:
The drive
and ball
thrower
modules
of the
Hoop-o-bot.

Like the ball thrower module, the hoop module is designed to present its backboard and hoop to a player on the left side of the robot. The *Constructopedia* drawings show the hoop module laying on its right side with its backboard and hoops facing up. The view is from the module's lower-rear corner. You don't stand the module up into its proper orientation until time to attach it to the robot.

Step 26

In this step, you use a pair of regular connector pegs to join two 1x6 perforated blocks, as shown in the *Constructopedia*.

1. Insert two regular connector pegs into a 1x6 perforated block.

The connector pegs go into the top hole and the next-to-the-bottom hole.

Figure 4-14:
The
Hoop-o-bot
hoop
module.

   2. **Attach a second 1x6 perforated block to the first so that the two
      blocks are side by side, held together by the pegs.**

Step 27

In this step, you add a pair of regular connector pegs and a pair of long connector pegs to the module, as shown in the *Constructopedia*.

   1. **Add a regular connector peg to each side of the module.**

      The connector pegs go into the middle holes of the blocks.

   2. **Add a long connector peg to each side of the module.**

      Insert the short end of a long connector peg into the bottom hole of
      each block.

Step 28

In this step, you add two more 1x6 perforated blocks to the module, as
shown in the *Constructopedia*.

   1. **Add a 1x6 perforated block to each side of the module.**

      The result is four 1x6 perforated blocks held together with connecting
      pegs to form a 4x6 composite block with a connector peg sticking out of
      each of the lower corners.

The large composite block not only creates a secure attachment point for the posts that hold the hoop module above the ball thrower module of the robot, it also supplies a large surface area of pegs to which you attach a pair of 6x10 plates to serve as the backboard of the hoop module.

Step 29

In this step, you add a pair of long perforated blocks to the module to serve as posts. Attach the posts to the module with a pair of 2x6 plates and insert two connector pegs into each leg, as shown in the *Constructopedia*.

1. **Add a 1x12 perforated block to each side of the module.**

   The top hole of each 1x12 block attaches to a connector peg at the lower corner of the module.

2. **Add a pair of 2x6 plates to the module.**

   The plates attach to the module spanning the junction of the posts and the large composite block.

3. **Insert two connector pegs into each of the post blocks.**

   The connector pegs go into the fourth and sixth holes from the bottom of each post. Insert the pegs from the outside of the posts.

Step 30

In this step, you construct the front side of the hoop and attach it to the module, as shown in the *Constructopedia*. This is the hoop that's on the left side of the backboard when you're in playing position on the left side of the robot.

Step 31 instructs you to build the right side of the hoop, which uses identical pieces. So, while you're gathering pieces, go ahead and get double quantities of everything so you have all of the pieces out for both steps.

1. **Place the top side (cross bar portion) of an end-axle tee onto the top end of a size 5 axle.**

2. **Slip an 11-hole double-angle beam and two 3-hole beams onto the other end of the axle.**

   The axle goes through the end hole in the long side of the double-angle beam. The long side of the beam should be parallel to the tee, and the short side of the beam should point to the right. The two short beams attach to the end of the axle below the larger beam. The short beams should be perpendicular to the long side of the large beam and should point to the right.

3. **Insert a size 4 axle into the other end of the 3-hole beams and slide a mid-axle tee onto the axle.**

   Insert the axle into the bottom side of the beams. Orient the tee on the axle so that it's parallel to the long side of the double-angle beam.

4. **Slide a 9-hole angle beam and another mid-axle tee onto the lower axle.**

   Use the hole in the end of the long side of the angle beam. The long side of the beam should be parallel to the long side of the other large beam and the angled end should point to the right, just like the larger beam. Align the tee to match the one on the other side of the angled beam.

5. **Attach the assembly to the left side of the module.**

   The holes in the two tees on the lower axle snap onto the two pegs on the outside of the left (front) post of the hoop module.

Step 31

In this step, construct the right side of the hoop and attach it to the module, as shown in the *Constructopedia*. Simply repeat the procedure from Step 30, but swap the left/right orientation of the pieces to create an assembly that's the mirror image of the one in Step 30.

Step 32

In this step, you construct the rim-attachment assembly and add it to the module, as shown in the *Constructopedia*.

1. **Stick a size 6 axle into one end of a short pipe section and stick a size 8 axle into the other end of the pipe.**

2. **Add an axle-tip tee and a number 6 elbow to each end of the axle assembly.**

   The tees go onto the axles first with the axle-tips pointing to the front of the backboard (the left side of the robot). The elbows go onto the ends of the axles with the empty ends pointed up.

3. **Slip two mid-axle tees onto a long piece of green flexible tubing and then bend the tube into an arc and stick the ends into the elbows.**

   After inserting the ends of the tubing into the elbows, slip the tees down next to the elbows and rotate the tees so that the holes in the tees are on the outside of the arc.

4. **Insert short, button-end connector pegs into the holes in the elbows and tees.**

   The short end of the pegs should stick out to the front of the assembly (what will become the left side of the robot).

5. **Add the rim-attachment assembly to the hoop module.**

   The rim-attachment assembly goes onto the back side of the module (the right side of the robot). The axle-tips of the tees on the horizontal axle of the rim-attachment assembly plug into the tees atop the axles on the left and right hoop assemblies.

Step 33

In this step, you construct the backboard assembly and attach it to the hoop module, as shown in the *Constructopedia*.

1. **Use a 2x8 plate to join two 6x10 plates side-by-side.**

   The 2x8 plate attaches to the back side of the larger plates spanning the joint at its top end.

2. **Add six 1x4 plates to the face of the larger plates.**

   Position the 1x4 plates so that they're indented one peg from the top, left, and right side of the backboard assembly. These pieces are just decorative, but they're a nice touch, especially if you take care to use the pieces made of teal plastic.

3. **Attach the backboard assembly to the hoop module.**

   The lower portion of the backboard snaps onto the composite blocks at the top of the hoop module. The bottom edge of the blackboard should be adjacent to the 2x6 plate attaching the composite block to the posts.

Step 34

In this step, you add the rims to the front of the hoop module and also add double-head connector pegs to the posts, as shown in the *Constructopedia*.

1. **Bend a short green flexible tube into an arc and stick the ends into the pegs in the elbows of the rim attachment assembly.**

2. **Bend a yellow flexible tube into an arc and stick the ends into the pegs in the tees of the rim attachment assembly.**

3. **Insert a double-head connector peg into each of the bottom two holes of each post.**

   Insert the pegs from the outside. Don't push them all the way in yet.

Step 35

In this step, you mount the hoop module onto the ball thrower module of the Hoop-o-bot, as shown in the *Constructopedia*.

1. **Align the lower ends of the hoop module's posts with the upper ends of the ball thrower module's posts.**

2. **Push in the four double-head connector pegs in the hoop module's posts to lock the two modules together.**

Step 36

In this step, you pivot the ball containment tubes from the ball thrower module up into place, as shown the *Constructopedia,* and load the hoop-o-bot with a yellow foam ball.

1. **Pivot one of the yellow flexible tubes from the ball thrower module and insert the connector peg on the end of the tube into a hole in the lower beam of the hoop module.**

   The connector peg goes into the second hole in the short arm of the beam.

2. **Repeat the process for the other yellow flexible tube.**

3. **Drop a yellow foam ball through the hoop and into the ball cradle of the ball thrower module.**

Your Hoop-o-bot is complete and ready to play ball. It should look like the robot shown back in Figure 4-9.

Changing the game

Programming the Hoop-o-bot to play ball is a simple matter. Just make sure the Scout is turned on and try the following programs:

- ✔ If you run no program on the Scout, the Hoop-o-bot presents a stationary target that you can use to practice throwing the yellow foam ball through the hoop.

- ✔ Select motion program Loop A to instruct the robot to move back and forth, giving you a more challenging moving target.

- ✔ Select motion program Loop B to instruct the robot to throw the ball back to you after you make a hoop.

   The Loop B program runs the ball thrower module motor back and forth. If the ball lands in the ball thrower when the throwing arm is back, the robot will throw the ball to you when the throwing arm swings forward. However, if the ball lands in the ball thrower while the throwing arm is forward, the robot will do its best to hold onto the ball by swinging the throwing arm down onto the top of the ball and holding it there.

- ✔ Select motion program Loop AB to instruct the robot to perform both motions.

With a little programming ingenuity (and the proper lighting conditions), you can have the Light Sensor on the Scout trigger the action of the throwing arm when it detects the presence of the ball in front of the sensor. Here's how you do it:

1. **Position a strong light on the front side of the Hoop-o-bot so that the light falls on the Scout's Light Sensor.**

   The position of the light relative to the robot is critical, so you may want to disconnect the motor in the drive base (disconnect the connector wire from Port A) to make sure the Hoop-o-bot doesn't move.

2. **Select motion program Loop B and light program WaitFor.**

   See Chapter 7 for information on how to select programs on the Scout.

3. **Press Run to start the program.**

   When you drop a ball into the ball thrower module, the ball shadows the Scout's Light Sensor. When the Scout detects the change in light level, it activates the motor in the ball thrower module, which kicks the ball out to you.

Chapter 5

Building the Invention Bots

*I*f you're looking for the biggest and baddest robot-building kit, the LEGO MINDSTORMS Robotics Invention System is it. The Robotics Invention System is the kit of choice for the serious robot hobbyist and everyone wanting the maximum in power and versatility in their MINDSTORMS kits.

The Robotics Invention System contains more pieces than any of the other LEGO MINDSTORMS kits, and its microprocessor brick — the RCX — is more powerful and versatile than the Scout and Micro Scout processors found in the other sets. The Robotics Invention System is the only LEGO MINDSTORMS set that includes an application for your Windows-based computer that enables you to create your own programs and download them to the RCX via an infrared transmitter (which is also included in the set). The optional expansion kits — Exploration Mars, RoboSports, and Extreme Creatures — require the Robotics Invention System as their base. That's a lot of power and versatility packed into one box.

More so than the other LEGO MINDSTORMS sets, the Robotics Invention System enables you to explore the full robot development experience. Building robots with the Robotics Invention System is a three-phase process:

1. **Build the robot.**

   Assemble the LEGO blocks and pieces around the RCX microprocessor to create a robot with feelers, arms, and wheels, or whatever it needs to perform the tasks you have in mind.

2. **Create the program that controls the robot.**

   RCX programming is the topic of Chapters 8 and 9.

3. **Test your robotic invention.**

   Download and run your program and observe your robot's behavior. If you like what you see, you have a finished robot. Otherwise, you revise and rework the robot construction or programming (or both) until the robot works the way you want it to.

The focus of this chapter is on the first phase — building the robots. The chapter complements the *Constructopedia* that comes with the Robotics Invention System and includes detailed instructions for building three sample robots:

- ✔ **Pathfinder:** A simple two-wheeled robot designed for initial testing of your RCX microprocessor brick and RCX-programming setup.

- ✔ **RoverBot:** A mobile robot with bumpers or a Light Sensor that you can program to explore its environment.

- ✔ **InventorBot:** A stationary robot with arms that can sense or throw things.

The Robotics Invention System *Constructopedia* also includes instructions for building another robot, the AcroBot, as well as several variations on the RoverBot, AcroBot, and InventorBot. However, the available space in this book doesn't allow us to print detailed instructions for building everything in the *Constructopedia*.

As you build the sample robots, you have an opportunity to see the many LEGO MINDSTORMS pieces in use, and you can observe the construction techniques for building robots and robot components. After building a couple of the sample robots, you'll be ready to begin designing and building your own robotic inventions.

The drawings of MINDSTORMS pieces in the box beside each step number in the *Constructopedia* indicate what pieces you will need for that step. A number with an x beside a piece indicates how many of that piece you will need. So 2x means that you need two identical pieces to complete the step. A blue number beside an axle indicates the length of the axle. For example, a 4 beside an axle means that the axle is the same length as a block with four pegs on its top. In this chapter, we identify blocks and plates by the number of LEGO pegs on the top of each piece, using numbers to indicate the number of rows of pegs and the number of pegs in each row. For example, a 2x8 plate has two rows of pegs with 8 pegs in each row for a total of 16 pegs. Examine the *Constructopedia* drawings carefully to make sure you're using the correct pieces for each step and that you install them in the proper position and orientation. Axles, connector pegs, tee fittings, and other pieces come in slightly different sizes and configurations that are easy to confuse with one another.

If you lost your copy of the *Constructopedia* book, don't despair. You can order a replacement copy of the *Constructopedia* from LEGO Consumer Affairs by calling 800-422-5346. There is a service charge for replacing lost LEGO MINDSTORMS set pieces such as the *Constructopedia*.

Preparing for Robot Building

Before you begin building robots with the Robotics Invention System, we have a few housekeeping chores to get out of the way. It's basic stuff like inserting batteries to power the RCX unit and making sure you know how to connect the motors and sensors to the RCX.

- ✔ Insert six AA batteries in the RCX. Pry off the back cover of the RCX to expose the battery compartment.

- ✔ The gray pegs just above the display on the front of the RCX are the sensor ports. There are three sets of four pegs labeled 1, 2, and 3 (see Figure 5-1). You can connect Touch Sensors or Light Sensors to any of the sensor ports. You can also use the sensor ports to connect the Rotation Sensors and Temperature Sensors that are available separately.

- ✔ The three sets of black pegs just below the display on the front of the RCX are the *output ports*. They're labeled A, B, and C. (Refer to Figure 5-1.) Output ports are normally used for connecting motors to the RCX, but they can also power other devices (such as the LEGO Light) that are available separately.

- ✔ You use connecting wires (two special 2x2 plates joined by a length of wire) to connect motors and Touch Sensors to the RCX. The plates on the connecting wires snap onto the pegs on the motors, sensors, and the RCX just like any other LEGO building block (see Figure 5-2).

If you look closely, you can see small, gold-colored metallic contacts embedded in the pegs and holes of the connector wires, in the pegs on the tops of the motors and Touch Sensors, and in the pegs on the RCX's sensor and output ports. These contacts automatically make the required electrical connections when the connector wire plates snap into place.

- ✔ The electrical connections on the motor are in the four pegs centered over the axle, not the raised pegs over the rear of the motor or the pegs on the outer edges of the unit.

- ✔ The electrical connections on the Touch Sensor are in the four pegs on the button end of the unit.

- ✔ The Light Sensor has its own built-in connector wire. You don't need to use a separate connector wire with the Light Sensor. The plate on the end of the Light Sensor wire connects to the RCX sensor ports just like a connector wire from a Touch Sensor.

✔ The orientation of the connector wires on the motors and on the RCX output ports makes a difference in the direction the motor turns. In other words, you must be careful to pay attention to whether the connector wire is trailing off to the front, back, left side, or right side of a motor. The same thing applies to the way the connector wires attach to the output ports on the RCX. Reversing the orientation of the connector wire causes the motor to turn in the opposite direction.

✔ The orientation of the connector wires on the Touch Sensors and sensor ports doesn't make any difference.

✔ See Chapter 8 for more information on how to use the buttons on the face of the RCX to select and run programs.

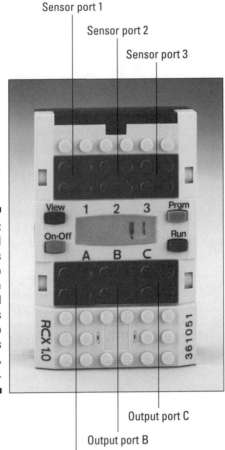

Figure 5-1:
Sensors and motors connect to the RCX via electrical connections built into special sets of pegs, called ports.

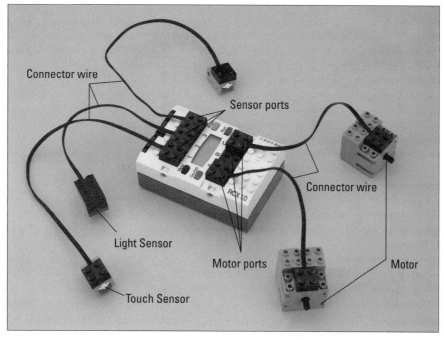

Figure 5-2:
The Scout
with Touch
Sensors and
motors
attached.

Paving the Way with the Pathfinder

The first robot project in the Robotics Invention System *Constructopedia* is the Pathfinder robot, as shown in Figure 5-3. The Pathfinder is a minimalist robot. It's really nothing more than a bracket for connecting a pair of motors to the back of the RCX. Add a pair of wheels, and voilà, you have a simple, self-propelled robot.

The Pathfinder can't do much — just move forward and back, and spin around in circles — but that's enough to complete the training missions that are part of the RCX setup and programming tests on the Robotics Invention System CD-ROM.

This robot is fast and easy to build, but it isn't very strong. It will probably hold together long enough to complete the training mission, but that's about all. Don't use this design as a template for future robot designs unless you want your robot to fall apart as it runs across the floor.

Note that the Pathfinder's motor bracket is cleverly designed to provide built-in balance tips at each end. They act like training wheels on a kid's bicycle — they keep the Pathfinder from tipping too far over to one end or the other. The bracket is narrow at each end to avoid creating too much resistance as it rubs on the floor. Thanks to this design, the Pathfinder gets by with only two wheels.

Step 1

Start with a base constructed of plates and a disk at each end, as shown in the *Constructopedia*. The base creates a bracket for the Pathfinder's two motors. The disk at each end creates a rub point to slide across the floor when the pathfinder moves. The *Constructopedia* drawings show the Pathfinder as viewed from the right-rear corner.

1. **Add a 2x4 plate to each end of a 2x8 perforated plate.**

   The 2x4 plates overlap the longer plate by two pegs lengthwise. The shorter plates go on top.

2. **Add a pair of 1x6 plates to the assembly.**

   The 1x6 plates go crosswise on the 2x8 plate, inside of and immediately adjacent to the 2x4 plates at each end.

3. **Add a small, 4-peg disk to the underside of the 2x4 plate at each end of the assembly.**

Step 2

In this step, you build a mounting column at each end of the base, as shown in the *Constructopedia*. The mounting column flairs out from the 2-peg wide base via a pair of wedge blocks to a pair of round blocks that attach to the back of the RCX.

1. **Add two 2x3 reverse wedge blocks to the end of the base assembly.**

   Put the two wedges together, thick end to thick end, so that they form a funnel shape. Attach them crosswise on the end of the base assembly.

2. **Add a 2x2 plate atop the wedge pieces, spanning the joint between the two wedges.**

3. **Stack a 2x2 round block on top of a 2x2 square block, and then set the stacked pair of blocks on one end of a wedge block.**

   Do the same thing on the other wedge.

4. **Repeat the process at the other end of the assembly.**

Step 3

In this step, you add two motors and connector wires to the assembly, as shown in the *Constructopedia*. The motors sit back to back across the mounting bracket.

1. **Attach two motors to the assembly.**

   The motors sit on the pair of 1x6 plates going across the assembly. The plates attach to the bottom edges of the motors. The motors mount back to back with the shafts sticking out to the sides of the assembly.

2. **Add a short connector wire to each motor.**

   Snap the plate at one end of the connector wire to the motor-contact pegs (the center pegs over the shaft). Make sure the connector wires from the motors are both going off to the sides of the motors. Both wires should go toward the same side, which becomes the back of the robot.

Step 4

In this step, you add the RCX to the assembly, attach the connector wires from the motors to the RCX's output ports, and add wheels and tires to the motor shafts, all shown in the *Constructopedia*.

1. **Mount the RCX microprocessor brick onto the assembly.**

   The RCX sits atop the four 2x2 round blocks. The RCX should be centered on the motor bracket assembly. Orient the top of the RCX toward the front of the robot.

2. **Connect the wires from the motors to the output ports on the RCX.**

Connect the left motor to output port A and the right motor to output port C. Make sure that the connector wires trail off from the connector ports toward the bottom end of the RCX.

3. **Mount a large solid wheel onto a small solid rim.**

   Build two of these.

4. **Mount a wheel/tire onto each motor shaft.**

   Press the wheel directly onto the shaft, concave side out.

That's all there is to it. The Pathfinder robot is ready for trial runs and training missions. Flip to Chapters 8 and 9 for more information on testing and programming the RCX.

Revving Up the RoverBot

The first full-fledged robot project in the Robotics Invention System *Constructopedia* is the RoverBot. (Yeah, we know the Pathfinder comes first. But that's really just a limited test construction, not a real robot.) The RoverBot, shown in Figure 5-4, is a mobile critter that can move around under its own power and avoid obstacles or follow a line on the floor.

Figure 5-4:
A RoverBot built with tracks and a single bumper module.

The RoverBot is composed of three modules: the driving base, a propulsion module, and a sensor module. The *Constructopedia* includes instructions for building three different propulsion modules and three different sensor modules, all of which will fit on the RoverBot in various combinations.

✔ **Driving base module:** A chassis that supports the RCX microprocessor brick and houses the drive motors. The driving base also provides attachment points for the various propulsion modules and sensor modules.

✔ **Propulsion module:** Takes power from the motors and uses it to move the robot. You can choose from the three following propulsion modules:

- **Wheel sets module:** Four standard wheels. The wheels certainly work well, but they're rather unimaginative.

- **Legs module:** Gives the RoverBot the ability to crawl around on crab-like legs (see Figure 5-5).

- **Tracks module:** Make the RoverBot look like a mini snow cat or bulldozer and give it almost as much rough-terrain capability. This is the option we chose for the version of the RoverBot shown in this book (refer to Figure 5-4).

Figure 5-5:
A variation on the RoverBot with legs and a double bumper.

✔ **Sensor module:** Provides input to the RCX program controlling the RoverBot to either detect obstacles in the robot's path or to detect changes in the light reflected from the floor. You have the following three choices for a RoverBot sensor module:

- **Single bumper module:** Uses a single Touch Sensor to detect obstacles in the robot's path. This is the bumper we chose to build for the RoverBot in this book (refer to Figure 5-4.)

- **Double bumper module:** Uses two Touch Sensors to detect obstacles in the robot's path. The dual sensors, combined with the appropriate programming, enable the robot to detect which side an obstacle is on. (Refer to Figure 5-5).

- **Light Sensor module:** A Light Sensor pointed toward the ground in front of the robot enables the robot to detect and follow a line on the floor (provided, of course, that you supply the appropriate programming).

You can mix and match propulsion modules and sensor modules attached to the same driving base to achieve nine different variations of the RoverBot. (Figure 5-5 shows just one of the variations.) And that's before you start adding any of the suggested enhancements from the back of the *Constructopedia* or incorporating any of your own ideas. There isn't room in this book to explore all the variations, so we include instructions for building the RoverBot with tracks and a single bumper.

Building the driving base

The foundation (or chassis) of the RoverBot is its driver base module shown in Figure 5-6. The driver base module includes the RCX — the brains of the robot — and the other modules attach to the driving base. With a couple of exceptions, the *Constructopedia* drawings show the driving base as viewed from the left-rear corner. Figure 5-6, on the other hand, shows the driver base from the left-front corner. The driving base is symmetrical except for the orientation of the RCX and the motor connector wires.

Step 1

Begin building the RoverBot by assembling plates, as shown in the *Constructopedia,* to create two lower end-rails for the module.

1. **Stack a 2x4 perforated plate in the center of a 2x10 plate. Make two.**

2. **Add a 1x2 plate and a 1x2 side-tab plate to each end of each long plate.**

   Each plate hangs off the end of the long plate by one peg length. The tabs at each end go on the same side. Arrange the end-rails side by side so that the tabs on one end-rail assembly point toward the tabs on the other end-rail.

Figure 5-6:
The
RoverBot
driving base
module.

Step 2

In this step, you add a pair of 1x2 perforated blocks to the ends of the side-rails, as shown in the *Constructopedia*.

1. **Add a pair of 1x2 perforated blocks to each end of each end-rail.**

   The blocks sit across the short plates so that the holes in the blocks align.

   Mount the inner block first and then press down on it as you mount the outer block on the unsupported ends of the plates.

Step 3

In this step, you stack more plates on the blocks at each end of the end-rails, as shown in the *Constructopedia*.

1. **Stack a 1x2 plate and a 1x2 side-tab plate on top of the pair of blocks at each end of each end-rail.**

   Mount the plates across the pair of blocks. The side tab goes on the same side as the tabs below the blocks.

2. **Stack a 2x2 plate atop the newly added plates at each end of each end-rail.**

Step 4

In this step, you add two motors to the module, as shown in the *Constructopedia*.

1. **Position two motors back to back about four pegs apart.**

2. **Slide the tabs of the side-tab plates on an end-rail into the slots on the sides of the two motors.**

   Repeat on the other side with the other end-rail.

   There is nothing holding the end-rails to the motors as yet. Simply set the pieces together in position.

Step 5

In this step, you build the central mounting grid assembly and add it to the modules, as shown in the *Constructopedia*.

1. **Insert four regular connector pegs and two axle-end connector pegs into a 1x16 perforated block and attach two blue multi-hole connector blocks to the 1x16 block.**

   The regular pegs go into the second and third holes from each end. All the pegs stick out on the same side. An axle-end peg goes into the fifth hole from each end, sticking out to the opposite side of the 1x16 block. One multi-hole connector block goes on each pair of regular pegs with the open end of the multi-hole connector block at the end of the 1x16 block.

2. **Insert a matching set of pegs into another 1x16 perforated block and attach it to the opposite side of the multi-hole connector blocks.**

3. **Stack a 1x4 plate on top of a 2x4 plate (make two). Mount one stacked plate unit across the two 1x16 blocks just above each pair of axle-end pegs. Stick a short pipe section over the exposed tip of each axle-end peg.**

4. **Attach the mounting grid assembly to the module.**

   The unit goes across the end-rails of the module in between the two motors. The 1x16 blocks snap onto the plates of the end-rails, locking them into place and holding them onto the motors. The pipe sections should align with the holes in the 1x2 blocks at each corner of the module.

Step 6

In this step, you add a pair of blocks and a pair of plates to the top of the module, as shown in the *Constructopedia*. Also add small gears to the motor shafts and insert four connector pegs into the module.

1. **Add two 1x8 plates to the top of the module.**

   The plates go on top of the motors, spanning from one motor to the other on the outer sides of the raised pegs.

2. **Add two 1x12 perforated blocks to the top of the module.**

   The blocks go on the outer corners of the module, parallel to the motors.

3. **Insert a pair of short connector pegs into each 1x12 block, in the third hole from each end.**

4. **Push a small 8-tooth gear onto each motor shaft.**

Step 7

In this step, you add four double-hole plates to the bottom of the module, as shown in the *Constructopedia,* and insert a connector peg into a hole in each plate. Note that the *Constructopedia* drawing shows the module turned over so that the bottom faces up.

1. **Turn the module over to access its underside.**

2. **Add four 2x2 double-hole plates to the end-rail plates.**

   The plates go on either side of each motor with one of the holes of each plate pointed out toward the end of the module, parallel to the long blocks of the mounting grid.

3. **Insert a short connector peg into the outer hole of each of the double-hole plates.**

Step 8

In this step, you add four beams to the module to lock the top- and bottom-rails together and add connector wires to the motors, as shown in the *Constructopedia.* The *Constructopedia* drawing shows the module back in its original orientation, with the top facing up and the view from the left-rear corner.

1. **Attach four 5-hole thin beams to the module.**

   Each beam goes from a peg in one of the 1x12 blocks on top of the module to a corresponding peg in a double-hole plate below it.

2. **Attach a short connector wire to each motor.**

   The plate at one end of the connector wire attaches to the pegs over the motor shaft. The wire should trail out toward one end of the module, toward a blue multi-hole connector block. Both wires should lead toward the same end of the module, which becomes the rear of the module.

Step 9

In this step, you mount the RCX on top of the module and attach the motor wires, as shown in the *Constructopedia*.

1. **Mount the RCX microprocessor brick onto the module.**

   The RCX goes parallel to the long blocks of the mounting grid so that the motor shafts stick out to the sides of the RCX. Center the RCX on the module and press it down to snap the holes in the back of the RCX onto the pegs on the top of the module. You must get the RCX properly aligned and then press down firmly.

2. **Attach the connector wires from the motor to the RCX's output ports.**

   The wire from the left motor goes to output port A, and the wire from the right motor goes to output port C. The wires should trail off to the bottom end of the RCX, not out to the sides.

That completes the RoverBot driving base module. After you construct a propulsion module and a sensor module, you can attach them to the driving base to complete the RoverBot robot.

Building the tracks

The Robotics Invention System *Constructopedia* offers three separate propulsion modules for the RoverBot: wheels, legs, and tracks. You can build and use any one of them. We chose the tracks (shown in Figure 5-7) as the most interesting to build. It's fun to send your track-equipped RoverBot over an obstacle course to see how it handles climbing over small books and binders.

Figure 5-7:
The
RoverBot
tracks
module.

The tracks module is composed of two identical units — one for each side of the RoverBot. The *Constructopedia* gives instructions for assembling one unit — the framework, gear train, wheels, and track for one side of the robot. Of course, your RoverBot needs two track assemblies, so you should either build two of everything as you go through the following steps or go through the steps to build one unit and then repeat the process to build the tracks for the other side.

The *Constructopedia* drawings show the left track assembly as viewed from the left-front corner so that you see the track module from the outer side, where the track itself will be. Figure 5-7 shows the left track assembly from the right-front corner so you can get a little better look at the inner side of the assembly, where the track will connect to the driving base module. The tracks module is composed of two identical track assemblies, so it's more appropriate to refer to the inner and outer sides of a track assembly than to the left and right sides.

Step 1

Start building the tracks module by using two 2x2 plates to join two 1x6 perforated blocks to a 1x8 perforated block, as shown in the *Constructopedia*.

1. **Attach a 2x2 plate to the bottom of each end of a 1x8 perforated block.**

   Of course, the plates are wider than the block. The extra pegs of both plates should stick out on the same side of the block.

2. **Add a 1x6 perforated block to each end of the assembly.**

   The shorter blocks overlap the longer block by two peg widths and snap onto the exposed pegs of the 2x2 plates.

Step 2

In this step, you build up the junction where the blocks overlap by stacking plates, as shown in the *Constructopedia*.

1. **Snap a 2x2 plate on top of each joint in the longer blocks.**

2. **Add a 1x2 plate on the middle pegs of each of the 1x6 blocks.**

   The 1x2 plates sit adjacent to the 2x2 plates, leaving the outer two end pegs of each 1x6 block open.

3. **Stack a 1x4 plate on top of each 1x2 plate.**

   The 1x4 plate extends over the 1x2 plate and half of the adjacent 2x2 plate.

Step 3

In this step, you add three axles to the assembly along with two more blocks, as shown in the *Constructopedia*.

1. **Stick a thin spacer ring on the tip of each of three size 8 axles.**

2. **Stick one axle through each of the holes where the blocks overlap.**

   Insert the axles from the 1x8 block side. The long end of the axles should stick out of the end hole of the 1x6 blocks.

3. **Stick one axle through the middle hole of the 1x8 block.**

   Insert the axle from the 1x8 block side so that it sticks out of the side where the 1x6 blocks are attached.

4. **Stack a 1x4 perforated block on top of each of the 1x4 plates.**

Step 4

In this step, you add two gears and a spacer ring to the axles, as shown in the *Constructopedia*.

1. **Slide a 24-tooth hat gear onto the center axle.**

   The smooth side of the gear goes against the block.

2. **Slide another 24-tooth hat gear onto the rear axle.**

   Which of the two axles on either side of the center axle is the front and which is the rear is an arbitrary designation. Actually it doesn't make any difference because the track module works the same whether the front wheel drives the track or the rear wheel drives the track. Just make sure that the gear train you start building in this step engages the gear in the wheel you add in Step 6, and everything will work as planned.

3. **Slide a thick spacer ring onto the front axle.**

Step 5

In this step, you add another gear to the center axle and secure the upper and lower blocks to each other with a pair of blocks mounted vertically with connector pegs, as shown in the *Constructopedia*.

1. **Slide a 24-tooth gear onto the center axle.**

   The teeth of the gear should mesh with the hat gear on the rear axle.

2. **Insert a regular connector peg into each of the end holes of a 1x4 perforated block.**

   Make two.

3. **Mount the blocks on the assembly vertically, near the ends.**

   The blocks mount on the inner side of the assembly, away from the gears. The peg in one end hole of the vertical block goes into the middle hole of the 1x6 block, and the peg at the other end of the vertical block goes into the hole in the outer end of the 1x4 block on top of the assembly.

Step 6

In this step, you assemble the axles wheels and gears that support the tracks, stretch the tracks over the wheels, and add the tracks to the assembly, as shown in the *Constructopedia*.

The *Constructopedia* drawings are a bit confusing at this step. You need to assemble two separate wheels — one for the front of the track and one for the rear end of the track. However, if you don't realize that the drawing is intended to show two separate wheels, you can easily misinterpret the drawing to be instructions for putting all the spacers, gears, and wheels on one axle.

1. **Slide two thick spacer rings onto a size 6 axle.**

   Position the spacer rings approximately one peg width from the end of the axle. This is the axle for the front wheel.

1a. **Slide a 24-tooth gear and a 16-tooth gear onto a size 6 axle.**

   Position the two gears approximately one peg width from the end of the axle, with the larger gear closer to the end. This is the axle for the rear wheel.

2. **Add a track wheel and a thick spacer ring to the front axle.**

   The wheel goes on first, and the spacer ring slides on to hold the wheel in place on the axle. The wheel should rotate freely on the axle.

2a. **Add a track wheel and a thick spacer ring to the rear axle.**

   The rim of the wheel should slide over the 16-tooth gear, and the gear should mesh with the raised spokes of the wheel. The gear prevents the wheel from turning freely on the axle. The spacer ring slides onto the axle to hold the wheel in place, meshed with the gear.

3. **Position the wheels into the ends of the loop of a piece of Caterpillar track.**

   Make sure you don't get one of the wheels turned around. The end of the front axle with two spacer rings should be on the same side of the track as the gears on the rear wheel axle. It's this side of the track subassembly that attaches to the rest of the track module.

4. **Add the wheel and track subassembly to the track module.**

   The tips of the axles go into the next-to-last holes in the lower blocks near the ends of the track module. The larger gear on the rear wheel should mesh with the hat gear on the rear axle of the module.

Step 7

In this step, you add a long block to the outside of the module to support the five axles and lock it in place with three thin spacer rings, as shown in the *Constructopedia*. You also add a pair of connector pegs that you use to attach the track module to the driving base.

1. **Slide a 1x16 perforated block over the protruding tips of the five axles.**

   The axles supporting the wheels go into the second hole from each end. The center axle goes into the center hole of the block, and the other two axles should naturally line up with the appropriate holes (third hole from the center in each direction). The three center axles should stick through the block.

2. **Slip a thin spacer ring onto the protruding end of each of the three center axles.**

3. **Stick a double-head connector peg into the hole at the end of each of the two 1x4 blocks on top of the module.**

   The pegs go into the end of the blocks closest to the center of the module. Don't push the connector pegs all the way in yet.

Step 8

In this step, you attach the track module to the driving base, as shown in the *Constructopedia*.

1. **Align a track module with the side of the driving base.**

   The corners of the driving base should fit into the corners formed by the 1x4 blocks on top of the track module and the vertical blocks connected to them. Slide the track module up onto the driving base from the bottom. The small gear on the motor shaft should mesh with the gear on the center axle of the track module, and the double-head connector pegs on the track module should align with the holes in the blocks on either side of the motor in the driving base.

2. **Press the two modules together to snap the pegs on the track module into the lower corners of the driving base.**

3. **Repeat the process to mount the track module on the other side of the driving base.**

Step 9

In this step, you lock the track modules to the driving base by pushing in the double-head connector pegs, as shown in the *Constructopedia*.

1. **Press all four double-head connector pegs in all the way to lock the track modules in place.**

With its track modules installed, the RoverBot is ready to move. See Figure 5-8.

Building the single bumper

The RoverBot's single bumper module, shown in Figure 5-9, is one of three sensor modules you can choose from. The other options are a double bumper module and a Light Sensor module. You can build any one of the three, but we chose the single bumper module for this RoverBot.

Figure 5-8:
The
RoverBot
with the
tracks
module
installed.

The single bumper module houses a Touch Sensor, positioned so that it's triggered by pressure on the pair of beams that form the bumper component. The bumper module employs a rubber band to keep the bumper off the Touch Sensor button until there is positive pressure on the bumper. A small mounting bracket for attaching the single bumper module to the front of the RoverBot completes the module. The *Constructopedia* drawings show the single bumper module as viewed from the left-front corner.

Step 1

Begin the bumper assembly by adding a spacer ring and a cam to an axle, as shown in the *Constructopedia*.

1. **Stick a thin spacer ring on the end of a size 5 axle.**

2. **Insert the axle through the hole in the small end of a cam piece.**

   Slide the cam down the axle to rest against the spacer ring.

Step 2

In this step, you add a dual thickness beam, another axle, and a connector peg to the module, as shown in the *Constructopedia*.

1. **Slide a 4-hole dual thickness beam onto the axle in the cam.**

The axle goes through the hole at the end of the thin end of the beam. The beam should be perpendicular to the cam with the flat side away from the cam.

2. **Insert the end of a size 4 axle into the hole in the thick end of the beam.**

   The axle sticks out away from the cam.

3. **Insert a short connector peg into the beam.**

   The peg goes into the hole next to the thick end of the beam with the longer end of the peg sticking out beside the protruding axle.

Step 3

In this step, you add a multi-hole connector block to one end of the module and a Touch Sensor to the other end, as shown in the *Constructopedia*. You also add another axle and a connector peg to the module.

1. **Mount a Touch Sensor onto the front axle of the module.**

   The front axle (the one that goes through the cam) goes through the horizontal hole at the rear of the sensor. The business end of the sensor (the button) sticks out away from the beam and the other axle.

2. **Add a blue multi-hole connecting block to the opposite end of the module.**

   The block slides over the rear axle and the connector peg in the beam. The open end of the block extends out to the rear of the module, opposite the Touch Sensor.

3. **Insert a short connector peg into the open front hole in the side of the multi-hole connector block.**

4. **Stick a thin spacer ring on the end of a size 5 axle and insert the axle into the cam.**

   The axle goes into the hole in the thick end of the cam and sticks out over the Touch Sensor.

Step 4

In this step, you add another beam to the open (left) side of the module and attach a connecting wire to the Touch Sensor, as shown in the *Constructopedia*.

1. **Add a 4-hole dual thickness beam to the left side of the module.**

   The hole in the thin end of the beam goes on the axle sticking out of the Touch Sensor. The hole in the thick end of the beam fits onto the axle sticking out of the multi-hole connector block.

2. **Attach one end of a short connector wire to the front four pegs on top of the Touch Sensor.**

The connector wire should trail off the back of the Touch Sensor and over the blue connector block.

3. **Slide a thick spacer ring onto the top axle.**

Step 5

In this step, you construct a spring-loaded hinge assembly and add it to the module, as shown in the *Constructopedia*.

1. **Slide a thin spacer ring and a number 5 elbow onto a size 4 axle.**

   The spacer ring goes all the way to the end of the axle, and the axle slips through the center hole of the elbow.

2. **Stick the axle through the corner hole of a 5-hole L-beam.**

3. **Add another number 5 elbow and thin spacer ring to the axle on the other side of the L-beam.**

4. **Insert a size 3 axle into each of the elbows.**

   Position the elbows so that their angles approximate the angle of the L-beam and insert the axles into the end of each elbow that lies alongside the short side of the L-beam.

5. **Slide two 3-hole beams onto the pair of axles protruding from the elbows and add a small white rubber band to the other end of the elbows.**

   The rubber band should go around both elbows and the long side of the L-beam so that it holds the ends of the elbows parallel to the long side of the beam.

6. **Attach the hinge assembly to the top axle of the module.**

   The hole in the end of the long arm of the L-beam goes onto the top axle of the module, positioned so that the hinge sits above the Touch Sensor and hangs down in front of the sensor's button.

Step 6

In this step, you add a spacer ring and cam to the left side of the module, as shown in the *Constructopedia*.

1. **Slide a thick spacer ring onto the top axle of the module.**

2. **Attach a cam to the two axles on the left side of the module.**

   The thick end of the cam goes onto the top axle.

Step 7

In this step, you add the two large beams that will serve as bumpers and lock the cam in place with a final pair of spacer rings, as shown in the *Constructopedia*.

1. **Add a pair of 11-hole double-angle beams to the axles protruding from the hinge.**

   Stick the beam onto the axle using the end hole of the long side of the beam. The long side of the beams should be perpendicular to the body of the bumper module with the short side of the beams angling back parallel to the body of the module.

2. **Add a thin spacer ring to the end of each axle sticking through the cam on the side of the module.**

Step 8

In this step, you attach the bumper module to the driving base, as shown in the *Constructopedia,* and attach a connector wire from the Touch Sensor to the input port on the RCX.

1. **Join the blue multi-hole connector block at the back end of the bumper module to its counterpart on the front end of the driving base using a double-connector peg.**

   Stick one end of a double-connector peg (the one that looks like yellow binoculars) into the pair of holes on the top of the blue multi-hole connector block on the front of the driving base. The other end of the double-connector peg goes into the bottom holes of the multi-hole connector block at the rear of the bumper module.

2. **Plug the connector wire from the bumper module's Touch Sensor into input port 1 on the RCX.**

Congratulations, you just finished building the RoverBot. With the construction phase complete, you can go on to the programming phase of robot development. See Chapters 8 and 9 for information about developing programs on your computer and downloading and running those programs on your robot. Chapter 10 contains an assortment of sample programs especially suited for use with the RoverBot.

InventorBot

The InventorBot is a strange-looking little dude that offers an interesting alternative to the typical wheeled robot. The InventorBot, shown in Figure 5-10, stands upright on a base that's motorized, allowing the robot to turn its body. One arm includes a Touch Sensor, and the other arm tips the InventorBot's hat politely.

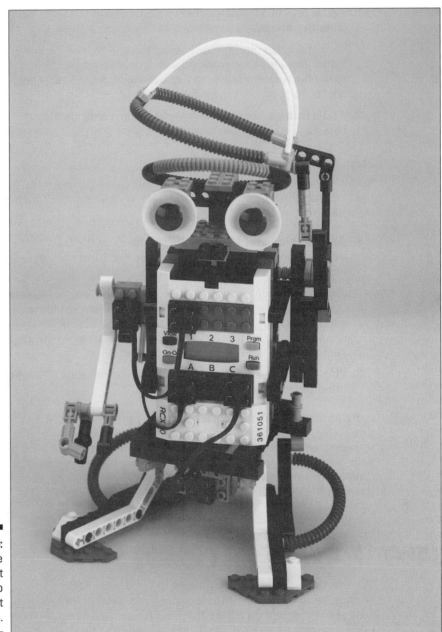

Figure 5-10:
The
InventorBot
with a slap
arm and hat
arm.

The InventorBot is composed of several modules:

- **Body:** In addition to the RCX microprocessor brick, the body module includes a motor to power the InventorBot's moving arm.

- **Standing base:** Holds the InventorBot body upright and includes a separate motor to rotate the robot's body on the base.

- **Head:** A decorative module that gives the robot some personality. The *Constructopedia* includes instructions for adding an optional Light Sensor to the head.

- **Right arm:** Includes a Touch Sensor. The *Constructopedia* offers two alternative arms:

    - **Slap arm:** Triggers robot actions when you give the InventorBot five. This is the option we chose to build for this book.

    - **Squeeze arm:** Squeeze the robot's hand to trigger the Touch Sensor.

- **Left arm:** The motorized arm gets its power from a motor in the body module. You can choose from two different arm configurations shown in the *Constructopedia:*

    - **Hat arm:** Holds a hat above the InventorBot head and tips the hat on command from your program. This is the arm we chose to build in this book.

    - **Thrower arm:** A simple spring-loaded arm that can catapult tires and other small objects across the room.

Building the body

The central core of the InventorBot is the body module (shown in Figure 5-11), which contains the RCX microprocessor brick. Basically, it's just a framework attached to the back of the RCX that houses a motor and gear train to power the left arm. The body module also provides attachment points for the other modules that make up the InventorBot. The *Constructopedia* drawings show the body module lying on its back as viewed from the robot's right side. In other words, you're looking at the module with its back lying on the table, its top to your left, its bottom to your right, and its right side closest to you.

Step 1

Start the body module by joining two perforated blocks with a pair of connector pegs, as shown in the *Constructopedia*.

Figure 5-11:
The
InventorBot
body
module.

1. **Insert a regular connector peg and a long connector peg into holes in the side of a 1x12 perforated block.**

   Insert the regular connector peg into the second hole from the bottom end of the 1x12 block. The peg sticks out to the right. Insert the short end of a long connector peg into the third hole from the end of the 1x12 block, beside the regular connector peg.

2. **Add a 1x4 perforated block to the module.**

   The middle hole of the 1x4 block goes over the long connector peg, and the bottom end hole fits over the regular connector peg.

Step 2

In this step, you use a 2x2 plate to attach a 1x2 perforated block to the other side of the long block, as shown in the *Constructopedia*.

1. **Stack a 1x2 perforated block on a 2x2 plate.**

2. **Snap the plate to the bottom of the 1x12 block.**

   The 1x2 block sits on the opposite side of the module from the 1x4 block. The hole in the 1x2 block aligns with the middle hole of the 1x12 block.

Step 3

In this step, you add a small plate and two axles with gears to the module, as shown in the *Constructopedia*.

1. **Add a 2x2 plate to the top of the module.**

   The plate attaches the 1x2 block to the 1x12 block.

2. **Stick a 12-tooth half-bevel gear on the end of a size 4 axle and insert the axle into the middle hole of the module.**

   The gear teeth go at the tip of the axle. Insert the axle into the 1x2 block and out the other side.

3. **Slide an 8-tooth gear onto a size 8 axle and insert the axle into the module.**

   Slide the gear to about the center of the axle. Insert the axle into the fourth hole from the top of the long block (the opposite end from the 1x4 block). Insert the axle from the left side of the module.

Step 4

In this step, you add gears to each of the axles and attach a small side-tab plate to the top of the module, as shown in the *Constructopedia*.

1. **Slide an 8-tooth gear onto the size 4 axle in the middle of the module.**

2. **Slide a 24-tooth clutch gear onto the size 8 axle.**

   The gear goes onto the right end of the axle and meshes with the 8-tooth gear you just added to the shorter axle.

3. **Attach a 1x2 side-tab plate to the front of the long block just below the 2x2 plate.**

Step 5

In this step, you add a long block to the left side of the module, as shown in the *Constructopedia*.

1. **Attach a 1x12 perforated block to the right side of the module.**

   The block snaps onto the long connector peg protruding from the shorter block. The end of the longer axle goes into the fourth hole from the top of the block.

Step 6

In this step, you add a pair of connector pegs to the right side of the module and stack some plates on the front, as shown in the *Constructopedia*.

1. **Stack a 1x2 plate on a 2x2 plate.**

2. **Stack another 2x2 plate on the remaining pegs of the lower 2x2 plate.**

3. **Add the stacked plates to the front of the module.**

   The plates span across the two longer blocks and mate with the 1x2 side-tab plate.

4. **Insert the short ends of two long connector pegs into the right side of the module.**

   One peg goes into the third hold down from the top (just above the long axle). The other peg goes into the fourth hole up from the bottom (just above the long connector peg and centered behind the plates across the front).

Step 7

In this step, you stack three small plates and attach them to the back of the module, as shown in the *Constructopedia*. Note that the *Constructopedia* shows the module turned over with the back side facing up, so that you can see where to place the plates.

1. **Stack a 1x2 side-tab plate on a 2x2 plate.**

2. **Stack another 2x2 plate on the remaining pegs of the lower 2x2 plate.**

3. **Attach the stack plates to the back of the module.**

   The plates sit directly behind a similar stack of plates on the front surface of the module. The side tab sticks out on the left side of the module immediately behind the corresponding piece on the front.

Step 8

In this step, you add another axle assembly with a gear to the module and position a motor with an attached gear, as shown in the *Constructopedia*. Note that the *Constructopedia* drawing shows the module back in its original orientation.

1. **Insert a size 6 axle into one end of a short pipe section.**

2. **Add a thick spacer ring and a 24-tooth hat gear to the axle.**

   Push the spacer ring and the gear all the way down the axle. The gear teeth should point toward the pipe section.

3. **Insert the axle and gear assembly into the module.**

   Insert the axle from the left side of the module. It goes in the second hole from the top of the module. The gear teeth should mesh with the 8-tooth gear on the adjacent axle.

4. **Add a 12-tooth half bevel gear to the shaft of a motor.**

5. Add the motor to the left side of the assembly.

The small tabs on the side of the module go into the slots on the side of the motor. The shaft end of the motor sticks up toward the top of the module so that the gear on the motor shaft meshes with the gear on the axle in the middle hole of the module.

Take a good look at the gear train of the InventorBot body module. First, the bevel gears change the axis of rotation 90 degrees. Then the gear train goes through two sets of step-up transitions with an eight-tooth gear driving a 24-tooth gear. As a result, the axle at the top of the module turns much slower than the motor driving it.

Step 9

In this step, you build another side piece and add it to the left side of the module, as shown in the *Constructopedia*.

1. Stack a 1x2 plate on a 1x2 side-tab plate and add it to the front of a 1x12 perforated block; add another 1x2 side-tab plate to the back of the block.

The plates go on the fourth and fifth pegs from the bottom of the block, with the tabs sticking out to the right side.

2. Insert the short ends of two long connector pegs into the left side of the 1x12 block.

One peg goes into the third hole down from the top, and the other goes into the fourth hole up from the bottom of the block.

3. Add the assembly to the left side of the body module.

The tabs from the plates go into slots on the left side of the motor, and the long axle from the module goes into the fourth hole down from the top of the left-side block.

Step 10

In this step, you add a pair of long plates to the back of the module and stack pairs of 1x1 plates on the top end ends of the module, as shown in the *Constructopedia*. Also attach one end of a connector wire to the motor.

1. Stack two 1x1 plates on the peg at the top end of each 1x12 block.

2. Add a 1x8 plate across the other end of the three 1x12 blocks.

3. Add another 1x8 plate across the back of the three 1x12 blocks.

4. Attach one end of a short connector wire to the motor.

The wire should extend out above the motor shaft and then bend to lead off to the right side of the module.

Step 11

In this step, you build up the module with a series of blocks, as shown in the *Constructopedia.*

1. **Stack a 1x2 perforated block on a 1x2 plate and insert a regular connector peg into the hole in the block.**

2. **Add the plate/block/peg assembly to the module.**

    The assembly mounts onto the 2x2 plate near the center of the module. The assembly sits on the upper pegs of the plate with the peg sticking down over the lower pegs. The connector wire from the motor runs under the peg.

3. **Add a 2x4 block to the front of the module.**

    One end of the block sits on a pair of pegs on the motor, just to the right of the connector wire. The block extends over to the right side of the module.

4. **Add a 2x2 block to the front of the module on the other side of the motor.**

5. **Add a 1x2 perforated block on each of the lower-front corners of the module.**

    The blocks go on either end of the 1x8 plate across the front of the bottom end of the module.

6. **Add a green 1x2 X-hole block to the middle of the plate between the two corner blocks.**

Step 12

In this step, you add another block and a couple of additional plates to the top of the module, as shown in the *Constructopedia.*

1. **Stack a 2x2 plate on the connector wire plate on the motor.**

2. **Add a 1x8 perforated block across the small stacked plates at the top ends of the three long blocks.**

3. **Add a 1x8 plate across the three 1x2 blocks at the bottom end of the module.**

Step 13

In this step, you add the RCX microprocessor to the module and stick four connector pegs into the sides of the RCX, as shown in the *Constructopedia.*

1. **Mount the RCX on the front of the module.**

Position the RCX on the front of the module with the bottom end of the RCX over the motor and the top end of the RCX over the gears. Press the RCX down firmly so that the pegs from the blocks and plates on the module fit into the holes in the back of the RCX.

2. **Insert the short end of a short connector peg into each of the four holes in the sides of the RCX.**

Step 14

In this step, you lock the RCX to the module with four beams and a pair of perforated blocks, as shown in the *Constructopedia*. You also plug the connector wire from the motor into an output port on the RCX.

1. **Add a pair of 7-hole beams to each side of the module.**

   One end of the beam goes on the peg beside the RCX's input port, and the other end of the beam goes on the corresponding long peg sticking out of the side of the module. Stack two beams on each side of the module.

   Slip one end of the beam onto the long connector peg first and then slip the other end of the beam over the shorter connector peg in the side of the RCX.

2. **Attach a 1x8 perforated block to the lower pair of pegs on each side of the module.**

   These blocks go on the pegs on either side of the RCX's output ports. The pegs on the blocks go up, toward the top of the module.

3. **Attach the connector wire from the motor to output port A on the front of the RCX.**

This completes the construction of the InventorBot body module.

Building the standing base

The InventorBot's standing base module, shown in Figure 5-12, provides a platform that holds the body module upright. But the standing base module is more than just a simple platform — it's a motorized turntable that enables the InventorBot to pivot and turn its body on the base. As a result, the standing base module includes a motor, gears, and pulleys.

The standing base module is composed of two subassemblies: the platform and the legs. You build the two subassemblies separately and then assemble them into the completed standing base module. Finally, you add the InventorBot body module to the standing base module.

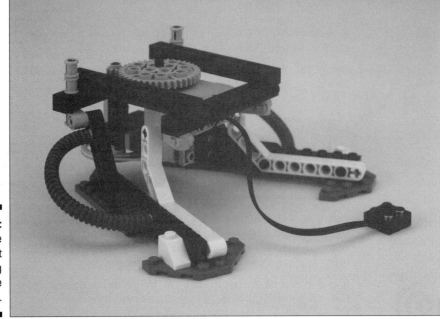

Figure 5-12:
The
InventorBot
standing
base
module.

Building the standing base platform

The standing base module's platform subassembly, shown in Figure 5-13, contains the motor and gear train that enable the InventorBot to pivot from side to side. The *Constructopedia* drawings for the platform subassembly show an unusual view of the assembly resting on its back and viewed from the bottom and slightly from the right side. This perspective provides a reasonably good view of the way the parts fit together, but makes it harder to visualize how the assembly relates to the finished robot. In contrast, Figure 5-12 shows the standing base module from the right-front corner, and Figure 5-13 shows the platform subassembly from the left-rear corner. You may want to view the module from different angles during construction in order to keep it properly oriented in your mind.

Step 1

You start building the platform subassembly by attaching a long block and a short block to a plate, as shown in the *Constructopedia*.

1. **Attach a 1x12 perforated block to a 2x4 plate.**

   Center the block on the end pegs of the plate. The 1x12 block becomes the upper-back side of the platform subassembly.

2. **Add a 1x4 perforated block, centered on the other end of the 2x4 plate.**

Figure 5-13:
The
InventorBot
motorized
standing
base
platform.

3. **Insert two regular connector pegs into the 1x12 block.**

   The pegs go into the second hole from each end of the block and stick out on the opposite side from the plate and the shorter block. The pegs stick up toward the top of the module and the plate, and the 1x4 block sticks down toward the bottom.

Step 2

In this step, you add two blocks and two plates to the assembly, as shown in the *Constructopedia.*

1. **Stack a 1x4 perforated block and a 1x4 plate onto the existing 1x4 block.**

2. **Stack another 1x4 perforated block on the center pegs of the 1x12 block and top it with another 1x4 plate.**

Step 3

In this step, you build a gear and axle unit supported by a pair of blocks and add the unit to the subassembly, as shown in the *Constructopedia.*

1. **Insert an axle-end connector peg into the center hole of a 1x4 perforated block.**

2. **Stick a short pipe section onto the peg and insert a size 4 axle into the other end of the pipe.**

3. **Slide the center hole of another 1x4 perforated block over the axle.**

4. **Press a 40-tooth gear onto the axle.**

5. **Mount the resulting unit onto the subassembly by stacking the 1x4 blocks onto the stacked blocks and plates of the subassembly.**

   The large gear sticks out over the long block at the top of the subassembly.

Step 4

In this step, you mount a motor onto the assembly, as shown in the *Constructopedia*.

1. **Push a thin spacer ring onto the motor shaft.**

2. **Snap a 1x4 plate onto each side of the bottom of the motor.**

3. **Mount the motor onto the stacked blocks of the assembly.**

   The plates on the bottom of the motor span across the two stacks of blocks so that the shaft of the motor is parallel to the axle supporting the gear. The motor shaft sticks out toward the bottom of the assembly, opposite the gear.

Step 5

In this step, you add a block (with a pair of connector pegs inserted) to the top of the motor and add an axle with attached fittings to each end of the long block at the back of the assembly, as shown in the *Constructopedia*.

1. **Attach a 1x10 perforated block to the top of the motor.**

   The block is centered across the pegs at the back end of the motor. This block becomes the top-front edge of the platform subassembly.

2. **Insert a long connector peg into each end of the block.**

   Insert the long ends of the pegs from the bottom so that they stick up through the top of the block.

3. **Slide two thick spacer rings onto one end of a size 4 axle.**

4. **Stick the axle through the end hole of the 1x12 block and cap the axle with a mid-axle tee.**

   Insert the axle from the gear-side of the assembly.

5. **Repeat Steps 3 and 4 at the other end of the block.**

Step 6

In this step, you add a pair of 1x10 blocks to complete the framework of the subassembly, as shown in the *Constructopedia.* You also add a belt and pulley to the assembly.

1. **Add a pair of 1x10 blocks to the top (gear side) of the assembly.**

   Each block spans the space between a connector peg on the 1x12 block and a connector peg in the end of the 1x10 block on top of the motor. These blocks become the left and right side pieces of the platform subassembly.

2. **Insert a size 6 axle into a single-spoke pulley.**

3. **Add the pulley to the assembly.**

   Insert the axle into the end hole of the 1x4 block at the back of the stacked blocks at the shaft end of the motor.

4. **Stretch a yellow belt (rubber band) over the single-spoke pulley and the thin spacer ring on the motor shaft.**

Step 7

In this step, you add a small gear and a connector wire to the assembly, as shown in the *Constructopedia.* The *Constructopedia* drawing for this step shows the platform subassembly in a more normal orientation — resting on its bottom and viewed from the right-front corner — so you can see the top of the assembly.

1. **Slip an 8-tooth gear onto the opposite end of the pulley axle.**

   The gear should mesh with the 40-tooth gear.

2. **Attach one end of a short connector wire to the motor.**

   The wire trails back over the top of the motor but is deflected by the block across the top of the motor.

This completes the platform subassembly of the InventorBot standing base module.

Notice the gear train that's incorporated into the InventorBot's standing base module. The small pulley on the motor drives a much larger pulley, thus reducing the speed of rotation. The belt and pulley arrangement also creates a certain amount of slip that acts like a clutch when the body module reaches the limit of its rotation. The small gear mounted on the other end of the axle from the pulley drives a 40-tooth gear, which reduces the rotation speed even more.

Building the standing base legs

The standing base legs subassembly, shown in Figure 5-14, provides a foundation for the platform subassembly and the rest of the InventorBot robot. The colorful pieces in the legs also help to enhance the InventorBot's appearance. The *Constructopedia* drawings show the pair of legs as viewed from the left-front corner. In the first few drawings, the legs appear to sit parallel to each other although they sit at an angle when installed on the platform to complete the standing base module.

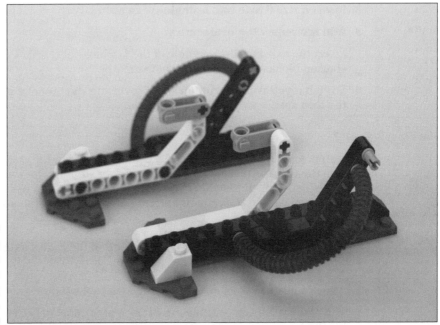

Figure 5-14:
The
InventorBot
standing
base legs.

The instructions in this section describe how to build the left leg of the InventorBot standing base leg subassembly. To make the right leg, repeat the instructions, but reverse any right/left references.

Step 1

To start, you build the foot section of the subassembly, as shown in the *Constructopedia*.

1. **Attach a 1x12 perforated block to a green 2x8 plate.**

   The block sits on the plate lengthwise on the right side of the plate. Leave two pegs of the plate open behind the end of the block.

2. **Add a 1x1 wedge block to the plate at the end of the 1x12 block.**

3. **Snap the other end of the 1x12 block onto a 3x6 triangular plate.**

   The long side of the triangular plate goes perpendicular to the 2x8 plate. The block attaches to two pegs to the left of center on the plate.

4. **Insert two regular connector pegs into the right side of the 1x12 block.**

   Pegs go into the front hole (the end over the triangular plate) and the middle hole.

5. **Insert three regular connector pegs into the left side of the 1x12 block.**

   Pegs go into the third, fifth, and seventh holes from the back end.

Step 2

In this step, you add leg and toe pieces to the foot, as shown in the *Constructopedia*.

1. **Add a yellow 1x1 wedge block to the triangular plate, just to the left of the end of the long block.**

2. **Add a 9-hole angled beam to the leg.**

   Attach the short side of the beam to the left side of the 1x12 block by slipping it onto the back two pegs on the left side of the block. The long side of the beam sticks up and back.

3. **Insert two connector pegs into the left side of the angled beam.**

   Insert an axle-end connector peg into the end hole of the beam's long arm. Insert a regular connector peg into the adjacent hole.

Step 3

In this step, you add a double angle beam to the leg, as shown in the *Constructopedia*.

1. **Attach an 11-hole double-angle beam to the right side of the leg.**

   The long side of the beam attaches to the pegs protruding from the right side of the 1x12 block. The short side of the beam sticks up near the center of the leg assembly.

2. **Insert a size 2 axle into the end hole of the beam's short side.**

   The axle should stick out to the right side.

Step 4

In this step, you add a tee and a length of flexible tubing to the assembly, as shown in the *Constructopedia*.

1. **Attach a long mid-axle tee to the axle in the end of the double-angle beam.**

   The tee goes parallel to the 1x12 block and sticks forward.

2. **Attach a piece of purple flexible tubing to the left side of the leg assembly.**

   Stick one end of the tubing onto the peg in the second hole of the angled beam. Stick the other end of the tubing onto the peg in the 1x12 block, just ahead of the angled beam.

Step 5

In this step, you attach the leg to the standing base platform subassembly, as shown in the *Constructopedia*.

1. **Slip the hole in the long connector peg (the one at the top of the yellow beam) onto the peg in the corner of the platform.**

   Position the platform so that the big gear is on the top and the pulley is on the bottom in the back. The peg you need is sticking out of the bottom of the left front corner of the platform.

2. **Snap the tee at the back-left corner of the platform onto the peg sticking out of the top end of the black angled beam of the leg.**

3. **Repeat the process to attach the right leg to the other side of the platform.**

Step 6

In this step, you mount the body module onto the standing base module, as shown in the *Constructopedia*.

1. **Seat the body module onto the tip of the axle sticking up through the large gear on top of the standing base module.**

   The hole in the green block in the middle of the bottom end of the body module fits onto the axle. Position the front of the RCX toward the front of the standing base module.

2. **Connect the wire from the motor in the standing base to output port C on the RCX.**

   The wire should trail down to the bottom of the RCX.

Figure 5-15 shows the InventorBot body module mounted on the standing base module.

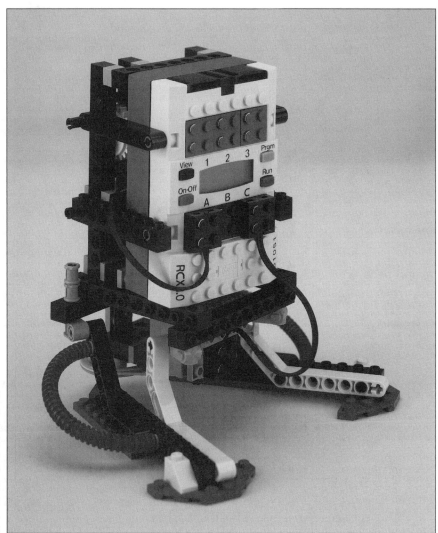

Figure 5-15:
The
InventorBot
with the
body
mounted on
the standing
base.

Building the head

The InventorBot head is mostly decorative, although the head does provide a suitable home for the optional Light Sensor, should you decide to install one. Even without the Light Sensor, the head, shown in Figure 5-16, looks like it should be able to see with those big eyes. The *Constructopedia* drawings show the head module as viewed from the right-front corner.

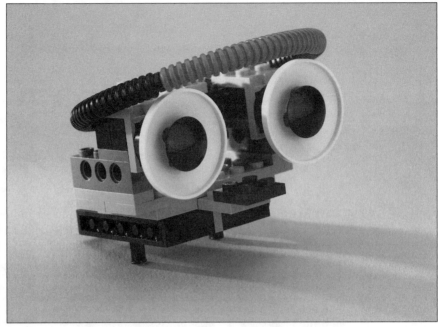

Figure 5-16:
The
InventorBot
head
module.

Step 1

Start building the head by laying three plates side by side, as shown in the *Constructopedia*.

1. **Lay a 2x4 perforated plate on either side of a 2x6 perforated plate.**

   The back ends of all three plates should be flush.

Step 2

Add a pair of 2x8 plates going across the module and add a 1x2 plate on the back edge, as shown in the *Constructopedia*.

1. **Lay two 2x8 plates across the first three plates.**

   The 2x8 plates stick out one peg width at each end because the plates are longer than the assembled module is wide. The plates are flush with the back edge, and the longer base plate sticks out two pegs in the front.

2. **Add a 1x2 plate to the module.**

   The plate stacks atop the back 2x8 plate, centered on the back edge.

Step 3

In this step, you add two plates and a pair of wedge blocks to the module, as shown in the *Constructopedia*.

1. Add two 1x4 plates across the ends of the 2x8 plates you added in Step 2.

2. Add a pair of 1x2 reverse wedge blocks to the module.

The wedge blocks sit side by side atop the 1x2 plate, with the wide part of the wedge going up and back.

Step 4

In this step, you add a pair of blocks and several plates to the module, as shown in the *Constructopedia*.

1. Stack a 1x4 perforated block atop the 1x4 plate at each side of the module.

Use the green 1x4 blocks.

2. Add a 2x2 plate atop each 1x4 perforated block.

The plate sits on the front two pegs of the block with the unsupported portion of the plate extending inward, toward the center of the module. Use the green 2x2 plates.

3. Stack a 2x2 plate atop the pair of wedge blocks at the rear of the module.

4. Add a blue 2x2 plate to the front of the module.

The plate mounts onto the front two pegs of the plate sticking out of the front of the module. The 2x2 plate sticks out another peg width to the front.

Step 5

In this step, you add five blocks and a pair of pegs to the top of the module, as shown in the *Constructopedia*.

1. Stack a pair of 1x2 perforated blocks atop the wedges and plates at the rear of the module.

The holes in the blocks go to the sides of the unit.

2. Insert a regular connector peg into each of the 1x2 blocks you just added.

3. Add a 1x2 solid block to each front corner of the module.

The blocks sit atop the green 2x2 plates, parallel to the front edge of the module.

4. Add a 1x8 perforated block to the top of the unit.

The block goes across the module, just behind the two 1x2 blocks you just added, spanning from one green plate to the other.

Step 6

In this step, you add two 1x4 plates and a pair of 2x2 corner bracket plates to the module, as shown in the *Constructopedia*.

1. **Add two 1x4 plates to the top of the module.**

   The plates span the gap between the blocks stacked atop the wedges at the rear of the module and the 1x8 block going across the middle of the module.

2. **Add a 2x2 corner bracket plate to each front corner of the module.**

   The 2x2 plate portion of the pieces sits atop the blocks at the front corners of the module. The pieces hang down in front of the module corners.

Step 7

In this step, you add a pair of round blocks and a pair of flexible tubes to the module, as shown in the *Constructopedia*.

1. **Attach a 2x2 round block to each front corner of the module.**

   The pegs of the round blocks snap into the vertical portion of the 2x2 corner bracket plates at each corner.

2. **Attach a pair of black flexible tubes to the module.**

   Stick one end of a black flexible tube over the peg protruding from the side of the block at the rear of the module. Stick a regular connector peg into the other end of the tube. Do the same on the other side of the module.

Step 8

In this step, you add the eyes to the front of the module and add another section of flexible tube to create a forehead, all shown in the *Constructopedia*.

1. **Attach a large white 1-peg disk to each of the round blocks at the front corners of the module.**

2. **Add a small black 1-peg disk to the center of each large disk.**

3. **Bend the black flexible tube pieces around to the front of the module and join them with a section of teal-green flexible tubing.**

Step 9

In this step, you build a mounting bracket for the head module and attach it to the underside of the module, as shown in the *Constructopedia*. The *Constructopedia* drawing shows the head module turned upside down so that you're viewing the bottom of the module from the lower left-front corner.

1. Stack a 1x2 block on one end of a 1x6 perforated block.

2. Add a 1x2 plate and another 1x2 block atop the 1x2 block you just added.

3. Add another 1x6 perforated block to the top of the stack and insert a pair of regular connector pegs into the unit.

   The 1x6 block sits atop the stack of blocks mirroring the bottom 1x6 block. The connector pegs go into the end holes of the two 1x6 blocks on either side of the stacked blocks.

4. Attach the unit to the bottom of the head module.

   The pegs on the unit snap into holes in the perforated plates that form the bottom of the head module. The stacked blocks go under the front edge of the module, and the 1x6 perforated blocks point toward the rear of the module.

5. Insert a regular connector peg into the middle hole of each of the 1x6 perforated blocks.

Step 10

In this step, you mount the head module on top of the InventorBot body module, as shown in the *Constructopedia*.

1. Attach the head module to the body by inserting the pegs on the bottom of the head into the holes in the perforated block at the top of the body.

   Be sure to center the head on the body.

Figure 5-17 shows the InventorBot, complete with its base, body, and head. Now the robot is ready to receive your choice of arms.

Building the hat arm

We chose to build the hat arm for the version of the InventorBot described in this book. There's just something appealing about a robot that tips its hat. Besides, the hat arm module, shown in Figure 5-18, includes an interesting linkage to a cam that creates the hat-tipping motion. The first few drawings in the *Constructopedia* show the hat arm module as viewed from the left-rear so that you're looking at the back of the arm and "hat."

Step 1

Begin assembling the hat arm module by building a bracket unit, as shown in the *Constructopedia*. The bracket holds the robot's tubing "hat."

Figure 5-17:
The InventorBot head added to the body and standing base modules.

1. **Place a size 4 axle into one end of a number 5 elbow.**

2. **Slip the hole of a mid-axle tee over the axle.**

   The tee sticks out in the opposite direction from the elbow.

3. **Stick the axle through the hole in the end of the long side of a 5-hole L-beam.**

   Position the beam so that the short arm points down. Insert the axle from the front side of the beam so that the elbow points away from the L-beam.

4. **Add another number 5 elbow to the end of the axle.**

   Position the elbow to mirror the elbow on the other end of the axle.

Step 2

In this step, you insert connector pegs into the elbows and tee, as shown in the *Constructopedia*.

1. **Insert axle-end connector pegs into the ends of the number 5 elbows.**

2. **Insert button-end connector pegs into the holes in the number 5 elbows.**

   Insert the pegs from the top.

3. **Insert an axle-end connector peg into the tee.**

   Insert the peg from the top.

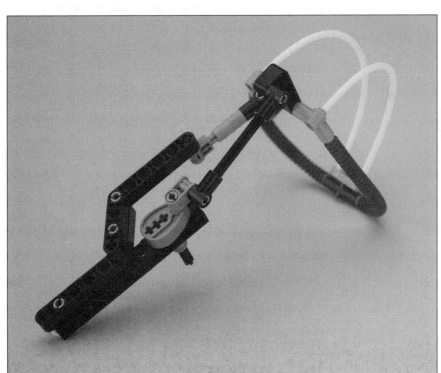

Figure 5-18:
The InventorBot hat arm module.

Step 3

In this step, you build the hat brim unit and attach it to the module, as shown in the *Constructopedia*.

1. **Insert an axle-end connector peg into each end of a number 2 elbow and a short connector peg into the center hole of the elbow.**

2. **Add two purple flexible tubes and a 3-hole beam to the unit.**

   Stick one end of a purple flexible tube onto the connector peg at each end of the elbow. Snap the center hole of the 3-hole beam onto the peg in the center hole of the elbow.

3. **Add the hat brim unit to the hat arm module.**

   Bend the ends of the two flexible tubes around and attach them to the pegs sticking out from the two number 5 elbows. Make sure the short beam on the hat brim unit is on the top.

Step 4

In this step, you build two linkage units and attach them to the module, as shown in the *Constructopedia*. Also add a pair of flexible tubes to serve as the crown of the robot's hat.

1. **Insert a size 2 axle into the end of a number 1 elbow.**

2. **Add a short pipe section to the other end of the axle.**

3. **Insert an axle-end tee into the other end of the pipe.**

   Make sure the holes in the tee and the elbow are parallel.

4. **Insert another size 2 axle into the tee.**

5. **Attach the upper linkage unit you just built to the module.**

   The hole in the number 1 elbow at the end of the unit slips onto the peg sticking out of the tee beside the L-beam. The axle at the other end of the unit should point up.

6. **Stick a number 1 elbow on each end of a size 6 axle.**

   Align the elbows so that the holes are parallel.

7. **Insert a regular connector peg into the hole in one of the elbows.**

8. **Attach the lower linkage unit you just built to the module.**

   The connector peg in the elbow goes into the hole in the end of the short arm of the L-beam. The linkage attaches from the rear of the module (the opposite side from the tee where the upper linkage attaches.)

9. **Install two pieces of yellow flexible tubing, arching across the top of the module.**

Insert one end of a tube into the button-end connector peg in one of the number 5 elbows. Insert the other end of the tube into one of the end holes of the 3-hole beam on the other side of the hat brim. Do the same with the other piece of yellow tube.

Step 5

In this step, you build the arm portion of the hat arm module and attach it to the linkages from the rest of the module, as shown in the *Constructopedia*. The *Constructopedia* drawing for this step shows the hat arm module lying on its back, as viewed from the top-left corner.

1. **Insert a pair of connector pegs and an axle into the holes in a 1x10 perforated block.**

   The connector pegs go into the bottom and middle holes of the block. Insert them from the left side. Slide two thin spacer rings to the middle of a size 5 axle. Insert the axle into the next-to-top hole from the right side of the block.

2. **Add two cam pieces and an axle-end connector peg to the module.**

   Stack the two cam pieces together so they work as a single unit. Push the center hole of the cams onto the left end of the axle sticking out of the block. Insert the axle-end connector peg into the hole in the narrow end of the cams.

3. **Add a 9-hole angle beam and a pair of connector pegs to the module.**

   The long arm of the beam attaches to the connector pegs sticking out of the left side of the long block. The angled arm of the beam sticks up and forward beside the cam. Insert two connector pegs into the short arm of the angled beam. An axle-end connector peg goes into the end hole. A regular connector peg goes into the hole next to the corner of the beam.

4. **Snap another 9-hole angled beam onto the left side of the module and add a tee to the cams.**

   The short arm of the new angled beam attaches to the short arm of the existing angled beam so that the long arm of the new beam extends off above the cam and parallel to the 1x10 block. Insert an axle-end connector peg into a mid-axle tee and attach it to the module. The tee attaches to the connector peg in the cams. The connector peg in the tee should point down or to the rear, but not up or to the front.

5. **Attach the linkages from the hat portion of the arm module to the arm unit you just built.**

   The axle in the end of the upper linkage goes into the hole in the top end of the angled beam on the arm. The connector peg in the tee connector on the cam goes into the hole in the elbow at the end of the lower linkage.

Step 6

In this step, you attach the hat arm module to the left side of the InventorBot, as shown in the *Constructopedia*. The *Constructopedia* drawing for this step shows yet another view, this time from the left side of the robot.

1. **Snap the hat arm module onto the connector pegs extending from the left side of the body module.**

   The axle from the cams in the arm module goes through the second hole from the top of the long perforated block at the back of the body and goes into the end of the pipe section on the other side of the block. This axle connects the hat-lifting mechanism of the arm to the drive train in the body module.

Figure 5-19 shows the courteous little InventorBot with its hat arm installed.

Building the slap arm

The InventorBot slap arm, shown in Figure 5-20, enables you to initiate behaviors by triggering the Touch Sensor built into the arm. So when you slap five with the InventorBot, the robot can respond. The *Constructopedia* drawings show the slap arm lying on its back, and the view is from the upper-right corner, looking down the outside of the arm.

Step 1

Start building the slap arm by inserting three axles into a 5-hole corner beam, as shown in *Constructopedia.*

1. **Insert a size 2 axle into the corner hole of a 5-hole corner beam.**

2. **Slide a thick spacer ring onto the middle of a size 5 axle and insert one end of the axle into the end hole of the beam.**

   Hold the beam so that the short axle sticks out of the left side of the beam and the arms of the beam stick down and away from you. (The part that sticks down is pointing toward the back of the module.) Insert the longer axle into the back hole from the left side.

3. **Stick a thin spacer ring onto the end of a size 6 axle and insert the axle into the other end of the beam from the right side.**

   Push the axle all the way through so that most of the axle length is sticking out on the left side of the beam.

Step 2

In this step, you add a 1x10 perforated block and another 5-hole corner beam to the module, as shown in the *Constructopedia.*

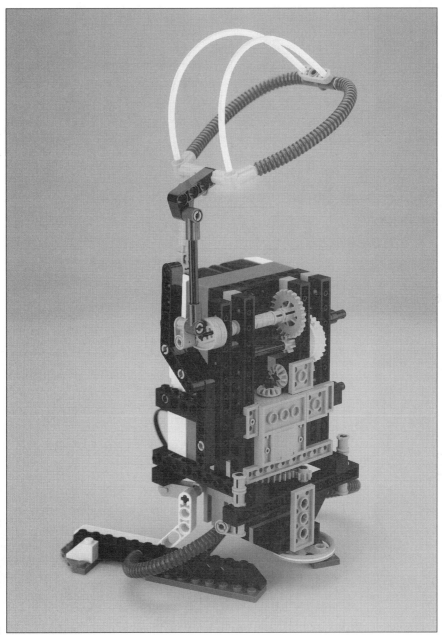

Figure 5-19:
The
InventorBot
with the hat
arm module
installed.

1. **Slide the top two axles through the holes on either side of the middle hole of a 1x10 perforated block.**

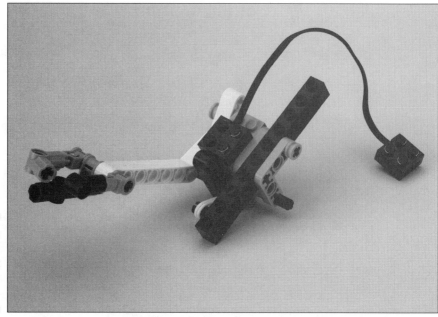

Figure 5-20:
The
InventorBot
slap arm
module.

2. **Add another 5-hole corner beam to the left side of the module.**

   Position the beam so that it engages all three axles and mirrors the beam on the other side of the module.

Step 3

In this step, you add a Touch Sensor and a 5-hole L-beam to the module, as shown in the *Constructopedia*.

1. **Slide a thin spacer ring onto the back axle.**

2. **Insert two regular connector pegs into a 5-hole L-beam and slide the beam onto the back axle.**

   Hold the beam so that the long side points up (toward the front of the module) and the short side points away from you (up). Insert a connector peg in the corner hole of the beam from the right side. Insert a connector peg from the left into the adjacent hole of the long side of the beam. Slide the hole in the short end of the beam over the axle.

3. **Insert a regular connector peg into the bottom hole of the 1x10 perforated block.**

   Insert the peg from the left side.

4. **Mount a Touch Sensor onto the module.**

Slide the hole through the Touch Sensor onto the long axle sticking out of the module. The Touch Sensor mounts parallel to the 1x10 block. The business end of the Touch Sensor (the yellow button) points down toward the bottom end of the module.

Step 4

In this step, you continue building the slap arm module by adding a spacer ring to lock the L-beam in place and spring-load the trigger with a couple of white rubber bands, as shown in the _Constructopedia_. Also add a connector wire to the Touch Sensor.

1. **Stick a thin spacer ring onto the end of the back axle.**

2. **Stretch a pair of white rubber bands between the connector peg in the corner hole of the L-beam and the connector peg in the end hole of the 1x10 block.**

3. **Attach one end of a short connector wire to the connections on top of the Touch Sensor.**

    The wire trails off over the back end of the sensor.

Step 5

In this step, you build the lower arm and hand portion of the slap arm module and add it to the rest of the module, as shown in the _Constructopedia_. The _Constructopedia_ drawings for this step show the lower arm as viewed along the outer (right) side of the arm from the fingers (pointing to the left on the page) up toward the elbow (on the right). The underside of the arm is up. The following instructions assume the perspective of holding the arm at the wrist with the fingers toward you and the bend of the elbow pointing down.

1. **Add a size 4 axle and two tees to the end of the long side of an 11-hole double-angled beam.**

    Stick the axle through the end hole of the long side of the beam. Holding the beam so that the long side points toward you and the short side points down, slide a mid-axle tee onto the axle on the right side so that the hole in the tee sticks up. Slide the cross portion of an end-axle tee onto the other end of the axle so that the open end of the tee points toward you.

2. **Add another tee along with axles and a connector peg to the end of the unit.**

    Add another end-axle tee to the right end of the axle. Make sure it points toward you, parallel to the tee on the other end of the axle. Insert a size 2 axle into each of the end-axle tees. Insert an axle-end connector peg into the other tee at the end of the unit.

3. **Add three elbow pieces to the end of the unit to act as fingers on the slap arm hand.**

   Stick a number 5 elbow on the axle sticking out of the right-most tee. Angle the elbow to the left. Stick a number 2 elbow onto the connector peg that's sticking out of the adjacent tee. And stick a number 1 elbow on the tee at the right end of the axle.

4. **Add the lower arm unit to the rest of the module.**

   Slip the middle hole of the short arm of the beam over the axle sticking out through the Touch Sensor. Lock the beam in place with a thin spacer ring on the end of the axle. To match the *Constructopedia* drawing, start with the forearm parallel with the long block that forms the upper arm and pointed up toward the top of the module. After you attach the lower arm to the module, rotate the hand and arm down toward the bottom end of the module so that the midsection of the beam makes contact with the connector peg that is sticking out of the right side of the L-beam, which serves as the trigger for the Touch Sensor.

Step 6

In this step, you attach the slap arm module to the right side of the InventorBot's body module, as shown in the *Constructopedia*. The *Constructopedia* drawing for this step shows the InventorBot and the slap arm from the right-front corner. Note that the lower arm portion of the slap arm hangs in its natural position when you pick up the slap arm module and position it in the proper orientation beside the robot body.

1. **Snap the slap arm module into place on the connector pegs protruding from the back edge of the body module.**

   The connector pegs go into holes in the 1x10 perforated block of the slap arm module. The top end of the slap arm module should line up with the top end of the body module.

2. **Attach the connector wire from the Touch Sensor to input port 1 on the front of the RCX.**

This completes the construction steps for the InventorBot. Figure 5-21 shows the InventorBot with the slap arm installed. Tapping the slap arm causes the spring-loaded trigger to momentarily lose contact with the button that's in the end of the Touch Sensor. With the proper programming, the RCX can detect and respond to a change in input from the Touch Sensor.

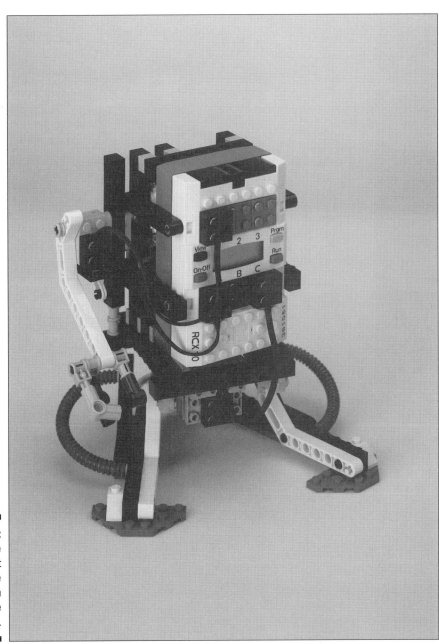

Figure 5-21:
The
InventorBot
with the
slap arm
module
installed.

Part III

Giving Your Bots Life through Programming

The 5th Wave   By Rich Tennant

Ever since I installed the "Dork Sensor," it won't leave my sister and her boyfriend alone.

In this part . . .

In this part, you find out how to make your robots move around and respond to changes in their environments — through programming. Whether you're selecting a predefined program on the Micro Scout microprocessor, doing some basic programming on the Scout microprocessor, or developing and downloading programs for the RCX microprocessor, you're giving your robot life!

Chapter 6

Scouting Out the Micro Scout

· ·

In This Chapter

▶ Exploring the face of the Micro Scout

▶ Running the built-in programs

· ·

*T*he Micro Scout sits at the heart of the robots that can be constructed from the Droid Developer Kit. The Micro Scout acts as the brains and power source for each robot.

You can build lots of different robots around the Micro Scout. The *Constructopedia* — the instruction book that comes with the Droid Developer Kit — contains pictures that help you build three different robots. Chapter 6 gives detailed instructions that go along with the *Constructopedia*.

Is It Really Programming?

The Micro Scout contains a bunch of programs so, in the strictest sense of the word, you don't have to do any programming to get your robots to move. However, you sort of program things by designing your robot to act and react in certain ways. That is, you build the robot so it will be controlled by the motor in the Micro Scout, and then you select a program that matches the sequence of activities you would like your robot to perform.

After you build your robot and hook its moving parts to the Micro Scout, your robot can respond to light, make noises, and move around. Exactly what your robot does depends on how you build it, and the way your robot does things depends on which of the seven programs you select.

How the Micro Scout responds to light

The Micro Scout has a light-sensitive eye (shown in the following figure) that's on the alert for a change in light. Inside the window is a readout that, when the Micro Scout is turned on, displays either a letter or a number. On each side of the display window, some little holes are used to emit the beeps and squeaks. Just below the display window are three buttons, labeled On-Off, Select, and Run, that are used to control your robot.

The eye can't really see things, but it can tell whether a light is shining on it. Each of the seven programs (covered in the "Playing With the Micro Scout Programs" section) responds to a change in the lighting in a different way. Some programs run the motor forward, some run it backward, some run it both ways, and some make noises.

If you're going to use a flashlight to control your robot, you need to make sure that the room isn't too bright and the robot doesn't run into the sunshine. The Micro Scout can't tell one light source from another and takes commands from a beam of sunlight just as well as it does from your flashlight.

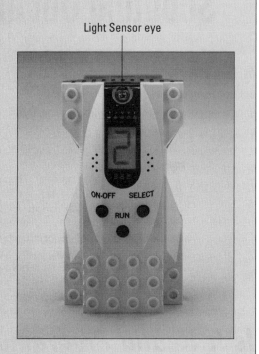

Light Sensor eye

The Programming Interface: Simplicity Itself

Three buttons control the robots in the Droid Development Kit.

- ✔ **The On-Off button powers up the robot.** When it first comes on, the letters L-E-G-O appear one after the other, and then a number from 1 through 7 or the letter P appears. The number that appears is the number of the program you ran last. The Micro Scout is ready to run the program number that's showing.

- ✔ **The Select button is used to switch from one program to another.** The robot can only be set to run one program at a time, and whenever the

Select button is pressed, the displayed program number changes. Each press of the Select button will cycle the program number from 1 to 7, then to P, then 1 to 7, and so on. If a program is already running, pressing the SELECT button stops it before switching to the next program number.

✔ **The Run button starts and stops the program.** You can tell when a program is running because the number in the window flashes. You can also tell a program is running because the little wheels turn and the robot scoots around the room. Press this button to start or stop the robot from running around.

The Run and Select buttons don't work unless you press the On-Off button first.

Playing with the Micro Scout Programs

Each of the eight programs makes your robot act a little different. Any of them can be used with any robot, but each one responds to the light in a different way.

✔ **Program 1 — One Direction:** When you first start this program, it makes a few beeps and starts the wheels turning. It puts the motor in reverse and backs up the robot for about five seconds, then stops and does it all over again. Then it does it one more time. After three short beeping serenades and three runs backward, the program stops.

If you build a robot that has its gears the other way round, the robot will go forward instead of backward. Also the R2-D2 Astromech Droid (covered in Chapter 3) has its power wheel on a swivel, so you really can't be sure which way it will go. If you remember in *Star Wars,* C-3PO had the same problem with R2-D2.

✔ **Program 2 — Two Directions:** This program is like Program 1 in that the robot performs a bit of beep song, takes off backward, stops to perform another song, and takes off again. The difference is that the second time, it takes off forward. It runs back and forth, singing between each run. In all, it goes backward three times and forward three times, with a little song between each run.

✔ **Program 3 — Seek Light:** With this program, the robot takes off backward. After about five seconds, it stops and beeps a couple of times and takes off again. As long as you don't flash a light on it, it backs up three times and the program stops running. If, at any point while it is backing away, however, you shine a light on it, it reverses direction and starts moving forward.

After it starts forward, the robot keeps moving forward as long as you shine the light on it. If you take the light off of it, the robot halts and starts backing up again. After it has backed up three times without going forward, the program stops, whether or not it has ever gone forward.

✔ **Program 4 — Light Control:** This program instructs the robot to move only when it can see a light. When you start the program, it sings a little beeping song and sits there waiting for some light. When it sees light, the robot starts running. When the light goes off, the robot stops. The robot does this just as long as you keep turning the light on and off.

The robot also understands a code. If you flash the light twice, the Micro Scout sings its little beeping song and reverses direction. If you flash the light twice again, it sings its song and reverses direction again. The robot keeps doing this as long as its batteries — and your batteries! — hold out.

✔ **Program 5 — Keep Alive:** When you start this program, the robot just sits there. Then, when you turn the light on, it still just sits there. But, when you turn the light off, it moves for just a second and stops. Each time you flash the light on and off, it moves for a second (or so). If you flash the light a bunch of times, it starts moving, keeps count of the flashes, and moves around one second for each flash. For example, if you flash the light five quick times, the robot will start moving on the first flash and continue to move for about five seconds.

You have to keep flashing the light to keep the robot alive. And a robot with a swiveled wheel, like R2-D2, turns its back on you so you may have to chase it around to keep it going.

✔ **Program 6 — Alarm:** This program starts with a couple of beeps and clicks and then sits and waits. It's waiting for a change in the light. When the light changes (either on or off), the robot plays a series of musical beeps and starts running back and forth quickly (or around in circles if the driver wheel swivels). It's like an alarm because it sits and waits for something to happen and, when it does finally happen, starts yelling and running around. After the "alarm" has gone off, the program stops and has to be restarted before the alarm goes off again.

✔ **Program 7 — Code:** This program emits a code sequence and waits for the light to respond with the same code. When the program first starts, there are a few little beeps and squeaks, and then there is a series of long and short beeps. Following this, there is a small click, and the robot waits for you to respond. If you respond by flashing your light at the robot with the same long and short code sequence, the robot moves forward just a bit. If you get the code wrong, it moves backward just a bit. This is a technique used by robots to program human beings. The easiest way to repeat the code is to use a flashlight and cover and uncover it with your hand. It still takes some practice, though.

✔ **Program P — Control:** This program does nothing yet but will work with future versions of LEGO MINDSTORMS.

Chapter 7

Programming the Scout

*T*he Scout is the power pack and collection of programming options that come with the Robotics Discovery Set, which you can use to create a number of different robots (see Chapter 4 for details). The Scout, which controls the motion of the robots in this set, is capable of detecting when the robot runs into objects or when a room becomes light or dark. Using these detectors, the Scout can then make decisions about what the robot should do next.

You can combine these detectors with a variety of programs that work together to allow your robot to operate in your room or yard. In fact, you can set up a collection of obstacles and then program your robot to work its way through the obstacle course. You can then adjust the program so that your robot tries different ways of going through the obstacles.

Understanding the Scout Display

Figure 7-1 shows the face of the Scout, which has a lot of stuff on it. The face has connection points for two Touch Sensors and two motors — the motor connections are important because the motors make the robot move. The face also has Light Sensor and Touch Sensor connections, which are used as input to the robot so that it can respond to its surroundings.

Power button

Connection for Touch Sensor 1

Select button

Indicator for Touch Sensor 1

Indicator for Touch Sensor 2

Connection for Touch Sensor 2

Run/stop button

Change button

Figure 7-1:
The face of
the Scout.

Power for motor A

Motor indicator lights

Power for motor B

The Touch Sensor indicators glow yellow whenever the Touch Sensor is touching something. The motor indicators glow yellow to indicate the direction (forward or backward) whenever a motor is running. The Touch Sensor connections and the motor power connections are square, so they can be plugged in four different ways. It doesn't matter which way the wires stick out when you plug in the Touch Sensors — they will always work the same.

On the other hand, which way you plug in a motor determines which way the motor runs when the power is turned on. This can be kind of neat because, after your robot is running, you can change these connections around and make the robot go different directions.

There is also a Light Sensor. (When you first look at the Scout from the top, it looks like there are two Light Sensors, but there's only one.) That's okay, however, because all it's capable of doing is detecting whether a room or area is dark, and you can certainly do that with only one "eye" from one sensor.

Figure 7-2 shows where the Light Sensor is located. There is also an indicator that lights up whenever the Light Sensor is triggered. At the very top center of the Scout is an infrared communications dome that can receive commands from either a Remote Control unit or the RCX unit from the Robotics Invention System. The communication indication light flashes whenever an infrared message is coming in.

The red light on the front of the Scout indicates an error of some kind. If the robot becomes confused for any reason, the light flashes. For example, if the robot has been instructed to turn right when the left sensor is touched and turn left when the right sensor is touched, and then both sensors are touched, the robot is supposed to turn both right and left at the same time. In this case, the light will flash.

The display window on the front of the Scout, shown in Figure 7-3, is divided into six areas. You program the Scout by making a selection from each of the areas. The six areas are shown in Figure 7-3.

- The upper-left corner of the display contains the motor commands. The motor can be set to run the wheels forward, in a zigzag pattern, in a circle to the left, or in a circle to the right. It can also be set to run one or both of the two motors back and forth in a random pattern.

- The top center of the display contains a list of the possible actions that can be taken when one of the Touch Sensors is triggered. The action may be to cause a running motor to reverse itself, back up and go another direction, or just stop. You can also set the Scout so that the robot won't move until after a Touch Sensor has been triggered.

Light Sensor — ┌─Communication indicator

Light Sensor indicator ── ┌─ Infrared communication ┌─ Red light error indicator

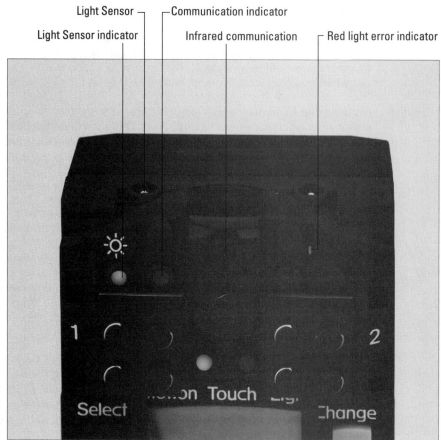

Figure 7-2:
The top of
the Scout.

✔ The top-right corner of the display contains the list of optional actions the robot can take when the Light Sensor is triggered. You can set the robot to seek the light or avoid it. You can also set it to start running only after the light changes or continue to run until the light changes.

✔ In the lower-left corner of the display, you can see a number of dots. These dots correspond to the speed of each activity. The more dots showing, the more time these activities take. For example, if your program is set to zigzag back and forth, it will zigzag fast with one dot showing and zigzag slowly with three showing. See the "Altering time with the time dots" section for more information.

✔ At the bottom-right corner of the display, printed with the letters "FX," is a collection of special effects that you can choose. These effects include both sound and motion and are named Bug Mode, Alarm Sounds, Random Movements, and Geiger Counter (see the "Using special effects" section later in this chapter for more information). Try them out to see what they make your robot do!

✔ At the center of the bottom of the display window is the power indicator. Whenever the power to the Scout is turned on, a little box, with some other little boxes inside it, shows on the display. There is also something that looks like a lightning bolt that can be set to indicate the Power Mode. The Power Mode does nothing yet, but it is designed to work with a future LEGO product called the Scout Booster Set.

There is actually a seventh area right in the middle of the screen below the touch area. A bunch of little arrows move from left to right whenever a program is running. (You can usually tell when a program is running because the robot is wandering around the room, but it is possible to set the programs in such a way that the robot is sitting still while waiting for something to happen. In this case, the only things moving are the little arrows on the display.)

Also, in this middle area is a battery indicator, but you won't see anything there until the batteries get low. When your batteries start to give out, you'll see a picture of a battery with an X drawn through it. This little picture doesn't go away until you either replace the batteries or they go completely dead. You can also tell when the batteries are dead because the display is completely blank, there is no sound, the wheels don't turn, and your robot turns over on its back with its legs in the air. Okay, it doesn't turn over on its back, but it's dead anyway.

Figure 7-3: The display window on the Scout.

Scout Programming Concepts You Should Know

The Scout contains a bunch of little program parts that you can put together in different ways to make your robot do different things. To get your robot to make simple motions, you use just one of these programs. The more program parts you add, the more complicated your robot motion becomes. You may be surprised at how smart it gets sometimes. To be fair, though, there are times when the Scout does something really dumb.

Between selecting the motion to be made by the wheels, the speed the wheels are to turn, the way the Scout is to respond to light and touch, and the optional special effects, you have 3,600 possible programming combinations. That is, there are 3,600 unique programs that you can punch into the Scout. Add to this the variation of the mechanical gears, wheels, and Touch Sensors, and there is virtually no limit to the kinds of things you can make your robot do.

After you select all of the program parts, and after you first select the Run button, the robot starts running by obeying the motion command you select (if you select one). This continues until one of the other program parts interrupts your selection and changes the action. For example, if you select the Avoid program, which avoids objects that it touches, the robot will continue rolling until a Touch Sensor is triggered. At this point, the Avoid program of the Touch Sensor takes over. The robot backs up just a bit, turns a little, and then turns control back over to the original motion program so that the robot continues on its way.

The motion program runs all the time and completely controls the robot when everything is normal. If you choose, for example, to have your robot run in a circle but be sensitive to light, as long as the light doesn't change, the circling continues. If you turn a flashlight on the robot, it responds to the light by having your light program take over and control the motion. After the light program has finished doing whatever it does, the main motion program takes over again, and motion continues normally.

Sometimes, too much happens. For example, the right Touch Sensor can be set to cause the robot to turn to the left, and at the same time, the left Touch Sensor can be set to turn to the right. Whenever either of these sensors is touched, the robot turns and then continues on. However, if the robot gets itself lined up and goes directly into a wall, both of the sensors will touch at the same time. Now the robot has been commanded to do two opposite things at once. Just like Robby the Robot in *Forbidden Planet,* the robot freezes and starts flashing red. Unlike Robby, the Scout gets itself out of the quandary. The Scout flashes its red light for a few seconds, shuffles back and forth for a while, and, finally, picks one of the two Touch Sensor programs and obeys its commands.

Modules and interruptions

The kind of programming in the Scout is known as *modular* and *interrupt driven*. All modern computers and computer software use this stuff.

The Scout software is *modular* because it comes in pieces. These pieces are known as *modules* or *objects*. Each one is a stand-alone program part that's designed to do one specific job. For example, one module is designed to reverse the direction of the robot. If this module has been selected for the Touch Sensor, all it does is look to see which way the robot is set to travel and reverses the setting so the robot starts travelling in the opposite direction. The module doesn't know why it was asked to reverse direction, and it doesn't know how to do anything else, but it reverses direction every time you ask it to.

The Scout software is *interrupt driven* because it can be doing one thing and an event from outside causes it to do something else. For example, the Motion module may be running along fine, minding its own business and keeping the wheels turning, when — bang! — out of the clear blue, an interrupt comes in from a Touch Sensor. A wall has been hit! The motion program freezes (it has been interrupted), and the Touch Sensor program does its thing. As soon as the Touch Sensor program finishes, the motion program takes up where it left off and gets the wheels rolling again.

Playing with the Buttons

The face of the Scout has four buttons. These four buttons are all you need to turn it on and off, start it running, stop it, and select the program combinations.

Before you can do anything else, you have to press the On-Off button to turn the Scout on. Then, after you select a program, pressing the Run button will start the program running.

You can stop a program running by pressing the Run button again or by pressing the On-Off button. If the robot is racing around the floor, you may have difficulty pressing a button to stop it, but it can be done. But I should warn you; never try to stop your robot while it is in the vicinity of a cat because your hand can get caught in the attack.

The first time you ever turn on the Scout, it is in the default state. A simple little program runs the wheels forward and completely ignores the Light Sensor and Touch Sensor. After you select a program, it *persists* — that is, when you turn it on, it will still be set to your selected program.

If you want to return the Scout to its *initial state* (the settings it had before you turned it on for the first time), there are two things you can do. While it is turned on, you can press and hold the On-Off button for two seconds. You'll hear a short beep, and the Scout will be reset. The other way to do it is to remove all the batteries, let the Scout die, and then put the batteries all back in. It is probably easier to press the button.

Using the Select and Change buttons

The two buttons labeled Select and Change are used to program the Scout. The Select button chooses one of the six programmable areas of the display, and the Change button is used to switch from one option to the other within the selected area.

Turn the Scout on and look at the display. Something is flashing. Notice that the stuff in one, and only one, of the areas is flashing. This means that this area is the one that is currently selected. Press the Select button, and the stuff in another area starts flashing. Every time you press the select button, the stuff in a different area starts flashing. That's all the select button does.

There are two ways that an area can be flashing. There can either be one thing flashing in the area or everything in the area can be flashing. If there is only one thing flashing, it is the one that is currently active. If everything in the area is flashing, that means that nothing in the area is currently active.

You use the Change button to determine which selection inside an area is the active one. Once the Select button has caused the stuff in the area to flash, the Change button will switch from one to the next. Whenever there is only one thing flashing, it is the one that is selected. If everything in an area is flashing, nothing is selected.

The time-lapse setting in the lower-left corner is a little different. It shows up as one, two, or three circles. The amount of time that commands consume depends on how many circles are showing. One circle is the quickest, and three circles take the longest.

Then there's the Power Mode thing in the middle of the bottom of the display window. When you press the Change button, you hear some tones and the lightning bolt appears. This shows that the Scout is in Power Mode. The Power Mode turns off your other programming options but does nothing else yet. It is designed to work with a future LEGO product called the Scout Booster Set.

Anyway, if you get the Scout stuck in Power Mode, just press the Change button and it will pop right out again.

Pressing buttons for multiple commands

After you understand the control panel, you are almost ready to program the Scout so it will run your robot around the room. Okay, you and I both know that you've already done that. You just punched some buttons and came up with some kind of configuration, pressed the Run button, and the robot took off. Or maybe it didn't. Some combinations cause the robot to just sit there without moving. It's thinking about doing something, but you never told it what to do, so all it knows how to do is run down your batteries.

You must always have something selected in the Motion group (see the following section). If you don't tell the robot how you would like it to move, it won't. In fact, the simplest possible program is the one that comes up the first time you turn on the Scout — the Forward command. Select it in the Motion area, and when you press the Run button, it takes off and continues in a straight line until you stop it.

After you set the Motion command, you can mix and match any of the other settings. You can, for example, leave the Motion set to Forward and set the Touch command to Reverse. The robot will take off in a straight line until a Touch Sensor hits something, and then it backs up and continues until another Touch Sensor is triggered. When another Touch Sensor is hit, it starts going forward again. This continues until you stop it. Then you can turn on the Avoid command in the Light Sensor area, and the robot will do this same back-and-forth thing but will avoid going into places that are dark, or if it's in the dark, it will avoid going to places where there is light.

That's how you program your Scout. You pick the way you'd like the motor to run and then select the other things you want it to do. Some of these combinations may seem more interesting than others, but how well a combination works depends a lot on how your robot is designed. Remember that there are 3,600 possible combinations!

Motion commands

The two Scout motor controls are used to run the motor forward and backward. The touch commands, light commands, and FX commands all can be used to modify the basic motor configuration defined in this section.

Forward can be backward to your robot. The direction a motor runs depends on how the motor is plugged in to the Scout. If your robot takes off in the wrong direction, rotate one of the connectors on the power lead that connects the motor to the Scout. The connectors are square, so they can be plugged in four different ways, depending on which way you want your robot to go.

✔ **Forward:** In this mode, both motors run without changing direction. With this command, the robot runs continuously in one direction.

The Reverse command of the Touch Sensor (see the following section) reverses the direction of a robot set to continuously run Forward. You can, for example, have a Touch Sensor on both the front and back of the robot, and by setting the Touch Sensor to Reverse, you will cause the robot to change direction every time it runs into something.

Which way is forward depends on how you have the motor plugged in.

✔ **ZigZag:** This setting is like Forward except that only one motor runs at a time. This way, the robot works its way forward by waddling like a duck — one side moves and then the other side moves. Also, just like Forward, the Reverse command of the Touch Sensor reverses everything and causes the robot to waddle backward instead of forward.

✔ **Circle:** There are two Circle commands: One circles to the left, and the other circles to the right. To make the circles, the Scout runs both motors for a second or so, runs only one motor for a second, and then goes back to running both. With one motor running and the other staying still, the robot runs in a jerky kind of circle. The Reverse command of the Touch Sensor causes the robot to reverse its action and back up along the same circular path.

✔ **Loop AB:** On the face of the Scout, the connection for the motors are labeled A and B. Using these designators, there are three Loop commands:

- The Loop A command causes the A motor to run forward for a second, back for a second, and then stop for second. This whole sequence is repeated over and over until you stop it. The B motor never runs.

- The Loop B command is just the opposite of the Loop A command. The B motor is the one that runs back and forth while the A motor never runs.

- The Loop AB command runs both the Loop A and Loop B programs at the same time. When the wheels happen to be running at the same time in the same direction, the robot takes off either forward or backward. When only one motor is running, the robot makes the same kind of sharp turn it makes with the Loop A or Loop B program. If both motors are running but are running in opposite directions, the robot spins in one place.

Touch commands

Whenever a Touch Sensor is activated, a small command program is run. If there is another program running (such as a Motion command), it's suspended until the Touch command finishes.

✔ **Reverse:** This is really a tiny program. It doesn't do anything but reverse the direction of the motors. For example, if the Motion program is running both motors forward, this command stops the motors, reverses their direction, and lets them start running again. This causes the robot to back up whenever a Touch Sensor runs into an object.

If a motor is running backward, it's switched to forward; if it is running forward, it's switched to backward. Both motors have their directions reversed, even if they are currently running in opposite directions.

✔ **Avoid:** This is a cute little program that makes your robot look like it's really smart. Using this in combination with any of the Motion commands causes your robot to avoid running into things.

Whenever a Touch Sensor is triggered, the robot backs up for a second. If Touch Sensor number 1 is triggered, the robot motors run in opposite directions to spin the robot a bit to the right. If Touch Sensor number 2 is triggered, the robot spins to the left. The Avoid program quits running, which causes the interrupted Motion command to resume and the robot proceeds on its way. It has just avoided an obstacle.

This program does seem to have a temper. After it has bumped into a few things, it can get a little upset. When it gets angry, it squiggles back and forth and makes a few really rude squeaking noises after it backs up.

✔ **WaitFor:** This program starts running immediately when you press the Run button. But the robot doesn't do anything. It just sits there and waits. If you bump a Touch Sensor, the main Motion program takes over and starts moving the robot about the room. The robot continues to run until a Touch Sensor is bumped again. When this happens, you're right back where you started with the robot calmly waiting for the Touch Sensor to be bumped again.

✔ **Brake:** This program stops one of the motors when one of the Touch Sensors is being held down. It's like the brake on a car. As long as you hold down Touch Sensor number 1, motor A will not run; as long as you hold down Touch Sensor number 2, motor B will not run. After a Touch Sensor is released, its motor takes off again.

Light commands

The way the Light Sensor reacts to light is determined when the Scout is turned on. If you turn the Scout on in a lighted area, the sensor will trigger every time the light is taken away. If the Scout is turned on without a bright light, the sensor will trigger every time it detects a bright light.

To see what I mean, turn the Scout on while is it pointed toward a lamp or flashlight. Every time you cover the Light Sensor with your finger, the indicator will light up. Now turn the Scout on while your finger is over the Light Sensor, and you will see that the indicator lights up every time you *remove* your finger from the Light Sensor.

Here are some additional possibilities for the Light commands:

- ✔ **Seek:** This command causes the robot to spin in place until it's triggered by the light. Then the spinning stops. If you ask it to seek the light, and if you combine this with the Motion command called Forward, when you start it running, the robot first takes off in whichever direction it is pointed. It suddenly stops and spins around until it sees the light, and the spinning stops. The Forward motion takes over again, and the robot races toward the light. If it spins and doesn't find the light, it just gives up after a bit and continues on in whichever direction it happens to be pointing.

  You can also have it seek the dark. It does the same thing as it does when it's seeking light, except that the spinning stops when there is no light.

  If you use a motion other than Forward, the same kind of thing happens. That is, whatever motion you choose will occasionally stop while the robot spins looking for the light.

- ✔ **Avoid:** This command works very much like the Avoid command for the Touch Sensors. It runs according to the Motion command you've selected until it encounters a change in the light (from light to dark or dark to light). It stops, backs up, turns just a bit, and takes off again.

  Also, just like with the Touch Sensor, after it has to turn a few times, the robot loses its temper and does a little dance while yelling some squeaky noises. Then, like a good little robot, it continues to do the job you asked it to do.

- ✔ **WaitFor:** This program starts running immediately when you press the Run button. But the robot doesn't do anything. It just sits there and waits. Then, when you shine a light on it (or remove the light from it), it takes off with whatever motion you programmed for it. To make it stop, shine the light on it again (or remove the light again).

- ✔ **Brake:** When you start the program running, everything is normal and the robot obeys the Motion command you selected. This continues until the light changes. Changing the light causes the Light Sensor to trigger, and the robot freezes in its tracks until you change the light back. After the light is back the way the robot likes it, the motion continues.

Getting the Most Out of Your Scout

You can modify the actions of the basic commands without a lot of effort. This section gives you a few examples.

Altering time with the time dots

As described in the "Motion commands" section, the Motion command goes along doing its job when, suddenly, one of the other commands triggers and the Motion command freezes and waits for the other command to finish. Some of these other commands (such as Reverse) execute immediately and turn control back to the Motion command, but some of them do other things. For example, the Seek command takes some time to spin around looking for light. But how long does it spin?

That's where the time dots in the lower-left corner of the Scout display come in. If you want it to just make a quick, partial circle, set it so that only one dot (meaning not a lot of time will be spent on making the circle) shows. If, on the other hand, you want it to spin all the way around a time or two, set the display so that three dots are showing. If you want to take a medium amount of time, set it to show two dots.

These time settings can make a big difference in the way your robot behaves. Try it with a Motion of Forward and the Touch Sensor set to Avoid. The robot still works its way around obstacles, but it does so in a completely different way. Which speed performs better depends on the shape and size of the obstacles the Scout finds in its path.

Using special effects

The four special effects in the lower-right corner of the display definitely give your robot a different personality. Any one of these effects (pronounced FX) can be used in combination with any of the other settings.

- ✔ The Bug Mode allows your robot to run the way you program it, but every now and then it wiggles back and forth, dances a bit, makes some musical chirping sounds, and then continues on its way.

- ✔ The Alarm Sounds is probably the most vocal of all the settings. Sounds accompany every action. Whenever a Touch Sensor is triggered, a motor reverses direction, or if it's just running along the floor, sounds come out of it. Some of these sounds are just beeps and squawks, but some are little musical chirrups.

- ✔ The Random Movements selection is just what it says it is. Your robot runs as you program it, but every now and then it does some other stuff. This doesn't really go on very long (you control how long by using the time dots), but there is no way to know exactly which way it's going to go.

✔ The Geiger Counter adds a sort of clicking chirp sound to your robot as the program runs. This sound replaces the normal little cricket-like chirping sound that the Scout usually makes. (If you haven't heard the little cricket chirps, turn on the Scout and put your ear close to it.) The number of clicks per second is faster when the motors are running than when they aren't. If you have your robot programmed to pause or wait, you can hear the Geiger Counter change as the motion of the robot changes.

Using the Remote Control

You can purchase a hand-held Remote Control for your Scout (it doesn't come with any LEGO MINDSTORMS kits). This same Remote Control works with the RCX brick of the Robotics Invention System, so a couple of buttons don't mean anything, but most of them work just fine with the Scout. The layout of the Remote Control is shown in Figure 7-4.

To use the Remote Control, it is only necessary to turn the power on to the Scout and set it down in a place where it can move around. Use forward and backward buttons for the A and B motors to run the motors individually, or run them both at once. (The up-arrow runs the motor forward, and the down-arrow runs it backward.) To run the robot in a straight line, press and hold both the A and B buttons at the same time.

In the bottom-right corner of the remote is a button with a little speaker icon next to it. Pressing this button causes the Scout to respond with a couple of quick beeps.

The program buttons P1 through P5 each load a predefined program into the Scout and run it. The Stop button at the bottom-left corner of the remote will stop the program from running. These programs are all configured inside the Remote Control:

✔ **P1:** Sets Motion to ZigZag, Touch to Avoid, FX to Bug Mode, and Time to one circle.

✔ **P2:** Sets Motion to Forward, Touch to Avoid, Light to Seek, FX to Bug Mode, and Time to one circle.

✔ **P3:** Sets Motion to LoopAB, Light to WaitFor, FX to Alarm Sounds, and Time to two circles.

✔ **P4:** Sets Motion to LoopAB, FX to Random Movements, and Time to one circle.

✔ **P5:** Sets the Scout to Power Mode. This is for use with a future LEGO product called the Scout Booster Set.

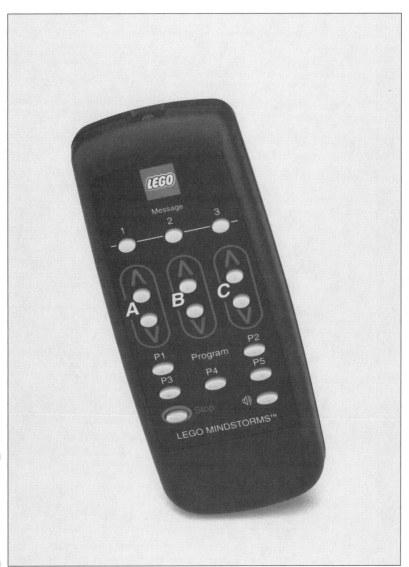

Figure 7-4:
The LEGO
MIND-
STORMS
Remote
Control unit.

Chapter 8

Beginning Programming with the Robotics Invention System 1.5

In This Chapter

▶ Starting up the RCX for the first time

▶ Building the trainer bot

▶ Running the built-in programs

▶ Creating your first program

---

*R*CX is the name of the most powerful controller in the LEGO MIND-STORMS family. RCX stands for Robotics Command System. (I guess they don't spell so well in Denmark.) With the Micro Scout (see Chapter 6), you can make your robot do a few things, but it's limited in that it has only seven programs and can't be taught new tricks. The Scout makes things a bit more interesting by giving you more options — thousands of program combinations and more control of your robot. But the excitement soon wears off and you realize that it can't do exactly what you want. But the RCX can be completely controlled by you. It's only limited by your imagination. By creating a program, you can teach your robot to walk in a straight line, run in circles, play a song, or find its way through a maze.

Not a software geek? No problem. LEGO makes programming as easy as building a model. It's just a matter of choosing the right programming blocks and sticking them together onscreen. As a matter of fact, it even looks like LEGOs on your screen. The whole process is made up of just four steps: build your robot, put the RCX code blocks together to create a program, load the program into the RCX brick, and run your program. This chapter shows you how.

Setting Up Your RCX Brick

Prepare your RCX brick by removing the back cover and installing six AA batteries. (Pay attention to the direction of the + symbol.) All six batteries go in the same way. LEGO recommends alkaline batteries, but unless you own stock in a battery company, I recommend using rechargeable batteries. They may give you a little less power, but the money you save can go toward buying that Temperature Sensor your robot has been asking you for!

Verify that everything is working by pressing the red On-Off button on the front of the RCX brick. If the display shows a number and a little man standing, everything is okay. If not, verify that you used fresh batteries and that all of the batteries are facing the right way. Now you can move on to building your robot.

It is never a good idea to mix battery types in the RCX. Always replace all six batteries with six brand new batteries of the same type.

If you're putting the RCX away for a long time, take the batteries out. If you leave them in and they leak, the RCX brick could be destroyed.

When replacing batteries, always move quickly. The memory of the RCX will stay intact for about 60 seconds without batteries. If you take longer than this, you will have to reload the firmware and any programs you've written. The *firmware* is the main operating system for the RCX (kind of like Windows for the PC) and must be loaded along with your program. We show how to do this in the "Setting up the Robotics Invention System Software" section.

Building a Trainer Bot

Before you can program the RCX, you need to build a simple robot, one that can move around with at least two wheels and a motor driving each of the wheels. The PATHFINDER or any version of the ROVERBOT is well suited for this (see Chapter 5). The PATHFINDER only uses about 30 pieces and can be built in a few minutes by following the building instructions in the Robotics Invention System *Constructopedia*.

If you have a little more time (and aren't in a hurry to get to the programming), try building one of the ROVERBOTs. The ROVERBOT is actually a family of robots. Start by building the Driving Base, as shown in the Robotics Invention System *Constructopedia*. Then add the Wheel Set, the Legs, or the Tracks. Although all three work on most surfaces, our favorite is the caterpillar-like tracks for going across carpets and bumps in floors.

Although you won't use the sensors until later, you can go ahead and build the Single Bumper, the Double Bumper, or the Light Sensor. We suggest building the Double Bumper, which gives you the ability to know on which side you bumped into something.

Getting to Know Your RCX Brick

The RCX Brick is the heart of the Robotics Invention System. This device can control up to three devices, such as motors or lights, and monitor up to three sensor devices, such as Touch Sensors, Light Sensors, Temperature Sensors, or Rotation Sensors. In addition, the RCX brick has a built-in counter that you can use to keep track of the number of times something happens, a built-in timer to tell your robot when to do things, and a communication system to talk to other RCX bricks.

The front of the brick has four areas, as shown in Figure 8-1:

✔ **Connectors for the motors:** The connectors for the motors are black LEGO connectors labeled A, B, and C and are found near the bottom of the brick. While these look like normal LEGO-style blocks, closer examination shows that small metallic contacts are molded into the LEGO pegs.

✔ **Connectors for the sensors:** The connectors for the sensors are gray LEGO connectors labeled 1, 2, and 3 and are found near the top of the brick. These also look like normal LEGO blocks, but also have the molded connectors.

✔ **Four control buttons:** The buttons are used for setting up and running your RCX programs.

✔ **A display:** Also used for setting up and running your RCX programs.

Buttons

The four buttons are labeled On-Off, View, Prgm (program), and Run, as shown in Figure 8-2, and can do the following:

✔ **On-Off:** As you may have guessed, the On-Off button turns power on and off in the RCX. If you forget to turn off the power, the RCX shuts down by itself after a few minutes.

✔ **View:** The View button lets you read the state of a switch, read the value of a sensor, or read the power level of a motor. This can be useful when your program isn't working and you need to find out what's wrong.

✔ **Prgm:** The RCX brick can hold five different programs in memory. You choose which program to use by pressing the Prgm button until the program number is shown on the right of the display. Pressing this button while a program is running stops it.

✔ **Run:** The Run button starts the program that you selected. Pressing the button one time starts the program. Pressing it a second time stops the program.

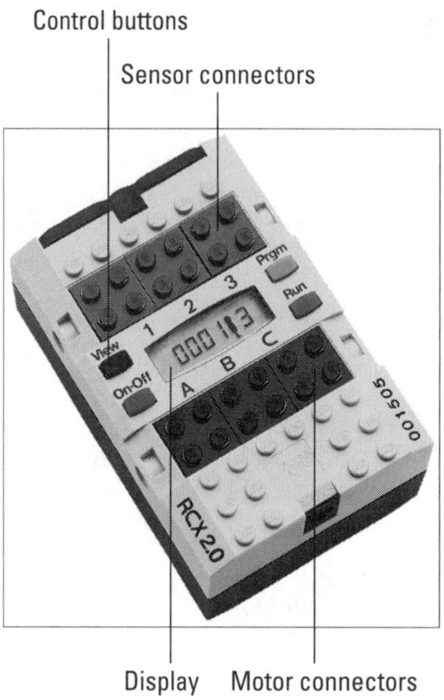

Control buttons

Sensor connectors

Figure 8-1:
The RCX has connectors for sensors and motors, control buttons, and a display.

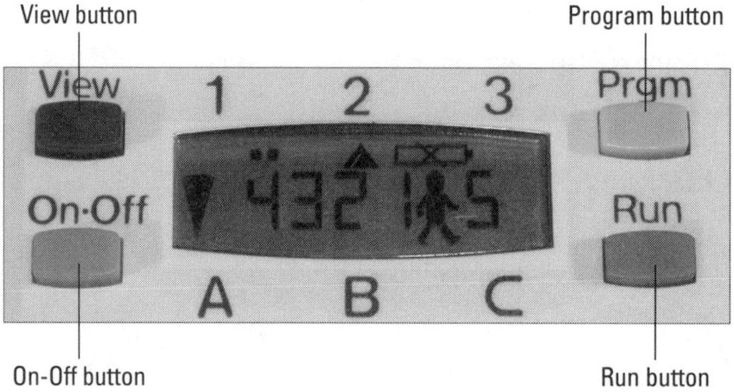

Display   Motor connectors

View button   Program button

Figure 8-2:
The front panel of the RCX has four control buttons.

On-Off button   Run button

Display

The display is made up of six areas: Numeric Display, Little Man, Program Number, Download Indicators, Status Indicators, and Low-Battery Indicator, as shown in Figure 8-3. Here's what they do:

✔ **Numeric Display:** The Numeric Display is blank until you download the RCX firmware. We explain how to download this in the "Setting up the Robotics Invention Systems Software" section, later in this chapter.

   After the firmware is installed, the Numeric Display shows either the number of minutes that the RCX has been powered on or the time of day. It is also used to display the state of a sensor or motor in the view mode. This is the mode in which you can see exactly what each of your sensors is doing (see the "Using the view function" sidebar).

✔ **Little Man:** The Little Man has nothing to do with a Louisa May Alcott book. Instead, it indicates whether or not your program is running. When the Little Man is standing still, your program is stopped. If his legs and arms are moving as if he is running, guess what? Your program is running!

✔ **Program Number:** To the right of the Little Man is the Program Number. You select the program to run by pressing the Prgm button. The RCX brick can hold up to five different programs, and these coincide with the numbers 1 to 5.

✔ **Download Indicators:** When you transfer a program from your PC to the RCX, you're downloading. The Download Indicators show up only when you transfer a program from your PC to the RCX brick. The first indicator is on the left of the display and looks like a cone. This tells you that a signal is being received. At the same time, a series of dots moves across the top of the display to indicate downloading progress.

✔ **Status Indicators:** Next to each sensor connector is a small triangle that turns on when the sensor is on. If you connect a Touch Sensor to connector 1 and press the switch, the small triangle next to number 1 will turn on. When you release the switch, the triangle will turn off. This can be a tremendous help when you're building a robot to test whether a sensor is working.

   The Status Indicators only work for Touch Sensors. Use the View button to see the value of the Temperature, Light, or Rotation Sensors.

   You'll find two small triangles next to each motor connector. When a motor is running, these triangles indicate which way the motor is going. If the motor is going forward, the triangle points to the right. If it's going backward, the triangle points to the left. If the motor is off, neither triangle shows.

✔ **Low-Battery Indicator:** At the upper right of the display is a Low-Battery Indicator that looks like a battery with an "X" through it. If this indicator turns on, the batteries are getting low. If it begins flashing and the RCX starts beeping, the batteries are very low.

Using the View function

The View function can be useful for finding problems with your robot. It lets you see what type of information is going into the RCX brick and what the RCX brick is telling your motors.

To use the View function, press the View button when the power is on. This makes a small arrow point at Sensor 1. Each press of the View button moves the arrow to the next sensor or to the next motor. After going through all three sensors and all three motors, one more press of the View button turns off the view mode.

✔ **Touch Sensor:** If the arrow is pointing to a Touch Sensor, the display shows a 1 when the sensor is pressed and shows a 0 when the sensor is released.

✔ **Light Sensor:** If the arrow is pointing to a Light Sensor, the display shows the brightness of the light. A completely dark room will display a 0 (but you'll never be able to see it unless you can see in the dark). The brightest light will display a 100.

✔ **Temperature Sensor:** If the arrow is pointing to a Temperature Sensor, then the display shows the current temperature in either °C (Celsius) or °F (Fahrenheit). You can choose

which mode to use during system setup in the "Setting up the Robotics Inventions System Software" section, later in this chapter.

✔ **Rotation Sensor:** If the arrow is pointing to a Rotation Sensor, the display shows the amount that the sensor has turned. The sensor counts 16 for every full turn of its axle. If you turn it one way, it counts up. If you turn it the other way, it counts down. The value of the Rotation Sensor is reset to 0 every time the program is run.

The Light, Temperature, and Rotation Sensors only work if they've been set up in an RCX program. Just plugging in a sensor doesn't let it work in the View Function. An RCX program that uses that sensor at that location must be downloaded and run first.

✔ **Motor:** If the arrow is pointing to a motor connector, the display shows the amount of power being sent to the motor. This number can vary from 0 to 8, with 0 being off, 1 being very low power, and 8 being full speed ahead. Aye, Aye, Captain.

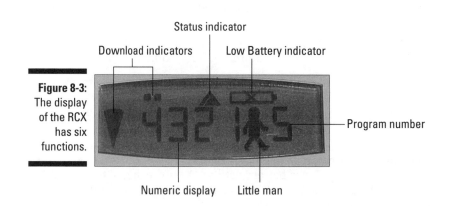

Figure 8-3:
The display of the RCX has six functions.

Status indicator

Download indicators

Low Battery indicator

Program number

Numeric display

Little man

View arrow

Light power display

Running the Built-In Programs

The RCX brick comes with five built-in programs. These are provided so that you can test your system before you get into programming.

✔ **It keeps going and going . . .:** Program 1 just makes your robot go forward. It does this by turning on motors A and C and leaving them on forever. Turn off this program by pressing the Run button. If your robot doesn't go or if it goes backward, verify that you have wired up the motors correctly.

✔ **Hey, stop!** To run Program 2, you need to attach two Touch Sensors to connectors 1 and 3. The program makes your robot move forward but when the Touch Sensor is pressed, the motor on that side stops. It does this by turning on motors A and C and then monitoring sensors 1 and 3. If sensor 1 turns on, motor A is turned off. If sensor 3 turns on, motor C is turned off. If the motors aren't stopping, verify that you're using Touch Sensors and that they're connected to connectors 1 and 3.

✔ **Follow that light:** To run Program 3, attach the Light Sensor to connector 2. The program makes the robot move forward whenever there is light on the sensor. It does this by monitoring sensor 2. If the Light Sensor on port 2 has light hitting it, power is applied to motors A and C. If not enough light is hitting the sensor, power is turned off. If the robot isn't moving, verify that you're using the Light Sensor and that it's attached to connector 2. The best way to light up the sensor is with a flashlight.

✔ **Get out of my way!** Program 4 is a little more complicated and doesn't need any sensors hooked up. The program moves the robot around in a random pattern. It does this by randomly turning on motors A and C for varying lengths of time. When only one of the motors is on, the robot turns.

✔ **Bumper car:** Program 5 is the smartest of the built-in programs. With a single touch-sensor bumper connected to connector 1, the robot moves around and tries to avoid obstacles. It does this by turning on motors A and C, making the robot go forward while monitoring sensor 1. If sensor 1 turns on (meaning your robot ran into something), motors A and C are reversed, making your robot back up. Then motors A and C are run in opposite directions to make the robot turn. Finally motors A and C are turned on forward again to make the robot move forward.

Setting Up the Robotics Invention System Software

Before you start programming, you need to set up the infrared transmitter and install the Robotics Invention System software. Then you can go through the built-in guided tour and finally configure your system for use. (This section covers all of that.) Whew . . . at that point, you'll finally be ready to write your first program.

Using the infrared transmitter

You can program your RCX to do almost anything using a language called RCX Code. You write programs on a standard PC running Window 95/98 and transfer them to the RCX with an infrared link. The infrared link sends information to the RCX brick in the same way that your TV remote sends signals to your TV.

Because your PC doesn't come with an infrared port, one is included in the Robotics Invention System kit. It's the other big thing in the kit besides the RCX brick itself. Start by placing a fresh 9-volt battery into the back of the infrared transmitter unit. Then plug one end of the 6-foot serial cable into the back of this unit and the other end of the cable into an unused COM port of your PC.

If your COM ports are the 25-pin type, you need a 25-to-9-pin converter. These are available at your local computer store for a few dollars.

Installing the Robotics Invention System software

You need to load the Robotics Invention System (RIS) software onto your PC. To do this, insert the LEGO MINDSTORMS CD into a computer running Windows 95 or 98. The installation program should launch automatically. If it doesn't, double-click the CD icon in My Computer and double-click the Setup.exe program on the CD. Now, follow the on-screen instructions to complete the installation.

After the software is installed, you're ready to run the Robotics Invention System software. An icon appears on your desktop called "Robotics Invention System," of all things. Double-click on the icon to start the program.

You must have the RIS CD in the computer to run the software.

After a fancy start-up sequence, you see a screen (shown in Figure 8-4) that asks for your name. Because this is the first time you've run the program, click on "New User," type in your name, and click on "Enter." This starts the Guided Tour mode as described in the next section.

If this isn't your first time running the program, choose your name from the list and click on "Enter." If you've already completed the Guided Tour, the main RIS menu should be on the screen. If this is the case, you can skip the next two sections and jump right into the "Your First Program" section.

Guided mode

Guided mode is LEGO's way of teaching you about the basics of the RIS, by showing instructions on the screen and narrating in a Darth Vader-like voice. Guided mode is worth going through at least one time. Be ready to set aside a few hours to go through the entire training, though. When you're done (or when your patience runs out), move on to the "Set Up Options" section.

Figure 8-4:
The logon
screen is
where you
tell the RCX
who you
are.

If you enter the name of a new user (refer to Figure 8-4), you are taken directly to the guided mode. While this may be interesting to do one time, you certainly don't want to suffer through it again. Luckily, LEGO has created a hidden shortcut to skip the guided mode. After entering the name of the new user, click on the About button of the main menu while holding down the control key on your keyboard. Now you're ready to go.

Set Up Options

From the Robotics Invention System main menu, choose Getting Started. This takes you to the Getting Started menu. From there, choose the Set Up Options menu item. You're greeted by the Set Up Options page, as shown in Figure 8-5. This is where you tell the PC a few of the following things about your system.

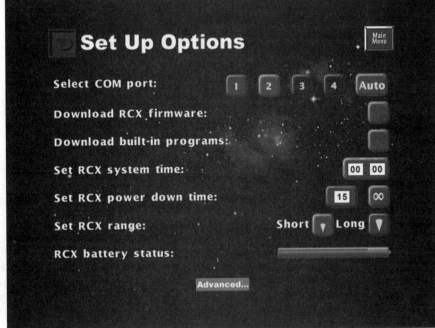

Figure 8-5:
The Set Up
Options
screen lets
you make
some basic
settings.

✔ **Select COM port:** This is the port that the infrared transmitter plugs into. You can either click on the COM port number or if you have no idea what a COM port is, click on the Auto button. This tells the RIS to find the infrared transmitter no matter what COM port it's plugged into.

✔ Before clicking on one of these buttons, make sure the infrared transmitter is set up (see "Using the infrared transmitter" section, earlier in this chapter); make sure the RCX brick is facing it (about six inches away); and be sure it's turned on. If the RIS can't find the infrared transmitter or if there is any type of problem, you're told what the problem seems to be (for example, the RCX is not in range or not switched on). You can either click the Continue button because you're smarter than the computer, or click on the Trouble Shooter button. This takes you to another set of screens and walks you through how to fix it.

✔ **Download RCX firmware:** The RCX brick can't do very much by itself. It's kind of like your PC without Windows — just an expensive paperweight. To make the paperweight more useful, a piece of software (called *firmware*) must be loaded onto it. To download the firmware, click on the solid black button. A small dialog box pops up and lets you know that the PC is "Initializing and downloading the firmware. Please wait . . .." This process takes a few minutes, so go ahead and fill your cup of coffee.

If the process works, you're rewarded with a message saying "Downloading complete." If it doesn't work, make sure that the infrared transmitter is pointing at the RCX brick, that the RCX is turned on and about six inches away, and that there are no obstacles between the infrared transmitter and the RCX. Then try again.

Downloading is just a technical way to say "transfer." In this case, downloading means transferring something from the PC to the RCX brick. *Uploading,* therefore, is just the opposite of downloading. It means transferring something from the RCX brick to the PC.

✔ **Download built-in programs:** Clicking this button reloads the original five built-in programs. This gives you a way to start over with a blank RCX.

Downloading the firmware or the built-in programs erases any programs that you have put in the RCX. They can be easily reloaded from the RIS if you want.

✔ **Set RCX system time:** Here's a really useful feature! Typing the current time into the boxes sets the display of the RCX to show the current time. Two points to remember: The time isn't loaded into the RCX until you return to the main menu (by clicking the blue box in the upper-right corner), and every time you turn off the RCX, you clear the time! You may want to play with this feature once to understand it, but don't bother with it too much.

✔ **Set RCX power down time:** The RCX brick is pretty smart. It knows when it's not being used and can be set to shut off and save battery power. This option tells the RCX how long to stay on when nobody is using it. You can set it to do this in 1 to 59 minutes. We found that leaving it at 15 minutes gives a good balance between saving power and being inconvenienced by the unit powering down too quickly.

If you don't like powering down, you can set the RCX to never power down automatically. You do this by clicking on the infinity symbol (∞). Just be prepared to use a lot of batteries because, chances are, you'll eventually leave the unit on by mistake.

✔ **Set RCX range:** The infrared transmitter can be set to work at short or long distances. We recommend using the long-range setting because it lets you place the RCX anywhere and still pick up the signal. The short-range mode is reserved for those times when many people are trying to talk to their RCXs, and you're worried about picking up their signals.

You need to do two things to set the units to long range: Select Long in the Set Up Options and find the switch on the bottom-front of the infrared transmitter, making sure it's in the long-range position (to the right).

✔ **RCX battery status:** The battery status shows how much power you have left in the batteries. The longer the green bar, the more power is left.

You can set a few more options from the advanced Set Up Options screen, as shown in Figure 8-6. You get to this screen by clicking on the Advanced... button at the bottom of the Set Up Options screen.

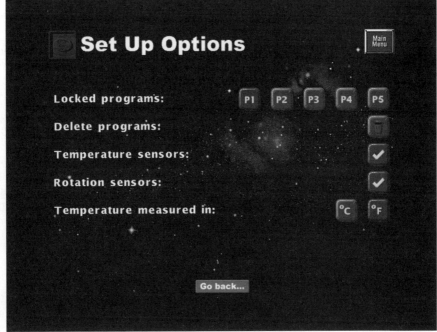

Figure 8-6:
The Set Up Options advanced screen is where you make advanced settings.

✔ **Locked programs:** Five slots in the RCX can hold programs. When you have a program that you'd like to keep, you can lock it. This keeps the program from being erased by a new program. By default, programs 1 and 2 are locked.

To lock or unlock a program, click on the numbered button. If the button is red, the program is locked. If it's black, the program is unlocked.

✔ **Delete programs:** To clear out your old programs, click the trash can button. You will be asked if you want to "Delete unlocked program slots?" Click the green check mark to delete all programs that haven't been locked. To leave all your programs alone, click the red X.

✔ **Temperature sensors:** If you've purchased a separate Temperature Sensor and want to use it in your programs, you must let the RIS know. To do this, click the black button with the yellow X. It changes to a red button with a yellow check mark that indicates that your system is ready to use the Temperature Sensor.

✔ **Rotation sensors:** The RIS must also be told about your plans to use Rotation Sensors. In the same way you did the Temperature Sensor, click the black button with the yellow X. It changes to a red button with a yellow check mark that indicates that your system is ready to use the Rotation Sensor.

There is no harm in telling the RIS that you have the Temperature and Rotation Sensors even if you don't. You won't get caught and end up behind tiny little bars at LEGO jail! But if you get the sensors later, you won't have to go back to the Set Up Options page.

✔ **Temperature measured in:** When you have a Temperature Sensor, you can choose to do your measurements in °C (Celsius) or °F (Fahrenheit). This affects how you write your programs and how the View mode reads the temperature.

If you're unsure of which system to use, take this simple test. If you think that 30° is cold, use the Fahrenheit setting. If you think that 30° is warm, use the Celsius setting.

When you're done setting up, click on the blue Main Menu button to save everything. If you made any changes, you'll be asked, "Do you want to save your changes?" To save your changes, click the green check mark. To leave all of your settings the way they were, click the red X.

Your First Program

You're ready to write your first program! Before going any further, make sure you have a functional two-motor robot, the Robotics Invention System software installed on your PC, a functional infrared transmitter, and the set up completed. If not, flip through this chapter for information on completing the needed steps.

Go to the main menu of the RIS and click on the brown Program RCX button. You're presented with the screen shown in Figure 8-7. From there, click on the middle RCX Code button. You're now in the main programming area for LEGO MINDSTORMS, as shown in Figure 8-8.

The first program you write will make the robot move forward for a few seconds and then stop. While this isn't very exciting, it gives you the chance to understand some of the basics of RCX programming. After you master these basic concepts, you can move on to Chapter 9 and get into the details of the programming area.

Figure 8-7:
The RCX
Code menu
is where
you get
to the
programming
area.

Figure 8-8:
The main
programming
area is
where you
write your
programs.

The Program block

Every RCX program starts with a block called the *Program block*. This block is the green one that is labeled "program UNTITLED" (refer to Figure 8-8). This block is like the base plate of a real LEGO creation. You build your program by attaching other blocks below this one. When the program is run, it begins at the program block and works its way down, one block at a time.

The block is currently UNTITLED because you haven't saved your program yet. When you do, the block will display the real name of the program. You will save your program in the "Saving your work" section at the end of this chapter.

Breaking down the program

When you write a program, you try to break the program into smaller pieces and then program those pieces. In this case, the program is really made up of three steps:

- **Motors on:** To make the robot move forward, turn on both motors that are attached to the wheels or treads.
- **Wait:** After the motors are running, leave them on for a while so that the robot has time to move.
- **Motors off:** To make the robot stop, turn off both motors.

Commands

Commands are all of the things that you can tell your robot to do: for example, turn on a motor, make a sound, and wait. Each command is located on a separate block. The command blocks are color-coded green and are located at the upper-left side of the programming screen.

Try clicking on the word "commands" on the screen. The LEGO block on the screen rotates and either hides or shows the commands available. Clicking on the other program elements (blue is for sensor watchers, red is for stack controllers, and yellow is for my commands) also rotates those items up or down. Click on commands so that the commands are showing like they are in Figure 8-9.

Scroll up arrow

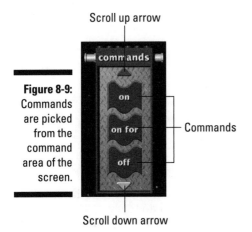

Figure 8-9:
Commands
are picked
from the
command
area of the
screen.

Commands

Scroll down arrow

There are 15 commands but only three are showing in the command area. To
see the other commands, you need to scroll up or down by using the scroll
arrows. Each press of the scroll arrow brings another command into view. For
now, scroll to the top of the list so that the "on" command is showing.

Stacking them together

The "Breaking down the program" section, earlier in this chapter, tells you
that the first step of the program is to turn on the motors. You do this by
using the On block. Move the cursor over the On block until the cursor turns
into a pointing finger. Click and release on the block to grab it. The cursor
turns into a grabbing fist, and the On block moves around with the cursor.
Move the block under the Program block and click again to release it. The On
block snaps into place below the Program block.

The new block is labeled "on ABC." This means that this block will turn on
the motors connected to connectors A, B, and C. Assuming your motors are
connected to A and C and not to B, you need to tell the program to leave B
alone. Actually, you need to know if your motor is connected to B or not to
B — that is the question.

In order to tell the On block to leave B alone, *flip it over* by right-clicking on it
so that it looks like Figure 8-10. Click on the X checkbox that's next to B. This
erases the X and tells the block to turn on only A and C. Flip the block back
over by clicking on the green check mark. Now the block is labeled "on AC."

Figure 8-10:
The back
of the On
block lets
you choose
which
motors to
turn on.

Figure 8-10:
The back
of the On
block lets
you choose
which
motors to
turn on.

The On block turns on the motors forever. The next step is to tell the program to wait a while and let the robot move forward. You do this with the Wait block. Scroll the commands down until the Wait block comes into view. Grab it by clicking on it in the same way you grabbed the On block. Drag it under the On block and click again to release it so that it snaps into place. The block is labeled "wait 1," meaning wait one second.

You want the robot to move forward for three seconds so right-click on the block to flip it over so that it looks like Figure 8-11. There are two ways to change the time: Click on the + and – keys or type in a new value. If you click on the + and – keys, the value changes by 0.1 seconds. If you're very patient, you can click the + 20 times to set the value to three seconds. If you aren't so patient, click on the value itself to highlight it. Now type in **3** and press enter. Click the green check mark to accept the changes. The block is now labeled "wait 3," meaning wait three seconds.

Figure 8-11:
The back of
the Wait
block lets
you set the
amount of
time to wait.

Finally, you need to tell the motors to turn off. Even the most casual observer may guess that this is done with the Off block. Scroll the commands up until the Off block is visible. Grab it and drag it under the "wait" block. Flip it over by right-clicking and uncheck the box next to the B. Click the green check mark to flip the block back over and keep the changes. The block now is labeled "off AC," meaning turn off the motors connected to A and C.

Your program should look like Figure 8-12. If it does, great! If it doesn't, you need to make some changes. If the labels are wrong (that is, it says "on AB" instead of "on AC"), right-click on the blocks with the errors and change the values. If the blocks are wrong or in the wrong order, simply move them. You do that in the same way you moved the blocks out of the commands area: Click on the block to grab it, move it to a new place, and click again to release the block.

You can leave blocks floating without being connected to anything without affecting your program. Use this to reorganize your commands. You can also drag blocks to the trash to delete them.

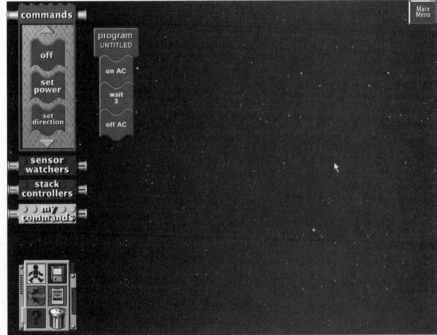

Figure 8-12: Your first program should look like this.

Downloading your program to the RCX

After you've written your first program, you need to try it out. Before you can run it, you need to download it to the RCX. The download button is located on the back side of the Program block. Right-click on the Program block to flip it over so that it looks like Figure 8-13. Make sure the RCX brick is turned on and is pointing at and sitting near the infrared transmitter. Click the download button to start transferring your masterpiece. A brief animation shows your program going into the RCX brick. When it is done, the RCX makes a chirping sound.

Figure 8-13:
The
download
button is on
the back
side of the
Program
block.

Testing your program

The time has come to try out your first program. Place your robot on the ground (robots don't like driving off the edge of tables) in a clear area. Make sure the power is on and then press the green Run button on the RCX brick. Your robot should move forward for three seconds and then stop. If it does, congratulations. If not, it's time for debugging.

✔ If your robot moved backward instead of forward, make sure the wires connecting your motors are installed identically to the *Constructopedia* drawings.

✔ If the robot turned or made a grinding noise, use your best judgment to determine whether you have a mechanical problem of some sort.

✔ If the program ran but didn't do what you expected, go back and verify that the program is identical to Figure 8-12.

Making a small change

Making a small change to your program (for example, changing the run time from 3 seconds to 10) is easy. Do this by following these steps:

1. **Return to your program and flip the Wait block over.**

2. **Change the value from 3 to 10.**

3. **Flip the block back over and verify that it's now labeled "wait 10."**

4. **Flip the Program block over and download the new program to your robot.**

   Test the program by running it. If it works, great. Otherwise, go back and verify your work.

What is debugging, anyway?

Debugging is just a fancy way of saying trouble-shooting. Anything wrong with your program is called a bug. As you try to figure out what went wrong and how you plan to fix it, you are debugging (literally taking bugs out of your program).

Saving your work

After you write and modify your first program, you need to save it to your hard drive for later use. Do this by following these steps:

1. **Flip the Program block over again.**

2. **Click on the Save As button.**

   This tells the RIS to save your program as a new name. This brings up the Program Vault that's described further in Chapter 9.

3. **Type a name for your first program.**

   Something creative like "My first program" will do just fine.

4. **Click on the "Save" button.**

   Your program is saved to the disk, and you're returned to the programming area. Notice that your Program block is now labeled "program My first prog." This shows that your program has been saved and lets you know what it's called.

5. **Click on the Main Menu button to get back to the main menu.**

6. **Click Exit to return to Windows.**

Chapter 9

More RIS Programming

*T*he heart of the Robotics Invention System is the RCX brick. This little yellow and gray block is stuffed with sophisticated electronics that control your robotic creations. Each RCX brick can control three devices (such as motors or a lamp) and respond to up to three sensors (Touch, Light, Temperature, and Rotation Sensors). The neat thing about the RCX is that it can be set up to do practically anything with these sensors and motors. You can build a robot that walks around the room avoiding obstacles, a robot that follows a line, a robot that can throw a ball, or anything else you can imagine.

How do you do this? By programming! Before you reach for your pocket protector and some tape for your glasses, consider this: Programming the RCX is easy. Unlike traditional programming that requires you to type out a series of arcane commands, the RCX is programmed right on the screen with graphics. By selecting, moving, and connecting blocks, you can set up your program to do almost anything. You have just four basic types of programming blocks and six simple tools to master on your way to becoming a robotics creator.

Programming with RIS 1.5

Before you can begin programming, be sure that your RIS software is installed and working properly (see Chapter 8). After it's installed, you start the Robotics Invention System software by double-clicking the desktop icon.

Getting to the programming screen

Log in to the system by selecting your name from the Logon screen. If this is your first time logging in, select New User from the Logon menu, type in your name, and click Enter. The first time you log in, you'll be in the guided mode, a training center through which you understand the basics of the RCX and RIS setup (see Chapter 8).

You can cancel the guided mode by holding down the control key and clicking the About button.

If this isn't your first time logging on, select your name from the list of users and click Enter. On the Main screen, click on the Program RCX button. When the RCX Code menu comes up, click on the middle button, called RCX Code. This brings up the programming screen.

The programming screen

The programming screen is where the real work will be done. As you can see in Figure 9-1, this screen has four sections:

- ✔ **Block selection:** Programming is accomplished by stacking blocks together on the screen. Each block represents a single command or decision. The programs start running at the first block on the top of the stack and work their way down the stack, doing the activities determined by the blocks one at a time until the last block is reached. Four basic types of blocks are available in RIS: Commands, Sensor Watchers, Stack Controllers, and My Commands. See the "Building Your Program with Blocks" section, later in this chapter, for more details.

- ✔ **Tools:** Six tools help with writing and debugging your program: Try-out, Copy, Help, Program Vault, Download/Save, and Trash. See the "Tooling Up with Tools" section, later in this chapter, for more details.

- ✔ **Main menu button:** To get back to the main menu, click on this button. If you make any changes to your program, you're given a chance to save your changes before going back.

- ✔ **Programming area:** This area is where you put your programming blocks and arrange them into stacks to run your program. Each *stack* is a program that instructs your robot how to behave. Many of your simple programs will fit into this area, but if your program is larger than the screen, the screen scrolls over automatically when you put the cursor near the edge of the screen. This allows you to see the area that was off the screen and hidden.

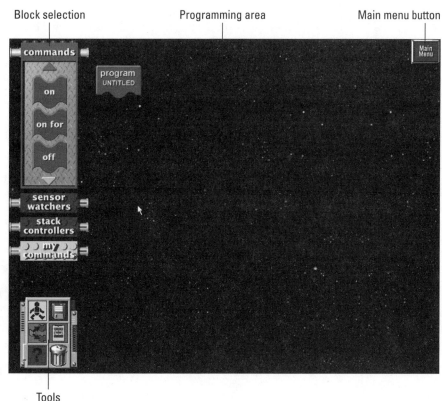

Block selection   Programming area   Main menu button

Figure 9-1:
The RIS
programming
screen.

Tools

Building Your Programs with Blocks

Blocks are the basic programming unit of the RCX system. Each block represents a command or an action that the RCX must do. The blocks are grouped together for convenience into four categories: Commands, Sensor Watchers, Stack Controllers, and My Commands.

Basic block techniques

A few basic rules apply to all programming blocks:

- ✔ **Where are they?** All the programming blocks are located in the four LEGO blocks in the upper-left side of the screen. The green block holds the commands, the blue block holds the Sensor Watchers, the red block holds the stack controllers, and the yellow block holds my commands. Each of these four blocks can be flipped up or down to show or hide the program blocks. Figure 9-2 shows the commands block flipped down and the other three flipped up. Flip the blocks up and down by clicking on their respective names.

Inside of these four blocks are the program blocks. Because only three program blocks can be seen at one time inside each group, you can scroll the commands up or down to see more. The small gray triangles at the top and bottom scroll the blocks up or down.

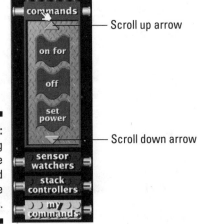

Scroll up arrow

Scroll down arrow

Figure 9-2:
Programming
blocks are
selected
from these
four groups.

✔ **Grabbing, dragging, and dropping:** Placing a program block into your program consists of three steps: Grab the block by clicking on it and releasing, drag the block by moving the mouse, and place the block by clicking again.

✔ **The descriptions change:** When you drag a block into the programming area, its name may change. For example, the On block becomes the On ABC block when dragged out. This is so that the block is more descriptive; that is, you can quickly see that this block will turn on outputs A, B, and C. If the name was On C, it would only be turning on output C.

✔ **Right click to flip:** Many of the program blocks have valuable controls on their backsides. To flip a block over, right-click on it with your mouse. When you're done with the flipped block, click on the green check mark to flip it back over. Figure 9-3 shows the backside of the On block, with controls for specifying which outputs to turn on.

✔ **Minimizing:** The Sensor Watchers, Check & Choose, and My Commands blocks are larger than the Command blocks. Clicking on the small box in the upper corner of the block reduces the size to make viewing your program easier. Clicking the small box again returns the block to its original size. The two sizes of a Check & Choose Touch Sensor block are shown in Figure 9-4.

Figure 9-3:
The backside of the On block has controls for choosing outputs.

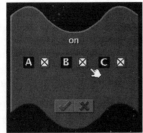

Figure 9-4:
Many blocks can be minimized.

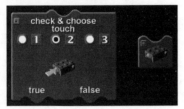

✓ **Rearranging:** Blocks in the programming area can be grabbed and dragged just as you may expect. When a block is grabbed, it takes all of the lower blocks in the stack with it. This lets you move an entire stack with a single action.

✓ **Random:** Many of the blocks need a value entered on their backsides to run properly. Some of these blocks allow a random value to be entered. For example, Figure 9-5 shows the backside of the Wait block. By clicking on the symbol of the die, the block is set to randomly choose a wait value of 0.1 to 1.0 seconds.

Figure 9-5:
Many blocks allow random values by clicking on the symbol of the die.

✓ **Floating blocks:** Blocks don't have to be attached to a stack. They can be dragged out to the programming area and left unattached. They won't actually do anything this way, but you can temporarily store a block or two while you're working on your program.

✔ **Saving:** Your program can be saved to the hard disk of your PC. Do this by right-clicking on the Program block, which is the first block of the stack. On the backside of this block is a button labeled Save and another one labeled Save As. If you're saving to your PC for the first time, click the Save As button. You'll be taken to the Program Vault (explained later in this chapter) where you can enter a name and save your program.

If you're not saving for the first time, you can click the Save button to save your program under its original name. After your program has been saved, the program block displays its name.

✔ **Downloading:** The backside of the program block has a button that downloads your program into the RCX brick. To download, make sure the RCX brick is on and then click on the download button. An animation shows your program's transfer to the RCX brick.

You can download to one of five program slots in the RCX brick. Choose which slot you want in the upper-left corner of the back of the program block.

✔ **Running:** After downloading your program, you can run it by pressing the Run button on the RCX brick.

✔ **Starting a new program:** If you want to start a new program from scratch and clear the programming area, flip over the program block and click on the Clear button.

Commands

Commands are all the blocks that tell the RCX to do something: turning on a motor, waiting for a second, and making a beeping noise are all examples of commands. The commands can be further broken down by function into output control, timing, sound, counter and timer, sensor, and communication.

Output control

These commands control the motors and lights connected to the RCX brick.

✔ **On:** This block tells the RCX to turn on one or more outputs. By right-clicking it and flipping it over, you can set it to turn on any combination of outputs A, B, or C. After an output is turned on, it remains on until specifically turned off with the Off block.

✔ **On For:** This block is just like the On block except that the output stays on for just a short time and then turns off. The time is set by flipping the clock over and using the + and – keys or typing in a new value. Any value can be set between 0.1 and 327.6 seconds (a nice, round number — see the "327.6?" sidebar for details). Using this block is just like creating a stack with an On block, a Wait block, and an Off block.

- **Off:** This block tells the RCX to turn off one or more outputs. Flipping it over lets you select which outputs to turn off.

- **Set Power:** This block sets the amount of driving power sent to the wheels. The outputs that you want to control and the power level are set on the back of the block. Power levels can be set from 1 to 8. Technically speaking, the power value represents the amount of time that the motor is on. So for a value of 1, the motor is on ⅛ of the time; for a value of 3, it's on ⅜ of the time; and for a value of 8, it's on ⅝ or all the time. You can't actually tell that the motor is turning on and off, but you can feel that the power of the motor is different at different power levels. When your program first starts up, the power level for all outputs is set to 8.

- **Set Direction:** This block is used to set the direction of each output. Although this only makes sense for motors and not for lamps (we've never seen a lamp running backward), it's very important for the control of your robot. You choose which outputs are going to be controlled and which direction to set on the back of the block. The chosen direction is set regardless of what direction the motor was running before.

- **Reverse Direction:** This block is similar to the Set Direction block in that it can be used to control the direction of a motor. However, unlike the Set Direction block, this block only changes the current direction of the motor. In other words, if the motor is going forward and this block is run, the motor will go backwards. If it is going backwards, it will reverse and go forward. As usual, you can choose which outputs to reverse on the back of the block.

Timing

There is only one timing block in the RCX: the Wait block. This block pauses the program for the amount of time set on the back of the block. When the time expires, the stack continues running. The wait time can be set to a value of 0.1 to 327.6 seconds.

327.6?

Where do programmers come up with numbers like 327.6? Why not 300.0 or 350.0 or something that looks more like a round number? Because 327.6 looks like a round number to a computer but not to you and us. It comes from the fact that inside the RCX brick, numbers are represented by a 16-bit binary number. That means that the number can be any value from -2^{15} to $+2^{15}$ or -32768 to $+32768$. Internally, too, the RCX timers count in 100ths of seconds. Of course, time can't go backward, so you get a timer that can go from 0 to 327.68. Because setting a timer to 0 makes no sense and 10ths of seconds are used for simplicity, you end up with a timer that times from 0.1 to 327.6 seconds.

Sound

Two blocks can generate sound in the RCX:

- ✔ **Beep:** This block generates one of six R2D2-like sounds. By flipping the block over, you can choose sound 1 (a simple beep), 2 (a double beep), 3(a falling tone), 4 (a rising tone), 5 (an error beep), and 6 (another rising tone).

- ✔ **Tone:** This block can generate a sound at a specific note and for a specific amount of time. With this command, you can actually get your RCX to play a tune. You can set the play time to be from 0.1 to 2.5 seconds and the note to play to almost any value, but most people can only hear notes between 50 and 14,000 Hz (cycles per second). If you're interested in really annoying your dog, play the notes at 15,000 and up and watch the reaction.

Counter and timer

Inside the RCX brick is a counter and a timer. The three following counter and time commands can be used inside your programs for keeping a count of events and keeping track of time:

- ✔ **Add to Counter:** This block adds one to the counter. When your program starts, the counter is set to zero. The first time the program runs an Add to Counter block, the counter goes to 1; the next time it goes to 2; and so on. Your program can use a Sensor Watcher or a Stack Controller block (explained later in this chapter in the "Sensor Watchers" and "Stack Controllers" sections) to check the value of the counter and use that to control your program. The maximum value for a counter is 32,766, but we doubt that you will ever need to count that high.

- ✔ **Reset Counter:** This block resets the counter back to zero.

- ✔ **Reset Timer:** This block resets the internal timer back to zero. There is not a corresponding Add to Timer block because the internal timer starts ticking all by itself. The timer starts at zero when the program starts and counts up to 327.6 seconds, or roughly 5½ minutes.

Sensor

There is only one sensor command, Reset Rotation. This block resets the rotation sensor to zero. The Rotation Sensor measures the amount of rotation of an axle. Every full revolution is 16 counts and can count as high as 32,766 (or 2,047 rotations).

Communication

Two RCX bricks or an RCX brick and a Scout can communicate with each other by sending messages on the infrared port. There are two communication blocks used to talk to other RCX bricks or Scouts.

✔ **Send to RCX:** This block sends a message numbered 1 to 255 out the infrared port. Messages are received by an RCX brick with the Check & Choose block or Sensor Watcher block.

✔ **Reset Message:** This block clears the last received RCX infrared command. Normally this block is placed after the Check & Choose block or the Sensor Watcher block that processed the message.

Sensor Watchers

Sensor Watcher blocks are special blocks that constantly monitor your sensors and start running a new stack when something happens to it. Sensor Watchers are a little different than other blocks because they don't attach to the bottom of a stack. Instead they attach to the side of the stack and actually become the top of another stack or two. You attach them by dragging the block to the right of the current stack and releasing.

You can use seven types of Sensor Watchers: Touch, Light, Temperature, Rotation, Counter, Timer, and RCX.

✔ **Touch:** This block can have two stacks attached to it. The stack on the left is started whenever the selected Touch Sensor is pressed. The stack on the right is started whenever the selected Touch Sensor is released. The input that the Touch Sensor is connected to is chosen by clicking 1, 2, or 3 at the top of the block.

Figure 9-6 illustrates the use of the Touch Sensor watcher. The On ABC block turns on the outputs and leaves them on. The Touch Sensor watcher waits for a Touch Sensor on input 1. When the Touch Sensor is pressed, the Reverse Direction ABC block runs, changing the direction of outputs A, B, and C. When the Touch Sensor is released, the Beep 3 clock runs, making a sound.

You can find the Touch Sensor program on this book's CD.

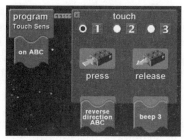

Figure 9-6:
This program runs outputs A, B, and C forward until Sensor 1 is pressed. Then the motors are reversed.

✔ **Light:** This block can also have two stacks attached to it, but unlike the Touch Sensor, the decision of which stack to run is not black and white. As a matter of fact, the Light Sensor can detect varying levels of light, from total darkness to very bright light. You must adjust the sliders or the values to the point where you want the device triggered. In other words, if you want the left stack to start when the light is dim (light level 40), set the left slider to 40. If you want the right stack to start only when the light is very bright (light level 60), set the right slider to 60. With the block set up like this, the left stack runs whenever the light level moves from 41 or higher to 40 or lower. The right stack runs whenever the light level moves from 59 or lower to 60 or higher. If the light level stays between 41 and 59, neither stack runs.

The program in Figure 9-7 shows the Light Sensor in action. There are no blocks in the main stack, so nothing happens there. The Light Sensor watcher waits for the light level on input 2 to drop below 50. When this happens, the On ABC block runs, turning on the motors. When the light level goes above 50, the Off ABC block runs, turning off the motors.

Look for the Light Sensor program on the CD that comes with this book.

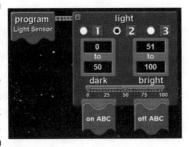

Figure 9-7:
This program runs the motors only when it's dark outside.

Every RCX brick and Light Sensor is a little bit different. A light level of 50 on a particular RCX-Light Sensor combination may register as 55 on the next unit. We always use the view function described in Chapter 8 to read the light levels that we're interested in before writing the program. This allows you to get real-life readings of the light level with your particular RCX and Light Sensor.

✔ **Temperature:** This block is just like the Light Sensor watcher except that it responds to the Temperature Sensor. It also has two stacks attached to it: one to run at low temperatures and one at high temperatures. The temperatures are set in either Celsius or Fahrenheit. This can be changed in your setup options, as explained in Chapter 8.

✔ **Rotation:** This block has only one stack attached to it. The stack will run whenever the Rotation Sensor enters the range displayed. The range is set in terms of 16 counts per full revolution. So a range of 16 to 32 means that the Sensor Watcher will run the stack when the Rotation Sensor has turned at least one and less than two full turns. Negative values can also be set in the block to indicate turning in the opposite direction.

✔ **Counter:** This block also has only one stack attached to it. The stack is activated when the internal counter enters the range chosen. For example, Figure 9-8 shows a program that uses the Counter Sensor watcher. There are no blocks in the main stack, so nothing happens there. The Touch Sensor watcher runs the counter block every time the Touch Sensor is pressed. The Counter Sensor block waits until the counter reaches ten, and when it does, it runs the Beep block.

Look for the Counter Sensor program on this book's CD.

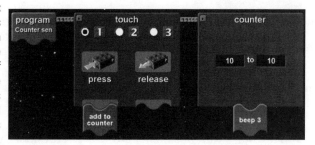

Figure 9-8: This program counts the number of times the sensor is pushed and beeps after ten.

✔ **Timer:** This block also has only one stack attached to it. The stack is activated when the internal timer is within the chosen range.

✔ **RCX:** This block also has only one stack attached to it. The stack is run whenever the RCX brick receives an infrared message in the range chosen.

Stack Controllers

Stack Controllers are the traffic cops of your program. They control how a program flows. All of the programs you've seen so far are just straight stacks. They run from top to bottom without repeating or stopping. With Stack Controller blocks, you can make your programs much more versatile and much smarter.

There are five Stack Controller blocks: Check & Choose, Repeat, Repeat Forever, Repeat While, and Wait Until.

✔ **Check & Choose:** This block is similar to a Sensor Watcher, but instead of starting a new stack, you can use this command in the middle of a stack. You use it to make decisions. One of two attached stacks is selected based on the condition you choose. For example, you can set up a Check & Choose block to look at a Touch Sensor and run the left stack if the sensor is on or run the right stack if the sensor is off.

When you first click on the Check & Choose block, you will be shown the box in Figure 9-9. Select the sensor you want by clicking on the picture of the sensor and then clicking the green check mark.

Figure 9-9:
The Check & Choose block needs to know what sensor to look at.

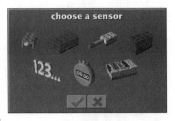

Figure 9-10 shows the Check & Choose block in action. This program will beep a high tone if the Touch Sensor is pressed when the program is run. It will beep a low tone if the Touch Sensor is not pressed when the program is run.

See the CD that comes with this book for the Check & Choose program.

Figure 9-10:
This program beeps high or low depending on the state of the Touch Sensor.

✔ **Repeat:** This block lets you run a section of your program many times, and is actually made up of two parts: the Repeat block and the End Repeat block. By inserting commands between these two blocks, you're telling your program to repeat them as often as you specify. The number in the top block indicates how many times to repeat.

The program shown in Figure 9-11 is an example of the Repeat stack controller. The program picks a random number between 1 and 5 and repeats the Beep and Wait blocks that many times. Run it a few times and make sure that each time you run it, you're getting a random number of beeps. The Wait block is needed here because without it, all of the beeps run into each other, and you wouldn't be able to count them.

Check out this book's CD for a copy of the Repeat Random program.

Figure 9-11:
This program beeps randomly from one to five times.

✔ **Repeat Forever:** This block is like the Repeat block, but instead of repeating a set number of times, it repeats forever. At first glance, this may seem useless, but it is quite common to surround your complete program with this block so that it continues to run forever.

Forever is not really forever. You can always stop your program by pressing the Run button on the front of the RCX brick.

✔ **Repeat While:** This block is like the Repeat block, but instead of repeating a set number of times, the commands are repeated while a certain condition exists. You can, for example, set up this brick to repeat a set of commands while the Light Sensor shows that the room is dark.

✔ **Wait Until:** This block is the opposite of the Repeat While block. It stops your program and waits until a certain condition happens. For example, it could have your program stop and wait until the counter has reached 10.

My commands

My commands are commands that you define yourself. You can create and name small programs and use them once or many times in your program. When you first start up the RIS software, the My Commands block has only one block, labeled New My Command. You can drag this block out into the programming area, add commands between its first and second blocks, name it, and then use it somewhere in your program.

Figure 9-12 shows a My Command block named Fwd wait. This block is made up of two commands: an On ABC For 1 block that tells the motors to turn on for one second and a Wait 1 block that tells the program to wait for one second. (This My Command block is not currently connected to a stack.) The main stack has three copies of the Fwd Wait block (all minimized). This stack will run the Fwd Wait command three times. Your robot will lurch forward for one second and stop for a second, doing this three times.

ON THE CD

You can find the My Command program on this book's CD.

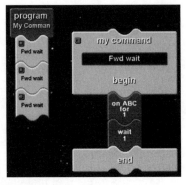

Figure 9-12:
This program shows that a new command block can be made.

Tooling Up with Tools

The six tools in the programming area — Try-out, Copy, Help, Program Vault, Download/Save, and Trash — are shown in Figure 9-13. The easiest way to learn each of their functions is by using them.

TIP

You can cancel the Try-out, Copy, and Help tools in three ways: by clicking on the tool again, by clicking on the space background of the programming area, or by pressing the Esc key on your keyboard.

Figure 9-13:
The tool palette has six tools that you use to modify and run your programs.

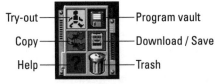

Try-out ——— ——— Program vault
Copy ——— ——— Download / Save
Help ——— ——— Trash

The following sections show you how to use each of the six tools in conjunction with a simple Beep block. To follow along with this example, drag a Beep block out of the green commands block (found by scrolling the commands down) by clicking on it to grab it, dragging it into the programming area of the screen, and clicking again to release the block.

The Try-out tool

The Try-out tool is used to instruct the RCX brick to run the block you clicked on right away. By using this tool, you can test small parts of your program without downloading your entire program and testing everything.

The Try-out tool is the one that looks like a little man with a yellow background. To try it out, click on the man. The cursor turns into a hand with a little man behind it. Now make sure the RCX brick is turned on and pointing at the infrared transmitter. Move the cursor over the Beep block, as shown in Figure 9-14, and click. This tells the RCX to do the command that you clicked on right away, so when you click, you'll hear a single, short beep. This is the Beep 1 command running on the RCX.

Now, right-click on the Beep block and change the beep setting to sound 4. Select the Try-out tool and click on the modified Beep block. You now hear a rising bubble sound from your RCX brick. You can use the Try-out tool on the following command blocks: On, On For, Off, Set Power, Set Direction, Reverse Direction, Wait, Beep, and Tone.

You can also use the Try-out tool on the Check & Choose, Repeat While, and Repeat Until stack controllers as well as on the Touch, Light, Rotation, and Temperature Sensor watchers. (When you use the Try-out tool on any of these Sensor Watchers, a small box is displayed in the middle of the block showing the current reading of the sensor. This gives you the same functionality as the view function of the RCX block itself.)

When the Try-out tool is pointing to a block that can be tested, the man opens up his arms and legs and looks like he's running. When the tool is pointing to a block that can't be run, the man just stands still.

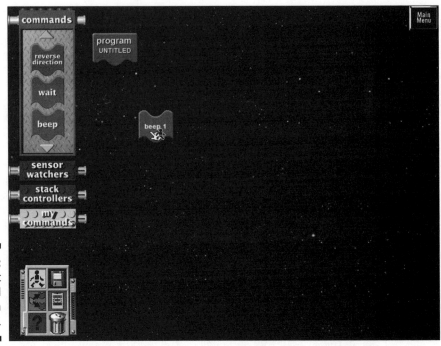

The Trace tool

The Try-out tool also turns on a hidden tool called the Trace tool. Tracing your program isn't something you do with crayons, but rather is a sophisticated way of seeing what is going on inside your program. With it, you can trace through your program one block at a time and see exactly what's working or not working in your program.

To see how this tool works, do the following:

1. **Make the Trace program shown in Figure 9-15 or load it from the CD.**

   This is just a simple program that plays one of each type of beep in a row. Create this program by dragging Beep blocks to the screen, flipping them over (by right-clicking on the block), and selecting the beep tone.

2. **Now comes the tricky part. Click on the Try-out tool, then click on the program block while holding down the control key on your keyboard (while you're doing this, rub your tummy and tap your head).**

   The trace controller shows up in the lower left-hand corner of the display, as shown in Figure 9-16. This controller lets you download your program into the RCX brick, set the run speed of the trace, and start and stop your program.

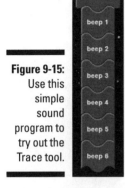

Figure 9-15:
Use this
simple
sound
program to
try out the
Trace tool.

Program number

Speed indicator

Figure 9-16:
The trace
controller
lets you
download
your
program
and trace it.

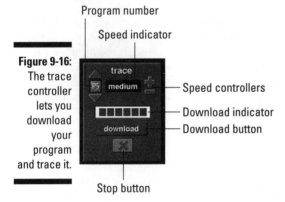

Speed controllers

Download indicator
Download button

Stop button

3. **Start the download by clicking the download button on the trace controller.**

   While your program is downloading, the word "downloading" replaces "download" and the download indicators flash green. When the download is complete, the RCX emits a tone and the download button displays "start." This loads a special version of your program that can be traced by the RIS software.

4. **Press the start button to see the trace in action.**

   A purple border with the number 1 is drawn around the current block, as shown in Figure 9-17. This border travels down the blocks until it reaches the end of the stack. If you push the stop button in the trace controller, the program stops running. If you push the red X in the trace controller, the trace is cancelled and the six programming tools are displayed again.

Figure 9-17:
When tracing, the current block is shown with a border around it.

If you have Sensor Watchers in your program, you may have two parts of your program running at one time. This means that your main stack is running but one of your sensors is also active and trying to run its stack. The tracing tool will show the second stack running with a blue border with the number 2 in the corner. In the same way, a third stack running will be highlighted in red with a 3 in the corner. This will keep going, but tracing more that one active stack at a time is too difficult to make it worthwhile. Try to stick to one or two.

The Copy tool

The Copy tool is used for copying stuff. (Pretty clever of those LEGO engineers!) Actually, the Copy tool can be very useful when you need to duplicate a part of your program and don't want to re-create the commands from scratch.

What is multitasking?

Multitasking is the technical way of saying that you're doing several things at once. You're multitasking when you talk on the phone and wash dishes at the same time or when you eat your lunch while driving.

A safer type of multitasking is what your RCX brick can do. It can actually run two different parts of the same program at once. Why would you want to do that? It is usually used for responding to a change in a sensor. In other words, if your main program tells your robot to move forward, it may bump into something. If it does, a second program starts to run and tells the robot to back up and turn. Then the main program takes over again and continues to tell the robot to move forward again. This will really simplify your program because your main program can be very simple (for example, Move Forward) and secondary programs can handle situations like bumping into a wall.

You activate the Copy tool by clicking on it: Your cursor turns into a hand with two gray arrows pointing to two command blocks. The gray arrows turn white when the cursor is over a block that can be copied. Use this cursor to click on the block you want to copy. As soon as you click, a copy of the block is created and you can drag it into place wherever you need it.

Try it out: Start by dragging a single beep block from the Command block. Instead of grabbing a second Beep block from the Command block, create a copy of the first one. Do this by clicking on the Copy tool and then clicking on the Beep block, as shown in Figure 9-18. Drag the copy of the block below the first one and release it, as shown in Figure 9-19.

Figure 9-18:
The Copy tool is used to duplicate blocks.

Figure 9-19:
After copying a block, drag it into place.

The Copy tool can also copy several blocks at once. It does this by copying the block that you clicked on plus all the attached blocks below the one you clicked. For example, if you have a stack of four blocks and use the Copy tool on the second block, not only will you make a copy of block two, but also blocks of three and four.

We use this feature quite often to make a copy of our entire stack. When we're debugging and we need to make changes to our stack, we drag a copy of the original stack off to the side and keep it around for reference while making changes to the original stack. That way, we can refer to it whenever we need to, and we can revert to the original if our debugging destroys the program.

The Help tool

The Help tool is your ever-handy reference manual. If you're ever in doubt about how a tool works or the functionality of a block, use the Help tool. Start the Help tool by clicking the question mark in the red button. This changes the cursor into a hand with a gray question mark. When the cursor is placed over an item that has help available, the question mark turns white. Using your cursor to click an object opens a help window that explains the object. Figure 9-20 shows the help information for the Beep block.

The help information is displayed in a standard Microsoft Windows Help dialog box. Links to related information are shown in green and are underlined such that, if you click on a link, you'll be taken to the related page. Click on the Back button to go back to the previous page. When you're done with the help window, you can close it manually or click on the programming area background to close it.

The Program Vault

The Program Vault is the place where you keep all your programs. Instead of using the standard file dialog box that's built into Windows, LEGO decided to create an entirely new (but not necessarily better) way of getting at your programs. For that reason, the Program Vault, shown in Figure 9-21, takes a little getting used to.

You get to the Program Vault by clicking on the floppy disk icon (the button has a blue background). If you're working on a program and have made any changes to it, you will be asked, "Do you want to save?" If you do, click on the green checkmark; if you don't, click on the red X and proceed to the programming vault without saving. If you want to continue working on the program and not proceed to the programming vault, click the Cancel button when you're asked about saving your program.

The top of the vault shows all of the folders that you have access to. Typically, you'll have folders for each registered user, the Robotics Invention System, the desktop, and the A: drive. Clicking a folder ("Peter" in Figure 9-21) brings up a list of all the programs that are in that folder. Clicking once on a program name (the Avoid program is selected in Figure 9-21) brings up the description of the program. This description is usually typed in when you first save your program and is used to describe your robot's name, what it looks like, what it can do, and any other information that will help you remember which program is which. You may change your program's description at any time. Always take the time to fill out a complete description of your program, because if you're anything like us, you'll end up with a bunch of programs in the vault and no idea what they are supposed to do or which robots they're supposed to go with.

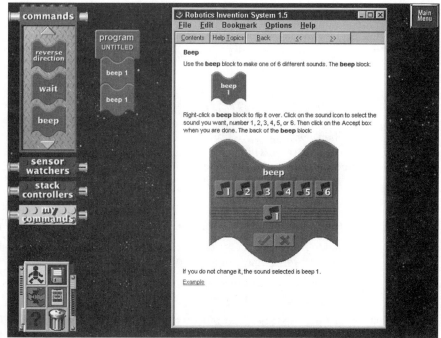

Figure 9-20:
The Help
tool display
information
about a
block.

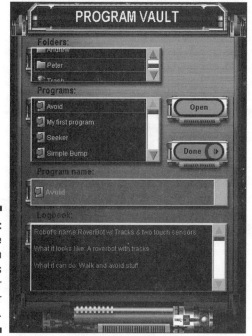

Figure 9-21:
The
Program
Vault holds
all your
programs for
safekeeping.

By double-clicking the name of your program or by clicking the name one time and pressing the Open button, you can go back to the programming area and open the selected program. Clicking the Done button takes you back to the programming area without opening any new programs.

The Download/Save tool

Using the Download/Save tool is exactly like right-clicking on the program block to flip it over. This gives you access to the Save, Save As, Clear, and Download commands. Activate the RCX tool by clicking on the small picture of the RCX brick in the green button.

- ✓ If your program is already named, the Save button will save the latest version of your program.

- ✓ Clicking the Save As button takes you to the Program Vault and allows you to enter a new name for your program.

- ✓ Clicking the Clear button asks if you're sure and then erases your current program so that you can create a new one.

- ✓ Clicking the Download button transfers your program to the RCX brick.

The Trash

The Trash is where you get rid of unused blocks from your program. This tool is the picture of the Trash can and is different from the other tools. Instead of clicking the tool to use it, you must grab the blocks that you want to delete and drag them to the Trash. When the cursor is directly over the Trash, the cover lifts slightly (don't blink or you'll miss it!). This means that you can let go of the block and delete it. We often drop the blocks near the Trash instead of in the Trash, so be careful.

After you have put something into the Trash, you can't get it back out. The only remedy for this is to save your program often so that you have a backup and to be very careful when throwing things away.

Part IV
Special Projects to Make You a Robot Scientist

The 5th Wave   By Rich Tennant

Well heck—that's just darn impressive! And you say it's programmed to sew up and dress the incision afterward, as well?

In this part . . .

This parts prepares you to go beyond the basics, with additional projects. You find out how to use some great programs that are on the CD, get in-depth information on using the various MINDSTORMS sensors, and find out how to go beyond the RCX programming language.

Chapter 10

Creating RoverBot Programs

• •

In This Chapter

▶ Making your robot move and turn

▶ Teaching your robot to sing

▶ Programming your robot to walk and avoid obstacles

• •

*B*y combining the mechanical elements of LEGOs with the electronic control of the RCX brick, you can create a robot that performs almost any function. The programs you write are transferred into the RCX brick and interact with motors and sensors to create a living, thinking robot. Of course, the mechanical construction of the robot plays a major role in the function of the robot, but the program is at least as important. Think of it this way: The program is the brain while the LEGO blocks are the body.

This chapter shows you how to put some smarts into that brain and make it take charge of the robot.

Move It

To run the Move It program, you need to build the RoverBot, as shown in the LEGO MINDSTORMS Constructopedia and in Chapter 5 of this book. Our preference is the RoverBot with tracks, because it runs well on most surfaces (including carpeting, grass, and so on) and travels relatively slowly so you can see your program function. It also keeps your robot from crashing into walls at high speeds and destroying itself! (Just make sure that you have the motors connected to outputs A and C.)

Purpose

The purpose of this program is to instruct the robot to move away from you in a straight line, turn around, and come back.

You can find the Move It program on this book's CD.

The program

The simplest way to make the robot move is to turn on both of its motors in the same direction. Do this with the On block. Because you have nothing connected to output B, flip the On block over and unselect output B. Your program should look like Figure 10-1. Download this program into your RCX and try it out.

Figure 10-1:
This program gets your robot moving.

When you use this program, what happens? The robot moves forward and then keeps going and going and going (hey, what type of batteries did you put in there, anyway?).

Your program now needs to tell it to stop. You can do this in two ways, both shown in Figure 10-2.

✔ The unconnected stack on the right in Figure 10-2 is the long way of getting the job done. The On block tells the motors to turn on, the Wait block pauses for three seconds, and the Off block tells the motors to turn off.

✔ The same happens with the stack on the left in Figure 10-2 but all in one block. The On For block tells the motors to turn on, waits 3 seconds, and tells the motors to turn off.

We use the left-hand version in this program. Download this program into your RCX and try it out. Your robot goes forward for three seconds and stops.

Figure 10-2:
You can tell the robot to stop in two ways.

Now you have to make the robot turn around. The easiest way to turn your robot around is to turn one motor on going forward and turn the other motor on going backward. Figure 10-3 shows how this can be done.

- ✔ The Set Direction block tells motor A to go forward and motor C to go backward. You make these setting on the back of the block, and your choices are shown on the front of the block by the small direction arrows.

- ✔ The On For block tells the motors to turn on and makes the robot spin. The value of your On For block may be different than the three seconds shown. This time is based on the condition of the batteries, the type of floor the robot is on, and so on.

Download the program into your RCX brick and see if it does a full 180° turn. If it does, great! If not adjust the last On For block. Make the time longer if you need more turning, shorter if you need less turning.

Figure 10-3:
Make the
robot turn
by reversing
one motor.

The last thing you need to do is make the robot come back to you. Make both motors go forward with the Set Direction block and then turn them on for three seconds with the On For block — see Figure 10-4.

Make sure you save your program if you want to use it later.

Figure 10-4:
The robot
walks away,
turns
around, and
comes back.

Square Dance

Like the Move It program, the Square Dance program is also best used with a RoverBot with tracks. You don't need bumpers, but make sure your motors are attached to outputs A and C.

Purpose

The purpose of this program is to instruct the robot to walk in a square pattern over and over and over.

The Square Dance program is on the CD that comes with this book.

The program

We start this program by making the robot move forward for four seconds.

1. **The On For block sets the time to 4.**

2. **The robot turns 90° by reversing one of the motors and running for enough time to turn.**

   • Reversing the motors is done with the Set Direction block.

   • The turn is completed with the On For block.

3. **A final Set Direction block sets both motors to forward again.**

   Even though this isn't needed yet, it will be useful later in the program because the next portion of the program assumes that the robot is set to go forward.

This first step is shown in Figure 10-5. The time of the last On For block may be different for your robot than in this example. This is due to differences in motors, batteries, and floor surfaces. If your robot doesn't turn 90°, experiment with the time value and make it longer to turn more, shorter to turn less.

Figure 10-5:
The robot walks away and turns 90°.

The LEGO MINDSTORMS version of Spirograph

Remember Spirograph, that cool toy with the xgears and pens that let you draw incredible shapes? I don't know if it's still available, but who needs it? You have in your possession the coolest version of a Spirograph ever. By building a chalk holder, you can let your RCX robot draw Spirograph-type shapes on your driveway. For example, the Square Dance program makes an interesting pattern to start off with; you can then change the On For times and the Turn times to make things really interesting.

Your robot is moving for four seconds and then making a 90° right turn. To make it go in a square, you simply have to instruct your robot to do this four times.

1. **Make a single copy, using the Copy tool (described in Chapter 9).**

2. **Grab a copy of your program and place it on the bottom of the stack.**

   Your program should look like Figure 10-6 and will then do half of the square.

Figure 10-6:
The robot travels two sides of the square.

You could keep tacking the go-turn sequence onto the end of your stack to make the square, but there is an easier way. Use the Repeat Stack Controller block instead.

1. **Get rid of the bottom four blocks of the program.**

   This leaves only the portion that moves and turns the robot one time. If you repeat this sequence four times, the robot will move in a square.

2. **Open the Stack controllers, grab a Repeat block, and place it in the programming area.**

3. **Grab the four commands that are in your stack and put them between the top and bottom of the repeat block.**

4. **Attach the Repeat block under the Program block.**

5. **Set the number of repeats to 4.**

   The robot now walks in a square. These additions are shown in Figure 10-7.

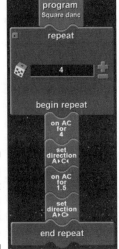

Figure 10-7:
This robot now travels a full square.

The robot probably doesn't walk a perfect square, though. This is because the angles aren't exactly 90° and small variations in the floor or carpet cause the robot to go off track a little bit.

The original purpose of this program was to make the robot walk in a square over and over and over. So far, your robot just does one square. The way to make your program run forever is to put it inside a Repeat Forever block.

1. **Drag a Repeat Forever block out to the programming area.**

2. **Put the Repeat block inside the Repeat Forever block.**

3. **Put the Repeat Forever block under the Program block.**

   It now looks like the program shown in Figure 10-8.

Figure 10-8:
This robot
now
completes a
full square
over and
over.

Alternatives

Another way to accomplish the task of making a square is to define a custom command for each side of the square and then put those four commands together.

1. **Drag a new My Command block into the programming area.**

2. **Place the four command blocks into it:**

   - On AC for 4

   - Set Direction A>C<

   - On AC for 1.5

   - Set Direction A>C>

3. **Name the My Command by clicking in the Untitled box and typing** Go and Turn.

   You have just created a custom command. The My Command's area now contains your new block.

4. **Drag four copies of this new command and place them on the Program block.**

   The program should look like the one shown in Figure 10-9 and makes your robot travel in a square.

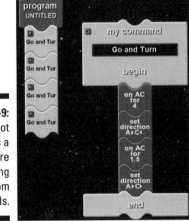

The Alternate Square program is on this book's CD.

Bump and Run

This program is based on the RoverBot, as shown in the LEGO MINDSTORMS *Constructopedia* and in Chapter 5 of this book. The RoverBot needs to be equipped with the double bumper so that the robot can detect when it bumps into something on the left or right. Make sure the motors are attached to outputs A and C and the Touch Sensors are attached to inputs 1 and 2.

Purpose

The purpose of this robot is to make a robot that can move around a room and avoid obstacles. It starts moving forward and backs up and turns when it runs into an obstacle. Then it continues on its merry way.

The Bump and Run program is on the CD that comes with this book.

The program

Start your program by making the robot move forward. This is done with an On block. Drag the On block from the Commands area, flip it over, and make sure only A and C are selected.

Because your robot will move forward forever, you need to make it respond to a Touch Sensor. This is done with a Sensor Watcher block. Flip down the Sensor Watcher area and drag a Touch Sensor Watcher block into the programming area. Your screen should look like Figure 10-10.

Figure 10-10:
The Bump
and Run
program
uses a
Sensor
Watcher.

The robot needs to back up and turn whenever the Touch Sensor is pressed.

1. **Use the Reverse Direction block to change the direction of outputs A and C. Place this block under the Press side of the Touch Sensor block.**

   Because the motors were turned on in the main stack and never turned off, the robot will start moving backward.

2. **Use a Wait block set to 2 seconds to let the robot back up.**

3. **Use another Reverse Direction block to change the direction of output A.**

   At this point, Motor A is running forward and motor C is still reversed so that the robot will start turning.

4. **Add another Wait block set to 2 seconds to allow the robot time to turn.**

5. **Use a Reverse Direction block to change the direction of output C.**

   This leaves both motors going forward again.

6. **Just for effect, add a Beep 4 block to the Release side of the Touch Sensor block.**

   This will run whenever the Touch Sensor is released and will make a sound. Your program should now look like the one shown in Figure 10-11. Download the program to your RCX brick and try it out.

At this point, only the left bumper is functional: The robot should start going forward, and when the left bumper is pressed, it will back up, turn right, and continue going forward. It also gives off a cute shifting beep every time the left bumper is released.

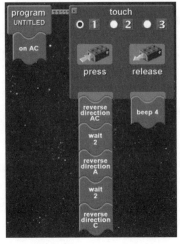

Figure 10-11:
The Bump and Run program now responds to the left sensor.

You need to make the right bumper functional. This is easy if you use the Copy tool and copy the Touch Sensor block.

1. **Drag the copy to the right of the program and drop it there.**

2. **Change the Touch Sensor block to look at input 3 by clicking the small circle next to the 3.**

3. **Change the first Reverse Direction block to reverse C and change the second reverse direction to reverse A.**

   This makes the robot turn left when the right bumper is pressed. Your program should now look like Figure 10-12.

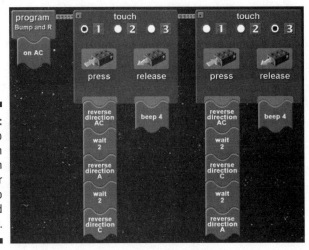

Figure 10-12:
The Bump and Run program allows your robot to avoid obstacles.

Download the program into your RCX brick and give it a spin. Every time your robot runs into something, it backs up, turns, and goes a different way. The amazing this is, your robot is responding to outside stimulus. It is actually making decisions on its own!

Alternatives

If you let your robot wander around long enough, you discover that it has a flaw. If both bumpers are pressed at the same time, such as when you have a head-on collision, the robot doesn't back up and turn. Instead it charges forward, oblivious to the object in its way. Why is this?

Even though both Touch Sensors appear to be touched at exactly the same time, one is actually touched a fraction of a second before the other. Suppose the left one is touched first. The first thing it does is reverse the motors to go backwards. Then the right bumper is touched. The first thing it does is tell the motors to reverse again. So now the robot is reversing the motors that are already reversed. Guess what . . . the robot is going forward again.

This is fairly easy to repair. Instead of using Reverse Direction blocks, replace them with Set Direction blocks, as shown in Figure 10-13. This way, the first Touch Sensor tells the motors to reverse. The second sensor also tells the motors to reverse, but they will be really reversing because you were specific with the Set Direction block and left nothing to chance.

Check out the Alternate Bump and Run program on this book's CD.

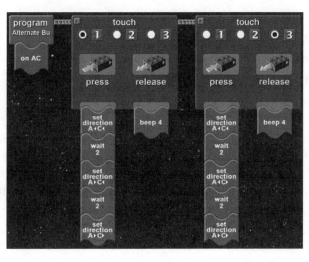

Figure 10-13: Fix the Bump and Run program's flaws by replacing the Reverse blocks with Set Direction blocks.

Better Beeps

This program doesn't need a robot at all, just the RCX brick and your ears.

Purpose

The purpose of this program is to make the RCX brick beep in a way that makes it sound like it's communicating. This requires making it produce a random number of sounds and tones.

Check out the Cool Beep program on this book's CD.

The program

Unlike some of the other commands, the tone command doesn't allow for random values to be entered. To make random tones, you need to use the Check & Choose blocks to select one of a few tones. This makes the tones appear to be random. Before you can use Check & Choose, however, you need to get a random value into the counter. The way this is done is kind of interesting.

1. **Create a new My Command and name it "Rand Cnt," which stands for random counter.**

2. **Add a Reset counter block into the Rand Cnt command.**

   This sets the internal counter to zero.

3. **Insert a Repeat block and set the number of repeats to 4.**

4. **Click on the die to set the repeat to a random 1-to-4 count.**

   This sets the repeat loop to repeat anywhere from 1 to 4 times.

5. **Inside the Repeat block, place an Add To Counter block.**

   This way, each time the block repeats, the counter goes up by one. The result of all this is that whenever the Rand Cnt command is executed, a random number between 1 and 4 is placed in the counter. The final custom command is shown in Figure 10-14.

   You can use the random value in the counter to select a tone to play.

6. **Minimize the Rand Cnt block and put it under the Program block.**

Figure 10-14:
The random counter command is used to select a tone to play.

7. **Select a Check & Choose block from the stack controller area.**

8. **When the selector pops up, choose the counter (the 123. . . symbol), click the green check mark, and drag the block to the bottom of the stack.**

9. **Set the values in the block to 1 to 2.**

   This means that if the value of the counter is either 1 or 2, the left stack runs; otherwise, the right stack runs. Your program so far should look like the one in Figure 10-15.

Figure 10-15:
The counter value is checked to find out its value.

10. **Add two more Check & Choose commands onto the first one. Make the value for the one on the left 1-to-1 and the value for the one on the right 3-to-3.**

    As shown in Figure 10-16, there are now four locations for stacks at the bottom of the Check & Choose blocks. The left-most location will run if the counter is equal to 1; the next location if it is 2; the third location if it is 3; and the last location if it is 4.

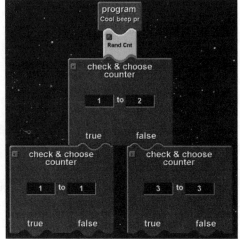

Figure 10-16: The counter value can be one of four choices.

11. **Add Tone blocks to the four spots on the bottom of the stack.**

    We've chosen tones that sound good to us, but you can use any values here. Our values for the Tone blocks are

    - 1000 for 0.1 seconds
    - 2000 for 0.2 seconds
    - 750 for 0.2 second
    - 500 for 0.3 seconds

    Flip each of the Tone blocks over and enter these values.

12. **After each of the Tone blocks, add a Wait block equal to the duration of the Tone block.**

    In other words, for the Tone 500 for 0.3 seconds, add a Wait block of 0.3 seconds. For more information on why you want to add a Wait block, flip to the "Why wait?" sidebar. Your program should now look like the one shown in Figure 10-17.

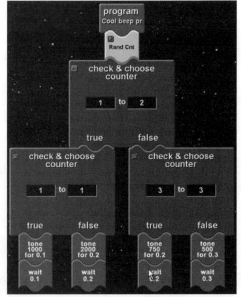

Figure 10-17:
Each of the
four choices
generates a
different
tone and
duration.

You can download the program to the RCX brick and test it out. Each time you run the program, one of the four tones is randomly chosen and played. Now all you have to do is put everything you've done so far inside a Repeat block to have several random beeps put together.

1. **Minimize the top Check & Choose block.**

2. **Drag a Repeat block out of the stack controller area into the programming area.**

3. **Set the value of the Repeat block to 10.**

4. **Click on the die to indicate a random value from 1 to 10.**

5. **Drag the two blocks away from the Program block and put them in the Repeat block.**

6. **Place the Repeat block under the Program Block.**

   The finished program is shown in Figure 10-18. Download and run the program to hear your RCX communicate with you.

Figure 10-18:
The RCX
brick
sounds as if
it's
communi-
cating.

Alternatives

You can put the new cool beeps inside a My Command block so that you can use it in other programs. This is quite easy to do.

1. **Drag a My Command block out to the programming area.**

2. **Name it "Cool Beep" and drag your entire stack inside of it.**

3. **Drag the Cool Beep block under the Program block.**

    The final result is shown in Figure 10-19 and runs in the same way as the previous program. The only difference is that Cool Beep can now be used in your other creations because it's a custom My Command block.

Use the Alternate 1 Cool Beep program on the CD that comes with this book.

Why wait?

Adding a Wait block after a Tone block may seem unneccesary — and it usually is. The Tone block plays the specified tone for the specified amount of time and doesn't need the delay. What's neat about the Tone block is that it will play the tone while your program has moved on to the next block. That means that the tone can be playing while you're telling your robot to move forward or do anything else. So if you play two Tone blocks in a row, the second one is saved and won't play until the first one is done. This works fine until you get to six tones in a row. The RCX brick can only remember five tones, so the sixth one gets lost. Then your sounds get all messed up.

That's what the wait is for. The Wait block makes your program stop and wait for the tone to finish before it moves on. That way, if you're playing more that five tones, you won't lose any of them.

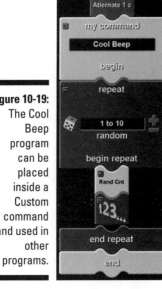

Figure 10-19:
The Cool Beep program can be placed inside a Custom command and used in other programs.

Another trick that you can try is to expand from four to eight the number of different tones that the program will create. This is a little harder to do on the screen because the Check & Choose blocks run into each other. The best way to add the extra blocks is to minimize the blocks before copying or moving. A version with eight tones (actually seven and a blank), called Alternate 2 Cool Beep Program, is included on the CD for reference.

It's Alive

This robot is based on the RoverBot, as shown in the *Constructopedia* and in Chapter 5 of this book. The RoverBot needs to be equipped with the double bumper so that the robot can detect when it bumps into something on the left or right. Make sure the motors are attached to outputs A and C and the Touch Sensors are attached to inputs 1 and 2. The program will use two custom My Commands: Cool Beep and Rand Cnt, both covered in the "Better Beeps" section of this chapter.

Purpose

The purpose of this program is much like the Bump and Run program; however, the goal is to give the robot more personality. For example, you can allow the robot to stop and sleep for a while or have it turn for no reason at all. What you're trying to build here is a robot that avoids obstacles but at the same time has a certain amount of unpredictability.

The program

Your main stack will be a Repeat Forever block. Grab this block from the Stack Controller area and place it under the Program block. If you created a My Command for the Cool Beep program, insert that inside the Repeat Forever block. If not, place a Beep block in it and select one of the six beep sounds and then place an On AC block and a Wait block with the time set to random and 1 to 15 seconds. The program should look like the one in Figure 10-20. If you download it into your RCX brick and run it, it will start by giving off a beep and then move forward. Every once in a while, the robot will give off a beep.

Figure 10-20:
The Alive program starts with a beep and a random run time.

After the robot has beeped and moved forward for a while, your robot is going to make a random choice between four things: turning right, turning left, spinning, and resting. You accomplish this the same way you created random beeps in the "Better Beeps" section of this chapter.

1. **Put a random value into the counter.**

   This is done by using the My Command named "Rand Cnt." (See the "Better Beeps" section, earlier in this chapter.)

2. **Drag the Rand Cnt command into the end of the Repeat Forever block.**

3. **Place a Check & Choose Counter block with a value of 1 to 2.**

4. **Attach a Check & Choose Counter block with a value of 1 to 1 on the left side and a Check & Choose Counter block with a value of 3 to 3 on the right side.**

   Figure 10-21 shows the blocks that you have just put on.

   You may now have run into one of the major problems with graphical programming languages such as RIS: Not much fits on the screen at once. You can scroll your display anytime you need by moving the cursor over to the edge of the screen.

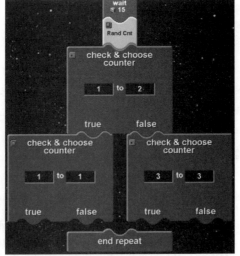

Figure 10-21: The Check & Choose Counter blocks pick one of four random actions.

Don't run this program yet because nothing is connected to the four stacks at the end. You need to add commands to make the robot choose one of four random actions.

5. **On the leftmost stack, add the following to define a right turn with a variable amount of turn:**

   - On AC block

   - Set Direction A>C< block

   - Wait Random 1-2 block

   - Set Direction A>C> block

   This random turning will add to the lifelike nature of the robot.

6. **On the second stack, add the following to define a left turn with a variable amount of turn:**

- On AC block

- Set Direction A<C> block

- Wait Random 1-2 block

- Set Direction A>C> block

Figure 10-22 shows what the end of your program should look like now.

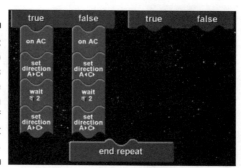

Figure 10-22: These two stacks define random amounts of right and left turns.

When you download and run the program, the robot moves forward for a random amount of time and then spins either right or left by a random amount before moving on. Each time the program runs through the Repeat Forever block, it beeps again. In this way, you can tell that it's starting another cycle of moving forward and doing something random.

The last two random things you need to program are a random spin and a random sleep.

7. **In the third stack position, place the following:**

- On AC block

- Set Direction A>C<

- Wait 4 Seconds block

- Wait Random 1-10 seconds block

- Set Direction A>C> block

This stack sets the motors to spin the robot, spins it for at least 4 seconds and up to 14 seconds, and sets the motors to go straight again.

In the last stack position, place an Off AC block and a Wait random 1-15 block. This stack tells the motors to stop running for 1 to 15 seconds, making the robot look like it's sleeping. The bottom of your program should look like Figure 10-23.

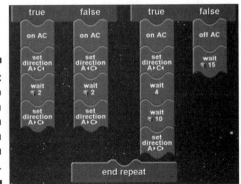

Figure 10-23:
The last two stacks add a random spin and a random sleep.

When you download and run the program, your robot will exhibit the four random behaviors. It will beep; move forward; or turn right, turn left, spin, or sleep; and then start over again. The only problem is that your robot doesn't know how to avoid obstacles. To solve this, you need to set up a Sensor Watcher block for each Touch Sensor.

1. **Minimize the Repeat Forever block to get it out of the way.**

2. **Drag a Touch Sensor block next to the Program block.**

   Make sure it is set to input 1.

3. **Under the Press label, place the following:**

   - On AC block

   - Set Direction A<C< block

   - Wait Random 1-4 block

   - Set Direction A>C< block

   - Wait Random 1-2 block

   - Set direction A>C>

   Whenever the left bumper is pressed, the robot will back up a random amount, turn right a random amount, and go forward again.

4. **For the right bumper, drag a Touch Sensor block next to the Program block. Set it to input 3.**

5. **Under the Press label, place the following:**

   - On AC block

   - Set Direction A<C< block

   - Wait Random 1-4 block

- Set Direction A<C> block

- Wait Random 1-2 block

- Set Direction A>C>

Whenever the right bumper is pressed, the robot will back up a random amount, turn left a random amount, and go forward again.

The final program (with the main stack minimized) is shown in Figure 10-24.

Use the Alive program that's on the CD that comes with this book.

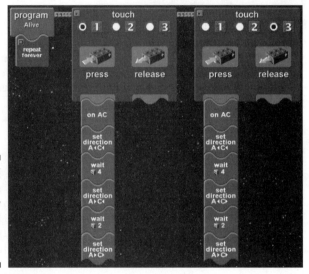

Figure 10-24:
The robot is now ready to prowl your living room.

Download and run this program to see your robot in action. You can fritter away quite a bit of time watching it wander around, bump into things, and make decisions.

Alternatives

You can easily build on this program. One way is to add more than four random actions to the main stack. This is done in the same manner as the alternative beep program did it, with another layer of Check & Choose blocks and four more command stacks.

Another way to modify the program is to add different random actions when a bumper is pressed. This is done by adding the Rand Cnt command followed by a few Check & Choose commands to choose the action. Examples of different actions after a bump are to back up for a long time before turning, go back and bump into the object a few more times before turning, or make a mad sound (beep 5).

ON THE CD

Playing music

Your RCX brick can play music, but it takes a lot of work. First, you need to know the frequency of the notes so you can set your Tone blocks correctly.

The following table shows the correct frequency value for each note.

	Very Low	*Low*	*Middle*	*High*	*Very High*
C	131	262	523	1047	2093
C#	139	277	554	1109	2217
D	147	294	587	1175	2349
D#	156	311	622	1245	2489
E	165	330	660	1320	2640
F	175	350	699	1398	2797
F#	185	370	741	1482	2963
G	196	392	785	1570	3140
G#	208	416	832	1663	3326
A	220	440	880	1760	3520
A#	233	466	932	1865	3729
B	247	494	988	1976	3951

We chose a value of 0.6 seconds to represent a quarter note, so an eighth note is 0.3, a half note is 1.2, and a whole note is 2.4. Always follow your Tone block with a wait block that is 0.1 seconds longer than the note. For example, to play a quarter note at middle C, use the Tone block set to 523 for 0.6 seconds followed by a Wait block of 0.7 seconds. The wait block is longer than the note so that you can hear the break between two notes of the same pitch.

A whole song is made by creating a stack with a Tone block and then a Wait block for each note of the song. Put the frequency value in for the note you want and a duration to match the type of note you have. A sample of *Mary Had a Little Lamb* is on the CD.

Chapter 11

Let There Be a Light Sensor

In This Chapter

▶ Detecting light and dark

▶ Programming your robot to follow lines on the ground

▶ Letting light run your robot

▶ Controlling your robot with light pulses

*T*he LEGO MINDSTORMS system allows many types of robots to be built. The mechanical structure of the robot is built with fairly standard LEGO- and TECHNIC-style pieces: blocks, wheels, axles, gears, and connectors. You use these together with some specialized pieces such as tractor treads to become the frame of your design. Motors are connected to the wheels to move the robot forward. As you can see in this chapter, Touch Sensors are used to detect when your robot has bumped into something.

But what about other senses? Humans have six senses: touch, sight, smell, hearing, taste, and humor. While no current devices can give your robot a sense of smell, hearing, or taste, much less a sense of humor (although you may find it funny when your latest creation goes zooming off the table), there is a device that allows your robot to see. It is called a Light Sensor. This chapter explores some of the uses for this sensor and how it can give your robot new functionality.

Stop Light

This program is based on the RoverBot with tractor treads, as shown in the *Constructopedia*. No Touch Sensors are needed, but the Light Sensor needs to be mounted. This doesn't need to be anything fancy: We just used the setup shown on page 102 of the *Constructopedia* and made the Light Sensor point forward. You could, of course, place the Light Sensor anywhere on top of the RCX brick and have it point forward.

The other end of the Light Sensor needs to be plugged in to input 2 of the RCX brick, and the motors must be connected to outputs A and C.

The Light Sensor is made of two parts inside the block. One is a photocell that can electronically measure the amount of light that's pointing at it. The other is a little red lamp that helps light up whatever the sensor is pointing to. The red lamp isn't needed when the sensor is facing forward, as in this project, but it will be on, anyway.

The sensor only works when the program indicates that a Light Sensor is connected to it.

Purpose

This program lets you control your robot with a flashlight. Whenever light is shinning on the sensor, the robot moves forward. When the sensor is dark, the robot stops.

The Stop Light program is on the CD that comes with this book.

The program

The program uses a Light Sensor block to control the motor. When the block sees light, it tells the motors to turn on; when it sees dark, it tells the motors to turn off. Here's how to build this program:

1. **Flip down the Sensor Watcher area, grab a Light Sensor, and drag it into the programming area.**

   The sensor automatically attaches itself onto the Program block. Click on the number 2 to let the RCX know that your Light Sensor is attached to input 2.

   The Light Sensor block is preset to see "bright" as any value over 51 and "dark" as any value under 50. These values work most of the time, but based on your RCX and your Light Sensor, you may want to adjust these numbers. Use the view function described in Chapter 8 to read the normal light level in the room and then read the level of the light when the flashlight is pointed at the sensor. Set your Light Sensor Watcher values to be between these measured extremes.

2. **Flip down the Commands area, drag out an On block, and connect it to the Bright side of the Light Sensor block.**

   Flip the block over and make sure that you're only turning on motors A and C.

3. **From the commands area, drag out an Off block and place it on the dark side of the Light Sensor block.**

Flip it over and make sure that it's also set to turn off motors A and C.

Your program should look like the one shown in Figure 11-1. Download it to your RCX brick and run it. Your robot will just sit still and do nothing until you shine a flashlight at the sensor. It moves forward until the light is removed.

Figure 11-1:
The Stop Light program gives you basic control of the robot with a flashlight.

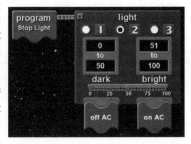

Follow That Light

This program is based on a RoverBot, with motors attached to outputs A and C and a Light Sensor attached to input 2. You can mount the Light Sensor any way that points it forward.

Purpose

This program shows how your robot can make independent thoughts. The purpose of this program is to have your robot search out and find a bright light (probably a flashlight). It does this by scanning the area and moving toward the brightest place.

The Follow That Light program is on this book's CD.

The program

The idea behind this program is to take a light reading to the right, to the center, and to the left. With these readings, the program decides which direction is the brightest, and the robot moves in that direction. This program really doesn't measure the brightest points but registers that the right, center, and left are either bright or dark, and then, based on Table 11-1, decides where to go.

Table 11-1	Direction decision table		
Right	*Center*	*Left*	*Direction*
Dark	Dark	Dark	Keep searching
Dark	Dark	Bright	Left
Dark	Bright	Dark	Center
Dark	Bright	Bright	Left
Bright	Dark	Dark	Right
Bright	Dark	Bright	Center
Bright	Bright	Dark	Right
Bright	Bright	Bright	Keep searching

If the robot sees a bright light to the right, a bright light straight ahead (center), and darkness to the left, it will turn to the right and move forward. Begin by creating My Commands blocks for a right turn, for a left turn, and for moving straight ahead.

1. **Begin by creating a My Commands block and naming it "Right."**

2. **Place a Set Direction block inside the Right My Commands block. Flip the block over and disable output B; set output A forward and output C backward.**

   This sets up the motors to turn right.

3. **Drag an On block below the Set Direction block. Flip it over and disable output B and set the time to 0.5 seconds.**

4. **Create another My Command block and name it "Left."**

5. **Place a Set Direction block inside the Left My Commands block. Flip the block over and disable output B; set output A backward and output C forward.**

   This sets up the motors to turn left.

6. **Drag an On block below the Set Direction block. Flip it over and disable output B and set the time to 0.5 seconds.**

7. **Create a third My Command block and name it "Fwd."**

8. **Place a Set Direction block inside the Fwd My Commands block. Flip the block over and disable output B; set outputs A and C to forward.**

   This sets up the motors to go straight.

9. **Drag an On block below the Set Direction block. Flip it over and disable output B and set the time to 1 second.**

The three My Commands blocks should look like those shown in Figure 11-2. You can either throw these three blocks away (they will still be available in the My Commands area) or minimize them and use them later in the program.

When you create a My Commands block, you're really creating a new command. This new command will always be available to use from the My Commands area. So even though you're throwing away this copy of the command, it's still available to use later.

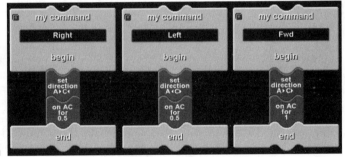

Figure 11-2:
Custom commands help ease programming later.

Now that you have the command ready, you build the program that samples the light in all three directions.

1. **Drag a Repeat Forever block out of the stack controller area and put it in the program stack.**

   This tells your program to go on searching forever.

2. **Inside the Repeat Forever block, put a Right block from the My Commands area.**

   This makes the robot turn to the right so that it can take its first light reading.

3. **Place a Check & Choose Light Sensor block below the Right block. Check number 2 to indicate that the Light Sensor is connected to input 2.**

4. **Place a Left block from the My Commands area on both the True and False sides of the Check & Choose block.**

The program should look like the one shown in Figure 11-3. If you download and run this program on your RCX, your robot will alternate between turning right and left.

Figure 11-3:
The first step is to look for light on the right.

So far, your program turns to the right, checks the light level, and then turns to the left so that it's facing the center. Next, you have to check the light at this location and then turn left again.

1. **Using the copy tool from the toolbox (see Chapter 10 for more information), make a copy of the Check & Choose Light Sensor along with the two Left commands. Place this copy to the side.**

   You'll use the copy in Step 3.

2. **Using the copy tool, make another copy of the Check & Choose Light Sensor along with the two Left commands. Place this copy on the True side of the Check & Choose Light Sensor block that you just copied.**

3. **Move the copy that you set aside in step 1 to the False side of the Check & Choose Light Sensor block.**

The program should look like the one shown in Figure 11-4.

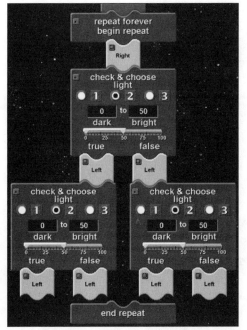

Figure 11-4:
The next
step looks at
light in the
center.

Now your program has the robot look for light on the right, turn, look for light in the center, and then turn again. Next, your program needs to instruct your robot to examine the light on the left. For this you need four more Check & Choose blocks.

1. **Drag a new Check & Choose Light Sensor block from the Sensor Watcher area. Attach this block to the far-left Left block. Make sure that the 2 is checked in this block.**

2. **Repeat step 1 for the other three Left blocks.**

The program is now too complicated for RIS to display properly, so RIS automatically minimizes blocks to make room for other blocks. Figures 11-5 and 11-6 show your program with opposite halves minimized.

What does your program do so far? It turns right and looks at the light level, turns to the left so that it's facing the center and looks at the light level, and turns left again and looks at the light level. This leaves you with eight stack locations at the bottom of your program. Each of these locations represents some combination of light level on the right, in the center, and on the left.

For example, the left-most stack represents the condition where it is dark on the right, in the center, and on the left. The sixth position represents the condition where the right is bright, the center is dark, and the left is bright.

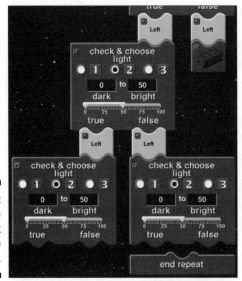

Figure 11-5:
The left side of the Check & Choose blocks.

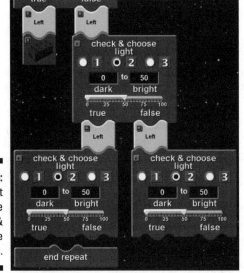

Figure 11-6:
The right side of the Check & Choose blocks.

Now it is just a matter of putting the proper commands at each of these stack locations. The action you want to take is the one described in Table 11-1. Remember that because of the way that the robot turns to look at the light, your robot is facing left.

1. **Place a Beep block at the first location. Flip the block over and set the beep sound to 5.**

2. **Place a Fwd block at the second location.**

3. **Place a Right block and a Fwd block at the third location.**

4. **Place a Fwd block at the fourth location.**

5. **Place two Right blocks and a Fwd block at the fifth location.**

6. **Place a Right block and a Fwd block at the sixth location.**

7. **Place two Right blocks and a Fwd block at the seventh location.**

8. **Place a Beep block at the eighth location. Flip the block over and set the beep sound to 5.**

These stacks are shown in Figure 11-7, unattached to their Check & Choose blocks.

Figure 11-7:
There are eight actions that the program can take.

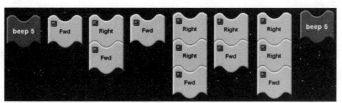

Download and try out this program on your RCX brick. Lay a flashlight on the floor pointing in the general direction of the robot. The robot turns and searches until it sees the light, and then it moves forward. Eventually, it will bump into the light.

Alternatives

Adding a bumper to the front of the robot allows the robot to know when it has reached its objective. When it does, the robot can stop or race around and celebrate.

The Alt 1 Follow That Light program is on the CD that comes with this book. In the program, notice the use of the counter to decide whether the robot is in seek mode or celebrate mode.

Another alternative is to give the robot something to do when it doesn't know where to go. If the robot sees dark or bright in all three directions, it just keeps looking. Instead, it could decide that after seeing nothing for ten tries, it will rush off to a new location and try again.

Check out the Alt 2 Follow That Light program on the CD that comes with this book. Again notice the use of the counter. It's used to count the number of times nothing is seen, but is also used to determine whether the robot is in seek mode or rush-off mode.

A Day at the Races

This program is specifically designed to run on a RoverBot with treads. If any other drive arrangement is used, the program will function, but the turn times will have to be adjusted. A Light Sensor must be mounted in the front center of the robot pointing down with about ¼ inch of clearance to the floor.

Purpose

This program is designed to make your robot follow a dark-colored track on the ground. A suitable track comes with the Robotics Invention System. The program senses when it's over the dark-colored track and moves forward. When it detects that it's not over the track, it turns back and forth to try to find the track again, and then it continues forward again.

The Day at the Races program is on the CD that comes with this book.

The program

The idea behind this program is to keep the Light Sensor over the dark-colored portion of the track. It is helpful to start the program on the track. Your program will first decide whether it's over dark or light and then make the following decision: If dark, continue the program; if light, beep and stop.

1. **Drag a Check & Choose Light block from the Stack Controller area. Make sure the 2 is selected indicating that the Light Sensor is connected to input 2. Set the values of this block to 45 to 100 and place it under the Program block.**

2. **Drag a Beep block from the Commands area and place it on the True side of the Check & Choose block.**

   This makes the robot beep when you start your program if the sensor isn't already over the dark-colored track.

3. **Drag an On block to the False side of the Check & Choose block. Flip it over and disable the B output.**

   This starts the motors for the duration of the program.

The program should look like the one shown in Figure 11-8. Download it and run it on your RCX. If you start the program over a white-colored area, the unit will beep and do nothing. If it is started over a dark-colored area of the track, it will begin moving forward.

Figure 11-8:
The program will only run the motors when started over a dark spot.

Next, you need to tell your program what to do if the robot drives off of the dark-colored track.

1. **Drag a Light Sensor Watcher from the sensor watchers area and place it next to the Program block. Click the button next to the 2 to indicate that the sensor is on input 2. Set the Dark value to 0 to 45. Set the Bright value to 45 to 100.**

2. **Drag a Turn Right block out of the My Commands area and place it on the Bright side of the Light Sensor Watcher.**

   If you didn't create this custom block in the "Follow That Light" section, create it now.

3. **Below the Turn Right block, add a Check & Choose Light block. Set the values to 0 to 45.**

   This block looks to see whether the area to the right is dark. If it is, the Check & Choose block does nothing, and the robot continues forward. If it is over a light area, the Check & Choose block runs the stack on the False side.

4. **Add two Turn Left blocks to the False side of the Check & Choose block.**

   If you didn't create this custom block in the "Follow That Light" section, create it now.

Your program should now look like the one shown in Figure 11-9. Don't run it yet because it may behave unpredictably.

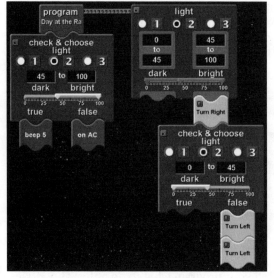

If the robot finds darkness on the right side, all is well. However, if it doesn't, it turns to the left. Your program needs to see if there is darkness on the left and then decide what to do next.

1. **Put a Check & Choose Light block below the Turn Left blocks. Make sure the 2 is checked and set the values to 0 to 45.**

2. **On the False side of the Check & Choose block, add an Off block. Flip it over and deselect output B.**

3. **Add a Beep block below the Off block. Flip it over and set the beep sound to number 5.**

The final portion of the program should look like the one in Figure 11-10.

Download and try out the program by setting it on the test pad. Make sure the Light Sensor is over the black track and start the program. Each time the robot goes off the course, you see it turn right and then turn left to try to find the track. If it can't find the track, the bot stops and beeps.

Based on your RCX brick, the condition of the batteries, the position of the Light Sensor, and dozens of other factors, you may need to adjust the amount of time used for the turn when turning left and right. If the robot seems to be swinging too far when looking left and right, go into the Turn Left and Turn Right blocks and shorten the turn time. If the robot seems to not quite turn enough, go into the Turn Left and Turn Right blocks and lengthen the turn time.

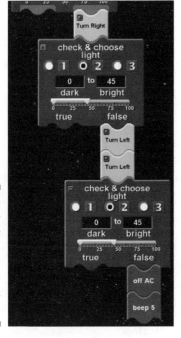

Figure 11-10:
The Sensor
Watcher
tries going
right and
then left to
find a dark
spot.

Alternatives

If you run the robot around the track in a clockwise direction, it does pretty
well. However, if you run it in the counterclockwise direction, it has a few
more problems. This is because the robot always looks right before it looks
left. This means that when it's going around the track counterclockwise, it
usually goes off the track to the right side. Instead of looking to the left
(where the track is), it looks to the right first and then finally looks to the left.

You can easily fix this by changing the program to look left first then look
right, but then the robot would have problems when going clockwise. The
real answer is to make the robot a bit smarter. If you have the robot remember which way it went off the track the last time and try that direction first,
the problem is solved. The secret is to use the counter as an indicator of the
last direction used and try that first.

The Alternate Day at the Races program is on the CD that comes with this
book. This program learns the last direction used and tries that direction
first.

Light Control

This program uses the same setup as the Stop Light program: a basic RoverBot with motors connected to outputs A and C and a Light Sensor attached to input 2.

Purpose

This program is an extension of the Stop Light program. In this program, you're designing the program to allow control of multiple functions with the flashlight. The number of flashes on the Light Sensor controls the response of the robot.

> ✔ **One flash:** Moves the robot forward
>
> ✔ **Two flashes:** Moves the robot backwards
>
> ✔ **Three flashes:** Turns the robot left
>
> ✔ **Four flashes:** Turns the robot right

After the robot receives the command, it will continue to do that command until it receives another flash to tell it to stop.

The Light Control program is on the CD that comes with this book.

The program

The basic idea of the program is quite simple: Use the counter to count the number of flashes, and then use that count to do the function.

1. **From the commands area, drag a Reset Counter block and attach it to the Program block.**

   The Reset Counter block sets the internal counter to zero so that you can start counting flashes.

2. **From the Sensor Watcher area, grab a Light Touch sensor and drag it into the programming area.**

   It automatically attaches itself onto the Program block. Click on the number 2 to let the RCX know that your Light Sensor is attached to input 2.

3. **Drag an Add to Counter block to the Bright side of the Light Sensor block.**

   This stack will run every time the RCX brick sees a flash of light, and the Add to Counter block will count that flash.

4. **Grab a Tone block and attach it to the bottom of the Add to Counter block.**

   The Tone block is a nice touch because it beeps every time your RCX brick sees a flash.

Your program should look like the one shown in Figure 11-11. Download it to your RCX brick and run it. Shine your flashlight at the Light Sensor. Each time the sensor sees the light, it will beep (it also is counting the flashes, but you can't see that).

Figure 11-11:
The Light Control program will count the number of flashes it sees.

Now comes the difficult part. Your main program needs to know when to look at the counter. You can't just set up a Check & Choose block to look at the counter value and do the function, because the robot won't know when the flashes are done. In other words, if you're looking for one flash, how does your bot know if it was one flash or the first flash of two flashes? What you need to do is to leave enough time for the flashes to come in before you act on them. The way to do this is to use the internal timer.

Each time a flash comes in, the timer will be reset to zero. The timer is always counting up, so if the timer ever reaches 1 second, you can be sure that it has been one second since the last flash. It is at this point that your bot sees how many counts there are and acts on it.

1. **Drag a Timer Reset block to the bottom of the program stack and another one to the bottom of the stack on the Light Sensor block.**

   These blocks reset the time to zero so that your program can tell how long it has been since the flashes came in.

2. **From the Stack Controller area, drag a Repeat Forever block onto the program stack.**

   This will make your program look for flashes over and over.

3. **Inside the Repeat Forever block, place a Check & Choose Counter block from the Stack Controllers area. Set both values in this block to 0.**

   When you pick a Check & Choose block, a small window pops up asking what type of Check & Choose block you want. Click on the 123... button to indicate that you want a counter type.

   The Check & Choose Counter block is included because you don't want your program to do anything when the counter is zero. The only time you want to do anything is when the counter is 1, 2, 3, or 4.

4. **From the Stack Controllers area, drag a Check & Choose Timer block and place it on the False side of the previous block. Set the values of this block to 0 to 1 second.**

   This time, when the Check & Choose block is clicked, click on the stopwatch to indicate that you want a timer type.

   This is the critical block. It's telling the RCX that you're not going to go on and look at the counter until one second has passed. One second from what? One second since the timer was reset in the Light Sensor stack; in other words, one second since the last flash came in.

5. **From the commands area, drag a Beep block and a Reset Counter block to the False side of the previous block. Flip the Beep block over and set it to sound 5.**

   These blocks are here only for demonstration and will be removed in the next list of steps (in this section).

The program should look like the one shown in Figure 11-12. Download and run the program on your RCX brick. You can flash the sensor as much as you want and receive a high beep confirming the flash. When you stop flashing for at least one second, the program assumes the flashing has stopped and a low beep is given.

Now all you have to do is tell your robot to go forward, backward, left, or right based on the value of the counter. This is done with Check & Choose Counter blocks.

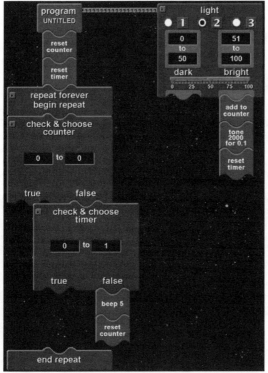

Figure 11-12:
The Light
Control
program
waits until
you're done
flashing.

1. **Remove the Beep and Reset Counter blocks from the program stack and set them aside.**

   You will use these in Step 8.

2. **Drag a Check & Choose Counter block from the stack controllers area and place it on the False side of the Check & Choose Timer block. Set both values in the block to 1.**

   This block will only run if the count is more than 0 and the timer is at more than 1 second, so the program is checking if the count is a 1. If it is, you're going to attach the commands to move forward to the True side. Otherwise, you attach more checks to the False side for other commands.

3. **On the True side of the last block, place a Set Direction block. Flip the block over and deselect the B output and set both the A and C outputs to forward.**

   This sets the robot up to move forward.

4. **Create a new My Commands block by dragging one out of the My Commands area and placing it under the Set Direction block. Name the command "Wait Light."**

The reason that the next section is placed inside a My Command block is because it will be used several more times in this program. Creating a My Commands block saves time later, and it makes the program more readable.

5. **Inside the Wait Light block that you just created, place an On block with A and C selected and a Reset Counter block.**

This turns on the motors and clears the counter. The counter is being cleared because the next command is going to wait until another flash comes in to turn off the motors. It uses the same flash counter as the rest of the program, so the counter must be cleared.

6. **Place a Repeat While Counter block with both the values set to 0.**

This tells the program to wait (potentially forever) for the counter to be something other than 0. The count will be something other than 0 when the next flash comes in.

7. **After the Repeat While Counter block (after it, not inside it), place a Reset Counter block and an Off block set to A and C.**

These commands turn off the motors and set up the program for the next command. Your Wait Light block should look like the one shown in Figure 11-13. You can now minimize the Wait Light block.

Figure 11-13:
The Wait Light block starts the motors and then waits for another flash to turn them off.

8. **Drag the Beep 5 and Reset Counter blocks that you set aside in Step 1 and attach them to the False side of the Check & Choose Counter block.**

The bottom of your program should look like the one shown in Figure 11-14. Download this program into your RCX brick and try it out. A single flash at the sensor will make the robot move forward. To stop the robot, give it another flash. More than one flash will result in the error tone.

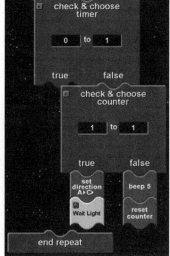

Figure 11-14: The first command tells the robot to move forward.

The next step to put your robot under your total domination is to add commands for going backward and turning left or right.

1. **Remove the Beep and Reset Counter blocks from the last block and set them aside.**

You will use these in Step 8.

2. **Place a Check & Choose Counter block on the False side of the Check & Choose Counter 1 to 1 block. Set both values of this new block to 2.**

This Check & Choose Counter block is the block that looks for a reverse command.

3. **On the True side of this block, place a Set Direction block and a Wait Light block. Flip the Set Direction block over, deselect the B output, and set both the A and C outputs to backward.**

4. **On the False side of the Check & Choose 2 to 2 block, place a Check & Choose Counter block. Set both values of this block to 3.**

This Check & Choose Counter block is the block that looks for the turn left command.

5. **On the True side of the last block, place a Set Direction block and a Wait Light block. Flip the Set Direction block over, deselect the B output, and set the A output to backward and the C output to forward.**

6. **On the False side of the Check & Choose 3 to 3 block, place a Check & Choose Counter block. Set both values of this block to 4.**

   This Check & Choose Counter block is the block that looks for the turn right command.

7. **On the True side of the last block, place a Set Direction block and a Wait Light block. Flip the Set Direction block over, deselect the B output, and set the A output to forward and the C output to backward.**

8. **Drag the Beep 5 and Reset Counter blocks that you set aside in Step 1 and attach them to the False side of the Check & Choose Counter 4 to 4 block.**

The end of your program should look like the one shown in Figure 11-15. Download it to your RCX brick and try it out. Your robot should now be totally controllable.

You may notice a slight problem with this program. Many times, it will miscount the number of flashes that you try to give it. This is because you can't hold your hand perfectly steady when you flash and a single flash may be read as a double or triple flash.

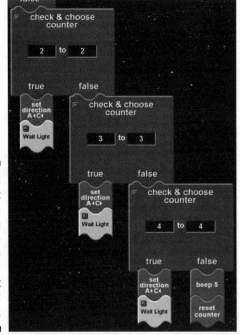

Figure 11-15: The last three commands make the robot go backward and turn it left and right.

You need to tell your program to ignore flashes that are too close together. Luckily, this is easy to do. You already have a timer that gets set to zero whenever a flash comes in. All you have to do is to reject any more flashes that come in before a minimum amount of time.

1. **Move the three blocks that are below the Light Sensor block out of the way.**

2. **Grab a Check & Choose Timer block and place it on the Bright side of the Light Sensor block. Set the values of this block to 0 to 0.5 seconds.**

3. **Grab the three blocks that you moved in Step 1 and put them on the False side of the Check & Choose Timer block.**

Now the flash counter must wait at least a half second between flashes. Your modified Light Sensor block should look like the one shown in Figure 11-16.

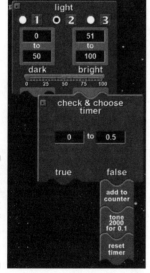

Figure 11-16:
The flashes must be at least a half second apart.

Download the program into your RCX brick and give it a final test.

Alternatives

It is quite a simple matter to expand the Light Control program concept and add a few more commands. You can, for example, set up a beep command for five flashes, for six flashes, and so on.

Another change that may be more useful is to have the robot run the command for as long as the light stays on the last flash. For example, on the backward command, give one flash and on the second flash, keep the light on the sensor. The robot will then move backward for as long as the light is kept on.

Making this change is just a matter of changing the Wait Light command that you created.

1. **Maximize one of the Wait Light commands in the program.**

2. **Replace the Repeat While Counter block with a Repeat While Light Sensor block. Set the values of this block to 50 to 100.**

Instead of the program waiting for another flash to end the command, it waits for the sensor to see darkness before it continues. The change is shown in Figure 11-17. Download this program into the RCX brick and run it. You should find it easier to control than the other version.

The Alternate Light Control program is on the CD that comes with this book.

Figure 11-17: The alternate Wait Light command keeps the robot running with the light on the sensor.

Chapter 12

Doing Other Cool Stuff

. . . .

In This Chapter

▶ Using the Temperature and Rotation Sensors

▶ Controlling your program with the remote control

▶ Talking to scouts and other RCX units

▶ Programming with other languages

▶ Using a Macintosh

. . . .

The LEGO MINDSTORMS system comes with a wide variety of equipment and features to design, build, and program sophisticated robots. The available sensors that detect touch and light meet the needs of many projects, and the RIS programming can do many things without getting too complicated.

But what happens when you want to conquer new territories? That's where you need to discover some of the other abilities of the RCX brick. It's able to measure temperature and rotation, talk to other robots, and be controlled by a remote control. After you master these elements, you can move away from the simple RCX Code programming and move on to more powerful languages. This chapter shows you how.

How's the Weather?

LEGO provides a stand-alone Temperature Sensor that can be connected to any input of the RCX brick. This sensor can measure the air temperature in either Fahrenheit or Celsius (see Chapter 8 for details on how to change this setting). Although there aren't that many uses for this device, it is kind of fun. The program explained here programs a robot to stay away from a hot fireplace but stay close enough to stay warm.

Purpose

This program is based on the RoverBot with tractor treads, as shown in the *Constructopedia*. No Touch Sensors are needed, but you need to mount the Temperature Sensor on the front of the robot facing forward and connect it to input 2. The robot will move forward if its temperature is less than 75°F, do nothing if the temperature is between 75°F and 85°F, and move backward if the temperature is above 85°F.

The How's the Weather program is on the CD that comes with this book.

The program

At first blush, the program seems easy enough — put in a Sensor Watcher that looks for the temperature to rise above 85°F and create a stack that tells the robot to move back. The problem with this approach is that the Temperature Sensor takes time to react. It's not instantaneous. This may cause the robot to walk right into the fireplace before the bot realizes that it is hot. You need to have your robot sample the temperature, make a small move either forward or backward, wait for the sensor to stabilize, and then repeat the process.

1. **Drag a Repeat Forever block to the bottom of the Program block.**

   This block will handle the repeat portion of the task.

2. **Inside the Repeat block, place a Wait block. Flip it over and set it to 5 seconds.**

   This is the delay that waits for the temperature to stabilize.

3. **Under the Wait block, place a Check & Choose Temperature block. Set the input by clicking on 2. Set the low temperature to 85 and the high temperature to 122 (the maximum temperature of the sensor).**

4. **Under the True side of the Check & Choose block, place a Set Direction block. Flip it over, turn off the B output, and set the direction for A and C to reverse.**

   This tells the robot to move backward when it's too hot.

5. **Under the Set Direction block, place an On For block. Flip it over, deselect output B, and set the time to 0.5 seconds.**

The program should look like the one shown in Figure 12-1. Download and run the program on your RCX brick. The robot will lurch backward every five seconds if the Temperature Sensor shows a temperature hotter than 85°F.

Use the view mode that's described in Chapter 8 to read the temperature on the RCX display.

Figure 12-1:
The How's the Weather program moves the robot away from extreme heat.

Now all you have to do is make the robot move forward if the temperature is below 75°F.

1. **Drag a Check & Choose Temperature block to the False side of the existing Check & Choose block. Set the input by clicking on 2. Set the low temperature to 0 and the high temperature to 75.**

2. **Under the True side of this new Check & Choose block, place a Set Direction block. Flip it over and turn off the B output.**

   This tells the robot to move forward when the robot isn't warm enough.

3. **Under the Set Direction block, place an On For block. Flip it over, deselect output B, and set the time to 0.5 seconds.**

The bottom of your program should look like the one shown in Figure 12-2. Download and run the program on your RCX brick. In addition to moving away from the very hot fire, the robot will now move toward the fire if the temperature gets too chilly.

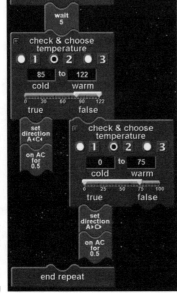

Figure 12-2:
The How's
the Weather
program
moves the
robot
toward heat
when it's
cold.

Steering Wheel

A Rotation Sensor is included in the Ultimate Accessory Set. This sensor can be used to precisely measure how much an axle turns. There are literally hundreds of uses for this sensor, from measuring exactly how far you've traveled to determining the precise angle of a turn to acting as an input device to choose a function based on angle. In this program, you use the Rotation Sensor to steer your robot.

Purpose

This program is based on the RoverBot with tractor treads, as shown in the *Constructopedia*. No Touch Sensors are needed, but the Rotation Sensor needs to be connected to input 2 with an extra-long connection wire. Place an axle through the Rotation Sensor and put a big wheel on the axle to act as your steering wheel.

The Steering program is on the CD that comes with this book.

The program

The Rotation Sensor raises its count by 16 for every complete turn of the axle. So if you turn it 90° (a quarter turn), it will read 4. If you turn it backward 90°, it will read –3. The concept of the program is simple — if the Rotation Sensor is less than –4, turn right; if it is between –3 and 3, go straight; if it is greater than 3, turn left.

1. **Drag a Rotation Sensor Watcher block into the programming area. Set the input by clicking on 2. Set the range to –100 to –4.**

   This checks to see that the Rotation Sensor is less than –3.

2. **Place an On block under the Sensor Watcher block. Flip it over and deselect B and C.**

3. **Place an Off block under the On block. Flip it over and deselect A and B.**

Your program should look like the one shown in Figure 12-3, and it will tell your robot to turn right when the steering wheel on the Rotation Sensor is turned right.

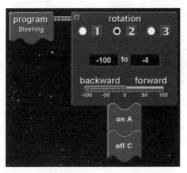

Figure 12-3: The Steering program looks for rotation of the sensor.

The next step is to instruct your robot to go straight.

1. **Drag a Rotation Sensor Watcher block into the programming area. Set the input by clicking on 2. Set the range to –3 to 3.**

   This checks to see that the Rotation Sensor is between 3 and –3.

2. **Place an On block under this Sensor Watcher block. Flip it over and deselect B.**

The final step is to add instructions to tell the robot to go left.

1. **Drag a Rotation Sensor Watcher block into the programming area. Set the input by clicking on 2. Set the range to 4 to 100.**

   This checks to see that the Rotation Sensor is more than 3.

2. **Place an On block under the Sensor Watcher block. Flip it over and deselect A and B.**

3. **Place an Off block under the On block. Flip it over and deselect B and C.**

The end of your program should look like the part shown in Figure 12-4. Download the program and run it on the RCX brick. The robot will move forward and turn when you turn the steering wheel on the Rotation Sensor. If the robot is turning in the opposite direction of the Rotation Sensor, just flip it over.

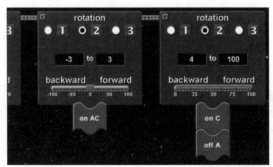

Figure 12-4: The Steering program steers in the direction of the Rotation Sensor.

Alternatives

The Steering program doesn't really give you very fine control of the robot. To give yourself more control, add more Rotation Sensor Watcher blocks and look for more positions of the Rotation Sensor. For example, you can make the robot turn hard left when the value is 5 or greater, turn left softly when the value is between 2 and 5, and so on. The amount of steering control is limited only by the number of stacks allowed in the RCX brick (which is ten, by the way).

The Alternate Steering program is on the CD that comes with this book.

RoboTalk

Another cool feature of the LEGO MINDSTORMS robots is that they can talk to each other. Each controller (RCX and Scout, but not Micro Scout) comes equipped with an infrared port that's normally used to download programs. This port can also be used to send messages to each other. An RCX brick can send a message to another RCX and tell it to turn, beep, stop, and so on.

The messages in the RCX aren't pre-defined — you make them up as you go along. For example, you may decide that when you send message 1, the second RCX should move forward. The first RCX uses a Send To RCX block to send message 1. The second RCX has an RCX Sensor Watcher block that looks for a message 1. When the second block receives message 1, it runs a stack that turns on the motors.

Remote Control

The Ultimate Accessory Set comes with a remote control. This device, also discussed in Chapter 7, is very handy. Here's what it can do:

- ✔ **1, 2, and 3 buttons:** These buttons send message 1, 2, or 3 to the RCX. The RCX does nothing with this information unless is has been specifically programmed to respond to these messages.

- ✔ **A, B, and C buttons:** These buttons directly control the outputs of your robot. Pressing the up button makes the motor on that output go forward and pressing the down button makes the motor go backward.

- ✔ **Program buttons P1, P2, P3, P4, and P5:** These buttons instruct the RCX to run the corresponding program (for example, P3 runs program 3).

- ✔ **Stop:** This buttons stops your program from running.

- ✔ **Speaker:** This button makes your RCX beep.

The CD that comes with this book contains a program called "Get the Message." It's designed to respond to the messages sent from the remote control. The program is based on a standard RoverBot, with the motors attached to outputs A and C. Message 1 tells the robot to go forward, stop, go backward, and stop on alternate presses. Message 2 tells the robot to turn right, and message 3 tells the robot to turn left.

Alternate Programming Languages

After a while, dragging bricks around the screen can become fairly cumbersome. There is just so much you can do with the cute little brick metaphor that LEGO gives you. In Chapter 11, you see that very complicated programs are hard to create within the RIS environment. It's difficult to build your program, understand the program's function, and document your program so that someone else can understand what was done. An alternative language can replace the RIS programming environment with something more powerful.

The RCX brick may have more capabilities than you think. It has 32 built-in counters instead of the one counter available in the RIS. It has a bunch of timers instead of the one that you can control with the block. Maybe future versions of the RIS software will let you get at these hidden features, but for now, you're either stuck with what LEGO gave you or you can use several alternative languages to unlock this hidden potential.

This section is not intended to be a complete tutorial of each alternative language, but it does give a basic overview and some reasons why you may want to choose one language over another.

Gordon's Brick

Gordon's Brick is a neat little program written by Malcom S. Powell. (I have no idea who Gordon is but let's not sweat the details.) This program takes you completely away from the brick metaphor of RIS and gives you an environment that's both simple and intuitive and gives you the power to access the RCX brick's hidden features.

Gordon's Brick is available on the CD included with this book.

Overview

Each program is divided into four sections:

- **Objects:** This area indicates what's connected to the RCX bricks — things like Touch Sensors and Temperature Sensors as well as timers, clocks, and messages are defined here.

- **Variables:** This is where variables are created. In the RIS version of the world, there is only one variable: the Counter. Here you can define up to 31 (we said 32 before, but Gordon uses one, so only 31 are left). With these variables, you can keep track of how many times you bumped into something or how many times you received a message.

- **Routines:** Routines are little pieces of program that can be used throughout your program. A typical routine may be to tell your robot to turn left. Then each time you need to turn left, you insert a call to your routine instead of inserting all of the individual commands to make your robot turn. The RIS version of routines is My Commands.

- **Tasks:** Tasks are where the action is — the main portion of each program. The RCX brick allows up to ten tasks to be running at one time. One task, for example, can be driving the motors, while another is monitoring the sensor inputs, and a third is waiting for commands from the Remote Control.

A program

A typical program is shown in Figure 12-5. One of the drawbacks of RIS is that there is no way to print out your program to keep for reference or to share with others. Gordon's Brick, however, does allow you to print out, but not quite the way you may expect. Instead of printing exactly what you see on the screen, you get a modified version. All the information is there; you just have to figure out the relationship between what's shown on the screen and what shows up in the printout.

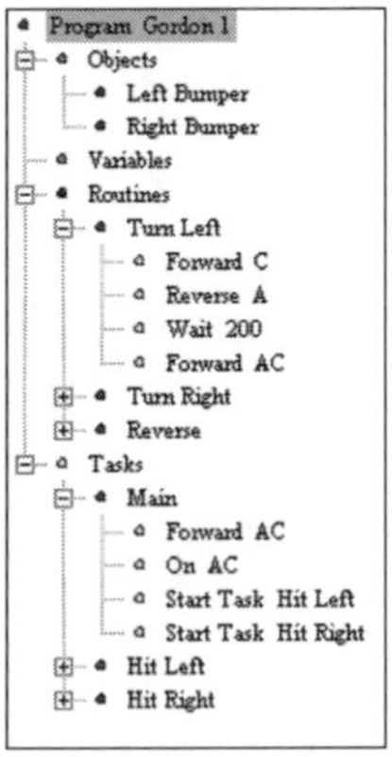

Figure 12-5:
Gordon's
Brick
programs
look simple
but can be
very
powerful.

The following is a printout for a program that moves the robot and causes it to back up and turn when an obstacle is encountered:

```
PROGRAM gordon_1;
        OBJECT left_bumper: TOUCH SENSOR(1);
        OBJECT right_bumper: TOUCH SENSOR(3);

        ROUTINE turn_left;
          FORWARD C;
          REVERSE A;
          WAIT 200;
          FORWARD AC;
        END;

        ROUTINE turn_right;
          FORWARD A;
          REVERSE C;
          WAIT 200;
          FORWARD AC;
        END;

        ROUTINE reverse;
          REVERSE AC;
          WAIT 200;
          FORWARD AC;
```

```
        END;
        INITIAL TASK main;
         FORWARD AC;
         ON AC;
         START TASK Hit Left;
         START TASK Hit Right;
        END;

        Task hit_left;
        LOOP FOREVER;
          IF left_bumper = 1
            THEN
                CALL Reverse;
                CALL Turn Right;
            ELSE
            END IF
          END LOOP
        END;

        Task hit_right;
         LOOP FOREVER;
          IF left_bumper = 1
            THEN
                CALL Reverse;
                CALL Turn Left;
            ELSE
            END IF
          END LOOP
        END;

  END.
```

Summary

Gordon's Brick is a good stepping-stone for beginning programmers who have outgrown the RIS software. It's still reasonably graphical, and commands never have to be memorized. You can make errors when entering the program because you're guided through each step. You have access to most of the advanced features of the RCX brick while being shielded from the complexity of those features.

Experienced programmers, however, may find the environment a bit too restrictive and safe and should look at NQC or PBForth, covered in the following sections.

NQC

Not Quite C (NQC) is a programming language for the RCX written by Dave Baum. It's based on the C programming language, which is known to thousands of programmers. With NQC, you can write a program as a text file and run it through an NQC compiler to convert it into something that the RCX can understand. This process can be quite complicated and is, therefore, enjoyable only to die-hard programmers!

Fortunately, Mark Overmars wrote a program called RCX Command Center that makes NQC a little simpler. You get the full power of NQC with some of the rough edges ironed out.

RCX Command Center (with NQC) is available on the CD included with this book. You can download it from `www.cs.uu.nl/~markov/lego/rcxcc/ index.html`.

Overview

NQC borrows its structure from the C programming language. It supports most of the structures available in the real language, but is limited by the functionality of the RCX brick itself. All the internal variables are available, as are all the timers. Virtually any useful math can be done on the variable to support counting or decision-making.

The programs are entered as text, but with the help of RCX Command Center, this task is simplified a little. One of the biggest hurdles to using the language is the strict syntax (see the "What is syntax?" sidebar). The syntax is quite complicated and must be perfect for your program to work. Leaving out a single semicolon will generate useful messages like

```
Line 4: Error: parse error
```

Making matters worse is that capitalization matters. In other words, the two commands

```
Wait(200)
```

and

```
wait(200)
```

are different. The first one will cause your program to wait two seconds. The second one generates another one of those useful error messages. Why? Because the C language pays attention to capitalization and treats uppercase and lowercase as different letters.

A program

A typical program is shown in this section. This program is similar to the Gordon's Brick program shown in the previous section. It makes the robot move forward until it runs into an obstacle. Then it backs up, turns, and goes on its way. Because the program is all text, the printout is identical to the screen version. You can also insert helpful comments anywhere in the program to explain what you're doing. This makes debugging and explanation of programs much easier.

```
task main()
{
  SetSensor(SENSOR_1,SENSOR_TOUCH);
  SetSensor(SENSOR_3,SENSOR_TOUCH);
  OnFwd(OUT_A+OUT_C);
  start lookLeft;
  start lookRight;
}

task lookLeft()
{
  while(true)
  {
    if (SENSOR_1 == 1)
    {
      OnRev(OUT_A+OUT_C);
      Wait(200);
      OnFwd(OUT_A);
      Wait(200);
      OnFwd(OUT_A+OUT_C);
    }
  }
}

task lookRight()
{
  while(true)
  {
    if (SENSOR_3 == 1)
    {
      OnRev(OUT_A+OUT_C);
      Wait(200);
      OnFwd(OUT_C);
      Wait(200);
      OnFwd(OUT_A+OUT_C);
    }
  }
}
```

Summary

NQC and the RCX Command Center are a good choice for experienced programmers. It also can be a good starting point if you want to learn a "real" programming language. You get full control of the RCX, but have to suffer through a long learning curve and endless attempts to fiX yOur capitaliZation.

What is syntax?

No, we aren't refering to a tax in Las Vegas (that would be a sin tax). Syntax describes the way a program must be written. You use syntax everyday when you speak and put sentences together. If you make a syntax error while speaking, the listener usually ignores it; he or she can still understand what mean you!

The problem is that computers aren't as smart as people are and don't allow for any mistakes.

So if you misplace a semicolon or misspell a word, your program just gives you a blank stare. With graphical languages such as RIS and Gordon's Brick, you can make syntax errors because you're never typing commands. Languages such as NQC and PBForth (covered in the following section), however, are picky about syntax and will constantly tell you that an error was made.

PBForth

PBForth (Programmable Brick Forth) was written by R. Hempel and is designed as a step above NQC. PBForth is based on the rather obscure language called Forth. The beauty of this language is that it overcomes all the limitations of the RCX brick.

PBForth is available on the CD included with this book.

Overview

Despite the fact that Gordon's Brick and NQC add a lot of power to programming, they are still limited by the RCX brick — actually, not by the brick itself, but by the firmware in the brick. (The *firmware* is the operating system of the brick.) The current version of firmware used with RIS 1.5 limits you to 32 variables, 10 stacks, and 8 routines, and has other limitations. PBForth eliminates these constraints and gives you the power to complete new tasks, such as directly controlling the RCX display.

The only catch is that the firmware in the RCX has to be replaced with new firmware. This is a painless process that can be reversed at any time by reloading the original firmware back into the brick. When the PBForth firmware is loaded into RIS, however, Gordon's Brick and NQC programs can't be used.

A program

A typical program is shown in this section. This program makes the robot move forward, turn left two times, and stop.

```
RCX_INIT

: GO
7 1 0 MOTOR_SET
7 1 2 MOTOR_SET ;

: STOP
7 3 0 MOTOR_SET
7 3 2 MOTOR_SET ;

: LEFT
7 2 0 MOTOR_SET
7 1 2 MOTOR_SET ;

: DELAY
0 0 TIMER_SET
BEGIN
   0 TIMER_GET 20 >
UNTIL ;

GO DELAY LEFT DELAY GO DELAY LEFT DELAY STOP
```

Summary

To really get the maximum power out of your RCX brick, PBForth is the language of choice. Be prepared for a long learning curve and a few temper tantrums as you try to get control of your robotics creation. But also be prepared to take your robot where no robot has gone before.

Can I Do This on a Macintosh?

The RIS system is designed to run only on a Windows-based PC and not on a Macintosh. The fact that most of the programs in this book were created on a Mac, however, should tell you that there is a way to work around the problem.

There are a few steps needed to do this.

1. **Run Virtual PC (or some other PC emulator) on your Mac.**

2. **Run the LEGOMac.exe program on the Virtual PC.**

   This makes a small software modification to the RIS software to allow it to work with Mac-style serial ports.

   The LEGOMac.exe program is available on the CD included with this book.

3. **Get a serial port adapter that plugs into a Mac serial port on one side and a 9-pin standard RS-232 port on the other. Plug the cable into the Mac and the IR transmitter.**

4. **Fire up the RIS software on the Virtual PC and start playing.**

Alternatively, you can program in NQC without needing a PC emulator. The Macintosh program Mac NQC is a full NQC development environment that has most of the functionality of Gordon's Brick. Or if you're really adventurous, you can try your hand at PBForth. After the PBForth firmware is downloaded into the RCX brick, any terminal emulator can be used to program the brick. That means that you can not only use a Mac, but you can also use virtually any computer platform such as Unix, Palm, DOS, and so on. Visit www. enteract.com/~dbaum/nqc/ for more information.

Part V
The Part of Tens

The 5th Wave   By Rich Tennant

"Do you remember which military Web site you downloaded your Bot software from?"

In this part . . .

In keeping with the ...*For Dummies* tradition, in this part, you'll find a couple of short chapters that you can speed through in a matter of minutes.

Chapter 13

Ten Embarrassing Bot Moments to Avoid

In This Chapter

▶ Laughing at our robot-building errors

▶ Finding out how to avoid such moments yourself

*H*ere, offered for your entertainment and enlightenment, are tales of a few of the silly moves and mistakes that Michael, one of your coauthors, made while working with LEGO MINDSTORMS robots.

The Sad Saga of the Self-Destructive Bot

I had just finished assembling my first LEGO MINDSTORMS robot from the Robotic Invention System and left it proudly perched on my worktable for all to see. Meanwhile, I turned to my computer to begin studying the programming software that would bring my robotic creation to life. I was exploring the training program on the CD-ROM when I downloaded the first sample program and activated it. Suddenly, I heard a whirring noise behind me and spun around just in time to see the robot making a battery-powered dash for the edge of the table where it plunged off into space.

Alas, robots can't fly. When my carefully constructed robot hit the floor, it promptly disintegrated into a heap of well-designed plastic pieces. (As Dr. McCoy would say, he's dead Jim!)

In a few short seconds, the robot had surged to life, only to meet an untimely death because I failed to provide a "safe" place for it to take its first steps. I didn't think about the robot reacting immediately to the sample program I was experimenting with on the computer, and I was surprised by how fast the robot moved. I learned my lesson.

Fortunately, one of the great things about LEGO MINDSTORMS robots is that the snap-together pieces make it easy to rebuild a broken bot without too much hassle. All it took was one author and a little time to put the robot back together again. Now the repaired robot responds to my every command. (But it stays on the floor unless it is safely switched off.)

The Robot that Ran Backsideward

Things were going along just fine. A fairly complicated robot had a fairly complicated program inside it, and it was really doing some neat stuff. Suddenly, I had an idea that would just make the whole thing perfect. To get it done, it meant taking everything apart and rearranging large chunks of the robot, but it was going to be worth it.

Two hours later, the rebuilt robot was ready to go. The new shape of the robot looked great! I pressed the start button, and the robot took off. But it started doing some really weird stuff. It was moving around, but it wasn't responding to the Touch Sensors in any reasonable way, and it kept making weird movements and getting itself stuck in places where it shouldn't get stuck.

After studying it for a little while, it became apparent that the wheels were turning backwards. How can that be? It was doing just fine before!

It turned out that, during the rearrangement of some of the parts, I had plugged the motor connector wires in at a different angle than the way they had been originally. There are four ways to plug in a motor, and two of them run the motor in the opposite direction. Whenever you change the motor connections, test and make sure the motor is turning the same way it did before. Or, better yet, experiment with the plugs and the motors to see which way they will turn when they are plugged in different ways.

One Piece Shy of the Perfect Robot

Several times, I've been working diligently to build a great robot when progress suddenly came to a screeching halt due to the lack of a critical piece. Bummer!

This really shouldn't happen when building one of the sample robots from a *Constructopedia* because the sample robots are carefully designed to be built with the pieces available in a given LEGO MINDSTORMS set (or rather, the parts inventory of the sets are designed to build the sample robots). You can safely assume that you won't run out of pieces building a robot from the *Constructopedia* unless you've lost or misplaced a piece. So discovering a missing piece usually prompts a frantic search of the floor as well as all the nooks and crannies around my worktable.

A few times I found the missing piece in the most unlikely place — in the robot I was working on. It seems that I had mistakenly picked up the wrong piece and used it in a previous construction step. The solution was to partially disassemble the robot and reconstruct it with the correct pieces.

If you're working on your own robot design, there's no assurance that the LEGO MINDSTORMS set you're using will have exactly the right number of pieces you need for the robot. So even a diligent search of your work area may not turn up the missing piece. The only solution to such a situation is to use your ingenuity to redesign your robot to use different pieces. Thanks to the modular nature of the LEGO MINDSTORMS pieces, that's often possible as long as the missing piece isn't one of the big specialty pieces such as R2-D2's head domes (but you weren't planning to build a two-headed R2D2 droid, were you?).

The Robot that Left a Trail of Pieces Across the Floor

After assembling a couple of sample robots, I thought I was ready to try building a robot of my own design. After all, I had spent countless hours snapping together traditional LEGO building blocks and this was the same thing, with the addition of motors and programming. So I started stacking blocks to create a robot. Everything went well and the finished robot looked pretty good until I turned it on and it started moving across the floor. That's when the robot started slowly disintegrating — trailing pieces behind it as it zigged and zagged and finally stumbled to a halt.

What I discovered was that robot building is fundamentally different from building castles out of LEGO blocks. There is more engineering required. The interlocking LEGO building blocks hold together remarkably well when they're part of a static model, but they aren't strong enough to withstand the twisting and turning forces of motorized movement. You must reinforce high-stress areas. It's not enough to snap together a stack of bricks — you need to add a beam alongside the stack to lock the top and bottom blocks together. (The sample robots in Part II provide many examples of such reinforced construction.) After I rebuilt the robot using some of the appropriate reinforcing techniques, it worked much better.

A Robot without Batteries

I remember excitedly opening one LEGO MINDSTORMS set box and immediately trying to see how the various pieces fit together. I couldn't wait to build my first robot! I opened the *Constructopedia* and hastily flipped to the page where the instructions began for a robot I wanted to build. I rooted around in the box for the required pieces and enthusiastically assembled them according to the diagrams. Time slipped by quickly as I built the robot. Finally, it was done and the robot looked perfect! I pressed the On button to bring the robot to life, but nothing happened. My elation at finishing the robot turned to disappointment when I realized what had happened.

In my haste, I had forgotten to put batteries in the microprocessor brick. As a result, I had built a static model instead of an interactive robot. What's worse, the microprocessor was completely engulfed in robot arms, legs, and body assemblies. There was no way to open the battery compartment of the microprocessor without disassembling much of the robot that I had so carefully constructed. But batteries are essential, so I had no choice but to break apart the robot, insert the batteries, and then rebuild the robot.

Now, I always turn on the microprocessor and check it to make sure the batteries are installed and the microprocessor is working before I incorporate it into a robot that I'm building.

Batteries Don't Last Forever — and Neither Do Battery-Powered Robots

I remember building one robot and developing a program for it. Everything checked out as I downloaded the program to the robot and began putting it through its paces. But when I tried to show off my handiwork, the robot seemed sluggish and unresponsive. Soon it stopped working altogether. I checked the program and I checked the motor and sensor connections, but everything was in order. Finally, I realized that the source of the problem was dead batteries. I had to partially disassemble the robot to get to the battery compartment of the microprocessor so that I could install fresh batteries.

Some robot designs leave the microprocessor in a position where it is reasonably accessible, so changing batteries is no big deal. Other robot designs bury the microprocessor so deep in surrounding assemblies that it's a challenge to reach the On/Off button, let alone the battery compartment. If you're working on such a robot, it's a good idea to put a fresh set of batteries in the microprocessor before you begin.

Chapter 14

Ten Fun Things to Do on the Internet

● ●

In This Chapter

▶ Finding like-minded LEGO MINDSTORMS fans on the Web

▶ Getting your questions answered

▶ Finding free programming help

● ●

*O*f course, the LEGO group has a corporate Web site. But did you know that there's a special section devoted just to LEGO MINDSTORMS robots? There's lots of information available on the Internet about LEGO MINDSTORMS sets and building MINDSTORMS robots. Check it out!

Exploring LEGO Worlds

As you know, the LEGO MINDSTORMS product line isn't the only thing from the land of interlocking blocks. You can find information on LEGO building blocks and all the other LEGO products at www.lego.com. Information about the LEGO TECHNIC sets is of particular interest to MINDSTORMS robot builders because many of the TECHNIC parts interconnect with MINDSTORMS parts.

Visiting the LEGO MINDSTORMS Web Site

There is a whole Web site (at www.legomindstorms.com) devoted to LEGO MINDSTORMS robotics. There's a lot to see and do at the official LEGO MINDSTORMS Web site. Just click on the icons across the top of the screen to get more information about one of the special interest areas:

- ✔ **Products:** Get online information about LEGO MINDSTORMS products, including a product selector grid. You can also find ordering information for Expansion Sets and individual parts that aren't sold in stores and are available only direct from LEGO Shop at Home.

- ✔ **Hall of Fame:** The best submissions from robot builders around the world are honored with a place in the monthly Hall of Fame. You can browse the current submissions and past winners to get ideas and cast your vote for which robots go into the LEGO MINDSTORMS Hall of Fame. You can even submit your own robot inventions.

- ✔ **Tips & tricks:** This is where you'll find the Tip of the Week as well as designs and building instructions for robots and robot components. You can also find tips for developing RCX programs to control your robots and instructions for building and programming robots and components such as a strong and versatile grabber arm.

- ✔ **Web missions:** Download online adventure games to play on your computer. You'll need to design and build Robotic Invention System robots to help you complete the game. Have fun!

- ✔ **FIRST LEGO League:** The FIRST LEGO League (FLL) is a joint project of FIRST (For Inspiration and Recognition of Science and Technology) and the LEGO Group. FLL sponsors competitions for teams of 9- to 14-year-olds to build LEGO MINDSTORMS robots to meet a challenge. Local teams participate in state tournaments, engaging in friendly competition and gaining recognition for creativity and leadership. Check out the FLL area to learn more about activities in your area.

- ✔ **Tech support:** Answers to installation and configuration questions in several languages.

In addition to the areas you can access by clicking icons, you can log in to participate in online forums where you can share your experiences using LEGO MINDSTORMS robots with other robot builders.

Going Unofficial

The Web site entitled Unofficial Questions and Answers about MIT Programmable Bricks and LEGO MINDSTORMS is a treasure trove of information. You can find it at `http://mevard.www.media.mit.edu/people/fredm/mindstorms/`.

Visiting LEGO MINDSTORMS Internals

This Web site is really an index to lots of LEGO MINDSTORMS-related sites and info. You can find it at `www.crynwr.com/lego-robotics/`.

Finding Out about the LEGO MINDSTORMS Web Ring

A Web ring is a series of linked Web sites that share a common theme. The LEGO MINDSTORMS Web ring is headquartered at http://members.tripod.com/~ssncommunity/webrings/legoms_index.html.

Go to the boxed Web ring links at the bottom of the page and click Next to go to the next Web site in the ring. Page through the ring to see an assortment of LEGO MINDSTORMS hobbyists' pages such as Sloth 1.0 (www.ismi.net/~phong/lego/sloth/), a design for a robot that walks like a dog.

Building a Spider Robot

Rene Schalburg's Web site gives fairly detailed instructions for building a walking spider robot with the Robotic Invention System. Check it out at http://schalburg.homepage.dk/Spider/Spider.html.

Meeting the Logo Turtle

The Machina Speculatrix Web site (www.plazaearth.com/usr/gasperi/walter.htm) demonstrates how to create a logo turtle (a three-wheeled robot designed for teaching robotics and programming) with LEGO MINDSTORMS kit pieces.

Engaging in Robot Combat

The Robot Arena Web site provides information about a group of robot builders who create LEGO MINDSTORMS robots that are designed to engage in autonomous combat against others of their kind. For more information, go to www.azimuthmedia.com/RobotArena/mainframe.html.

Dissecting the RCX

If you want to know what's inside the RCX microprocessor but don't want to tear it apart yourself, check out the RCX Internals Web site at http://graphics.stanford.edu/~kekoa/rcx/.

Appendix A

Parts Reference

*T*his appendix is designed to be a visual reference list of parts found in the main LEGO MINDSTORMS sets, including parts from the Droid Developer Kit, Robotics Discovery Kit, and the Robotics Invention System. That means that this reference covers all the available LEGO MINDSTORMS pieces except for a few specialized pieces found in some of the Expansion Sets.

This appendix also serves as a MINDSTORMS parts glossary that you can use to identify the parts we mention in the building instructions for the various robots described in this book. Because very few of the LEGO MINDSTORMS parts have official names, we made up some names of our own — mostly names that describe the piece or its function. This is where you can match a visual reference to the parts names used in this book.

Axles and Spacer Rings

The black sticks with the X-shaped cross-section are axles, which you use to mount wheels and pulleys and use as connector pins to join beams. Axles come in several lengths and are measured by the number of pegs that would be on a block of the same length. Variations on the basic axle include an axle with a molded end cap, a short axle with a ball tip (it looks a little like a trailer-hitch ball), and bendable axles made of flexible material. Figure A-1 shows an assortment of axle pieces.

- ✔ Size 12 axle (A)
- ✔ Size 10 axle (B)
- ✔ Size 8 axle (C)
- ✔ Size 6 axle (D)
- ✔ Size 5 axle (E)
- ✔ Size 4 axle (F)

- ✔ Size 3 axle (G)
- ✔ Size 2 axle (H)
- ✔ Cap-end axle (I)
- ✔ Ball-tip short axle (J)
- ✔ Size 19 flexible axle (K)
- ✔ Size 12 flexible axle (L)
- ✔ Size 11 flexible axle (M)

Spacer rings, as shown in Figure A-2, are small pieces that slip over an axle and act as spacers between beams, wheels, or other pieces. Spacer rings also serve as end caps to keep an axle from slipping out of a hole in a beam or other piece.

- ✔ Thin spacer ring (A)
- ✔ Thick spacer ring (B)

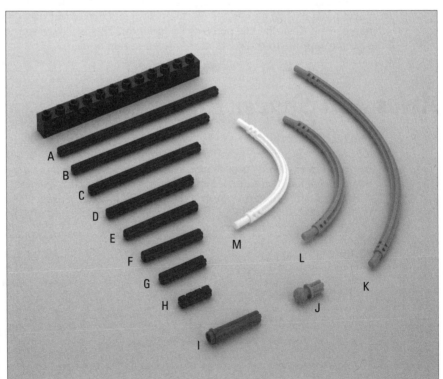

Figure A-1:
Axle pieces.

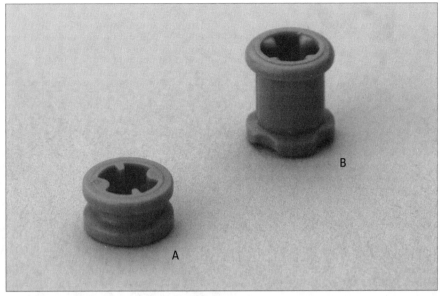

Blocks, Plates, and Beams

The primary structural pieces of the LEGO MINDSTORMS sets are the blocks, plates, and beams. The blocks, plates, and beams come in a variety of sizes and configurations.

Blocks

MINDSTORMS blocks have the most in common with the classic LEGO building blocks. As Figure A-3 shows, blocks come in a variety of sizes and shapes. They all have the distinctive LEGO pegs on the top. Block sizes are measured by the number of pegs on the top side — expressed as the number of rows of pegs and the number of pegs in each row: For example, a 2x4 block has two rows of four pegs. In addition to the pegs on the top of each block, many of the MINDSTORMS blocks are perforated with holes in the sides to accept axles and connector pegs.

Figure A-3:
Blocks.

> ✔ 2x6 solid block (A)
>
> ✔ 2x4 solid block (B)
>
> ✔ 2x2 solid block (C)
>
> ✔ 1x2 solid block (D)
>
> ✔ 1x2 2-hole perforated block (E)
>
> ✔ 1x2 perforated block (F)
>
> ✔ 1x2 X-hole perforated block (G)
>
> ✔ 1x1 perforated block (H)
>
> ✔ 1x4 perforated block (I)
>
> ✔ 1x6 perforated block (J)
>
> ✔ 1x8 perforated block (K)
>
> ✔ 1x10 perforated block (L)
>
> ✔ 1x12 perforated block (M)
>
> ✔ 1x16 perforated block (N)

In addition to the standard blocks, MINDSTORMS sets include several modified block pieces, including various wedge shapes and round blocks, as shown in Figure A-4.

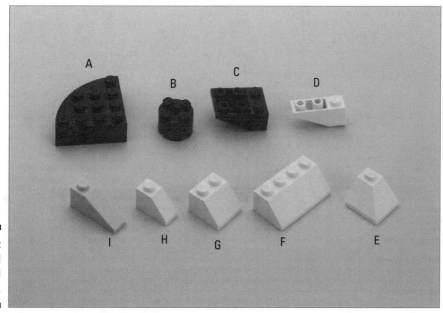

- 4x4 quarter round block (A)
- 2x2 round block (B)
- 2x3 reverse wedge (C)
- 1x3 reverse wedge (D)
- 1x1 corner wedge (E)
- 1x4 wedge (F)
- 1x2 wedge (G)
- 1x1 short wedge (H)
- 1x1 long wedge (I)

Plates

Plates are similar to blocks except that they are only one third the height of a standard block. Top plates are like regular plates except that they have no pegs — they are smooth on top. Figure A-5 shows the assortment of plates available in the MINDSTORMS sets.

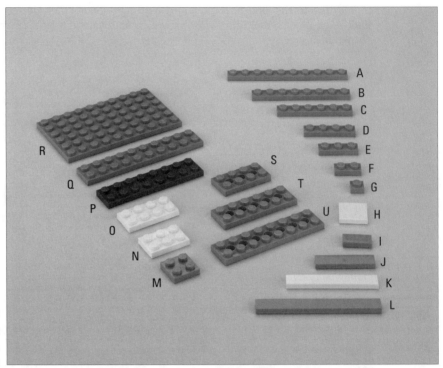

Figure A-5:
Plates.

- 1x10 plate (A)
- 1x8 plate (B)
- 1x6 plate (C)
- 1x4 plate (D)
- 1x3 plate (E)
- 1x2 plate (F)
- 1x1 plate (G)
- 2x2 top plate (H)
- 1x2 top plate (I)
- 1x4 top plate (J)
- 1x6 top plate (K)
- 1x8 top plate (L)
- 2x2 plate (M)
- 2x3 plate (N)
- 2x4 plate (O)
- 2x8 plate (P)

- ✔ 2x10 plate (Q)
- ✔ 6x10 plate (R)
- ✔ 2x4 perforated plate (S)
- ✔ 2x6 perforated plate (T)
- ✔ 2x8 perforated plate (U)

The MINDSTORMS sets include several variations on the standard plates, as shown in Figure A-6.

- ✔ 3x6 triangular plate (A)
- ✔ 3x3 triangular plate (B)
- ✔ 2x2 single-hole bracket plate (C)
- ✔ 2x2 double-hole bracket plate (D)
- ✔ 2x2 rotating-peg plate (E)
- ✔ 2x2 round plate (F)
- ✔ 1x2 side-tab plate (G)
- ✔ 1x2 single-peg plate (H)
- ✔ 1x2 grill-top plate (I)
- ✔ Small corner plate (J)

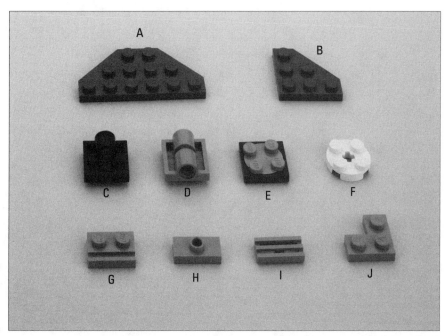

Figure A-6:
Plate
variations.

Beams

The other major grouping of structural pieces are known as beams — pieces that have no pegs, just holes for axles and connector pegs. The beams are sized by the number of holes and their thicknesses. See Figure A-7 for a visual inventory of MINDSTORMS beams pieces.

- ✔ 11-hole double angle beam (A)
- ✔ 9-hole angle beam (B)
- ✔ 7-hole beam (C)
- ✔ 6-hole beam (D)
- ✔ 5-hole beam (E)
- ✔ 4-hole dual thickness beam (F)
- ✔ 3-hole thin beam (G)
- ✔ 7-hole T-beam (H)
- ✔ 5-hole thin corner beam (I)
- ✔ 5-hole L beam (J)

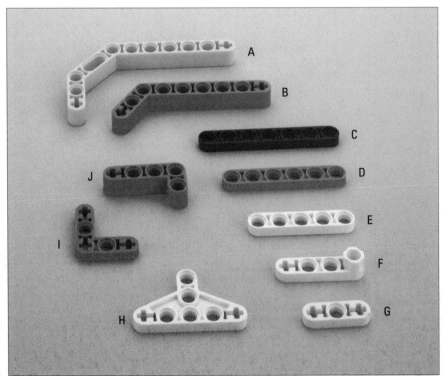

Figure A-7:
Beams.

Connector Pegs

You use connector pegs to join beams, perforated blocks, and other pieces. Figure A-8 shows the assortment of connector pegs and also the peg extender button.

- ✔ Double-head long connector peg (A)
- ✔ Long connector peg (B)
- ✔ Regular connector peg (C)
- ✔ Short connector peg (D)
- ✔ Button-end connector peg (E)
- ✔ Peg extender button (F)
- ✔ Axle-end connector peg (G)
- ✔ Double connector peg (H)

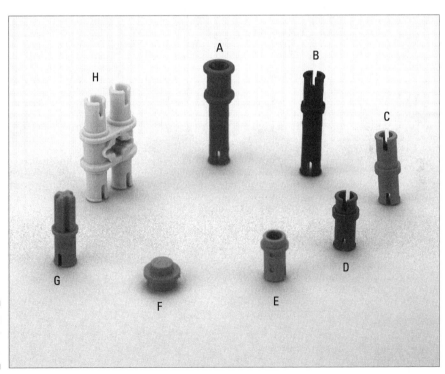

Figure A-8:
Connector
pegs.

Gears and Pulleys

Gears enable you to transfer the power output of motors to wheels, arms, and other robot appendages. By using the proper gear combinations, you can increase or decrease the speed and change the direction of a motor's rotation. Figure A-9 shows the MINDSTORMS gears, including some ungear-like gears, such as the worm gear and flat gear plate.

- Stacked double gear (16 & 24 tooth) (A)
- 24-tooth hat gear (gears turn back toward shaft) (B)
- 20-tooth full bevel gear (C)
- 12-tooth full bevel gear (D)
- 12-tooth half bevel gear (E)
- 8-tooth gear (F)
- 16-tooth gear (star center) (G)
- 24-tooth clutch gear (H)
- 24-tooth gear (4 holes) (I)
- 40-tooth gear (12 holes) (J)
- Worm gear (K)
- 10-tooth flat gear plate (1x4 plate) (L)

Gears aren't the only way you can transfer motion. You can also use pulleys and belts. Figure A-10 shows the pulleys and belts that are available in the MINDSTORMS sets.

- Small pulley wheel (spacer ring plus) (A)
- Single-spoke pulley wheel (B)
- 6-hole Pulley wheel (C)
- Rubber ring (D)
- Belts (rubber bands) (E)

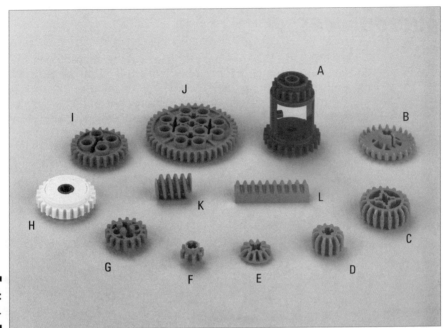

Figure A-9:
Gears.

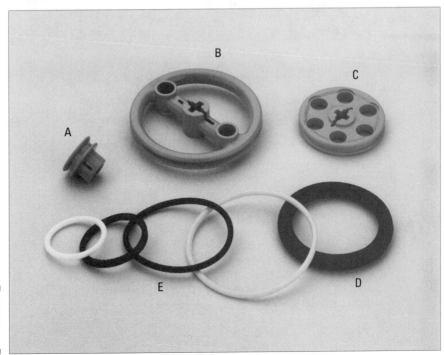

Figure A-10:
Pulleys and belts.

Microprocessor Bricks

The brains of any MINDSTORMS robot are in the microprocessor brick that processes input from sensors and controls the output of motors. Figure A-11 is a family portrait of the LEGO MINDSTORMS microprocessors, accompanied by the infrared (IR) transmitter and remote control that enable you and your computer to communicate with the microprocessors.

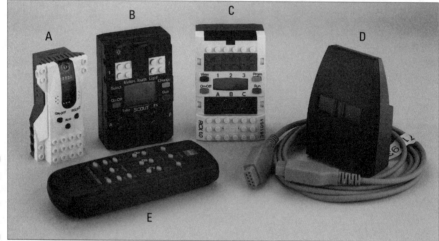

Figure A-11: Micro-processor bricks.

- ✔ Micro Scout (from the Droid Developer Kit) (A)
- ✔ Scout (from the Robotics Discovery Set) (B)
- ✔ RCX (from the Robotics Invention System) (C)
- ✔ IR transmitter and cable (from the Robotics Invention System) (D)
- ✔ Remote control (available separately) (E)

Pipes

Pipes are used to connect axles end to end. Corrugated pipe is flexible and serves a generally decorative purpose. The short sleeve is a tube that slips over an axle and allows the axle to rotate freely within the sleeve. Figure A-12 shows the MINDSTORMS pipe pieces.

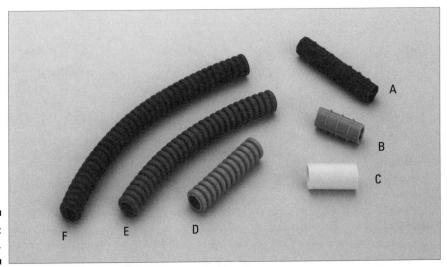

- Long pipe (4-peg) (A)
- Short pipe (2-peg) (B)
- Short sleeve (C)
- Corrugated pipe (4-peg) (D)
- Corrugated pipe (8-peg) (E)
- Corrugated pipe (10-peg) (F)

Sensors & Motors

The sensors and motors are what enable a MINDSTORMS robot to detect light and objects in its environment and to move or take other action according to its programming. Figure A-13 shows the standard sensors and motors and their connector wires.

- Long connector wire (A)
- Short connector wire (B)
- Medium connector wire (C)
- Touch Sensor (D)
- Motor (E)
- Light Sensor (F)

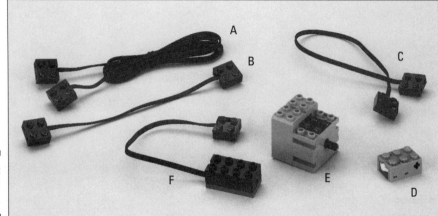

Figure A-13:
Sensors and
motors.

Tee Fittings and Elbows

The tee fittings and elbows shown in Figure A-14 enable you to join axles and connector pegs to other pieces in a variety of different configurations.

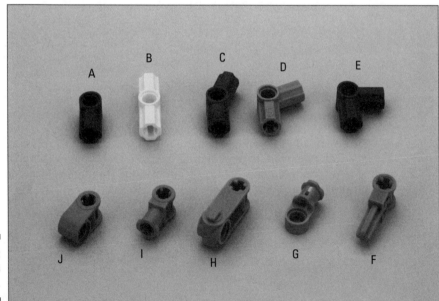

Figure A-14:
Tee fittings
and elbows.

✔ Number 1 elbow (A)

✔ Number 2 elbow (B)

- Number 3 elbow (C)
- Number 5 elbow (D)
- Number 6 elbow (E)
- Axle tip tee (F)
- Offset end-axle tee (G)
- Long mid-axle tee (H)
- End-axle tee (I)
- Mid-axle tee (J)

Tires and Wheels

The LEGO MINDSTORMS sets include a variety of wheels and tires that you can use to make your robots mobile. Check out Figure A-15 to see your options for putting robot rubber to the road.

- 81.6x15 bicycle tire (A)
- 6-spoke wheel (B)
- Medium 20x30 lug tire (C)
- Medium rim wheel (D)
- Large 49.6x28 smooth tire (E)
- Deep dish rim wheel (F)
- Caterpillar track (G)
- Track wheel (H)
- Small 30.4x14 smooth tire (I)
- Small rim wheel (J)
- Small solid wheel (crescent slots) (K)
- Small solid tire (L)
- Medium solid tire (M)
- Large solid tire (N)

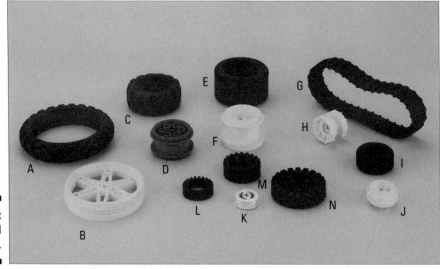

Figure A-15:
Tires and
wheels.

Uncategorized Special Pieces

The LEGO MINDSTORMS sets include many specialized pieces that serve a variety of special purposes ranging from specialized structural pieces to purely decorative pieces. Figure A-16 shows part of the assortment of special-purpose pieces.

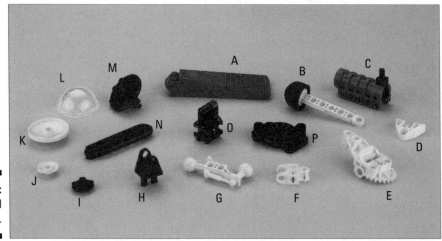

Figure A-16:
Special
pieces.

- ✔ Door stop wedge (A)
- ✔ Projectile (B)
- ✔ Launcher (C)
- ✔ Triangular side brace (D)
- ✔ Compound half gear piece (need left and right halves) (E)
- ✔ Mid-axle socket (F)
- ✔ Double-ball piece (G)
- ✔ Double-peg/double-hole hinge piece (H)
- ✔ Small 4-peg disc (I)
- ✔ Small 1-peg disk (J)
- ✔ Large 1-peg disc (K)
- ✔ Bug eye dome (L)
- ✔ Large 12-peg disk (M)
- ✔ Heavy arm beam (N)
- ✔ Multi-hole connector block (O)
- ✔ Lazy Susan pivot (P)

Figure A-17 shows some of the smaller special-purpose pieces that are part of the LEGO MINDSTORMS sets.

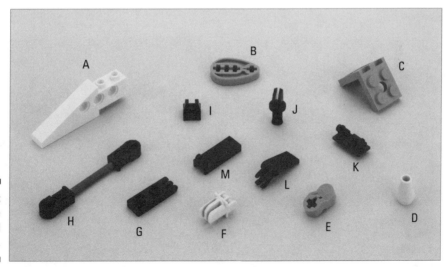

Figure A-17:
Some more
special
pieces.

- ✔ 1x2 perforated wedge (A)
- ✔ Cam (B)
- ✔ 2x2 corner bracket plate (C)
- ✔ Cone peg extender (D)
- ✔ Angled double axle end cap (E)
- ✔ Double hinge peg (F)
- ✔ 2-peg end-hinge plate (G)
- ✔ Connector rod (actually a connector rod, thin sleeve, and two ends) (H)
- ✔ 1-peg hinge plate (I)
- ✔ Small hinge peg (J)
- ✔ 2-peg hinge plate (K)
- ✔ Duck bill hinge (L)
- ✔ 2-peg end-hinge top plate (M)

Extra Decorative Pieces

The MINDSTORMS pieces shown in Figure A-18 serve no useful purpose whatsoever. However, they are part of the fun of making your robots look like something special, whether it's the R2-D2 droid of *Star Wars* fame or a beeping and buzzing insect.

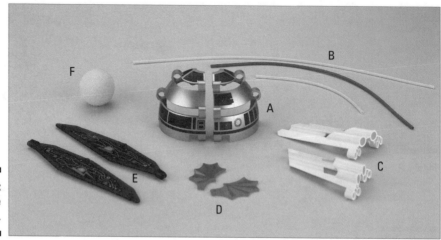

Figure A-18:
Decorative
pieces.

- ✔ Dome head piece (left and right) (A)
- ✔ Long flex tubing (12.8, 29.6, 36 mm) (B)
- ✔ Wings (left and right) (C)
- ✔ Pixie wings (D)
- ✔ Bug wings (left and right) (E)
- ✔ Foam ball (F)

Appendix B

RCX Reference

This appendix contains some handy information for programming the RCX brick. We also include a list of all of the blocks that are available when programming the RCX brick using the software that's supplied with the Robotics Invention System.

RCX Terminology

Every programming language has its own set of special terms, and the RCX programming interface is no exception. RCX programming is done by using the mouse to select blocks, flipping them over to adjust their settings, and placing the blocks in stacks. One or more stacks are combined to make up a program, and a program can be stored in the vault. It's really a simple process, but you have to know what all these words mean to be able to discuss it like a pro:

- **Block:** A block is the smallest possible unit in a program. Each block serves a single purpose within a program stack. A program stack is composed of a collection of blocks.

- **Command:** A programming block that contains an instruction to be obeyed by the RCX.

- **Counter:** An internal device that keeps a count of any event and can be read by your program.

- **Download:** In the context of the RCX, this term refers to copying a program from your PC to the RCX using the IR link.

- **Inputs:** Any device, such as a Touch Sensor or Light Sensor, that sends data to the RCX or Scout.

- **IR (infrared):** The data link connecting your PC with the RCX unit. IR is also used by the remote control to send signals to the RCX, and by RCX to send signals to the Scout of the Robotics Discovery Set.

- **Messages:** Information that can be sent between two RCX units, an RCX and a Scout, or an RCX and the remote control.

- ✔ **My Commands:** Custom commands that you create and use in your programs. Also called *subroutines*.

- ✔ **Output:** A device, such as a motor or lamp, that can be controlled by the RCX or Scout.

- ✔ **Program:** A collection of one or more stacks that can be downloaded, as a single unit, from your PC into one of the five program slots of the RCX.

- ✔ **Program Vault:** The storage location on your PC that's used to save programs so that they can be retrieved for modification and/or downloading into the RCX.

- ✔ **Sensor:** A device that's internal or external to the RCX device. Sensors represent connections to physical sensors that detect light, touch, temperature, and other changes in the robot's environment.

- ✔ **Sensor Watcher:** A block that monitors the status of a sensor and executes a stack depending on that status.

- ✔ **Stack:** A sequence of blocks connected one after the other to make up part of a program.

- ✔ **Stack Controller:** A programming block or pair of blocks that may alter the direction of logic flow through a stack. This block can be looping, branching, or pausing.

- ✔ **Timer:** An internal stopwatch that keeps track of time and can be read by your program.

- ✔ **Trace:** A troubleshooting tool that allows you to visually see your program run.

RCX Block Categories

A program can be written with the mouse by dragging and dropping blocks into one or more stacks. Each block has been placed into one of the categories shown in Table B-1. On the display, the category of each block can be distinguished by its color.

Table B-1		The Categories of the RCX Code Blocks
Block Type	*Color*	*Description*
Control	Green	A Control block is an instruction for the RCX to perform some specific action.
Sensor Watcher	Blue	A Sensor Watcher monitors and responds to either an internal or external sensor. A sensor can be an external device (such as a Touch Sensor) or can be internal (such as a timer).

Block Type	Color	Description
Stack Control	Red	A Stack Control block is capable of determining which block is executed next.
My Commands	Yellow	This type is assigned to any block that you create yourself.

RCX Block Reference

A program can be written using the mouse by dragging and dropping blocks into one or more stacks. The following is an alphabetical list and description of all of the different kinds of blocks.

✔ **Add to Counter:** This command (see Figure B-1) adds 1 to the value of the internal counter. The counter is a built-in sensor that always contains a number. When a program first starts running, the counter is initialized to 0.

Figure B-1:
Add to
Counter
block.

To test the value of the counter, see *Counter.* To set the value of the counter back to 0, see *Reset Counter.*

✔ **Beep:** This command (see Figure B-2) causes the RCX to make a sound.

Figure B-2:
Beep block.

The sound will be one of six beeping sounds that you select by flipping the block. The currently selected beep shows up on the block as the number 1 through 6, as shown in Figure B-3.

- Beep 1 is a short single tone.

- Beep 2 is a pair of tones.

- Beep 3 is a set of multiple tones descending in frequency.

• Beep 4 is a long set of multiple tones ascending in frequency.

• Beep 5 is a buzzing sound.

• Beep 6 is a short set of multiple tones ascending in frequency.

Also see *Tone.*

Figure B-3:
Flip side of
Beep block.

✔ **Check & Choose:** This stack controller is used to decide which of two possible stacks are to be executed. The decision is made based on the current status of a sensor. Any sensor (see Figure B-4) can be used.

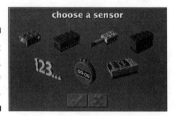

Figure B-4:
Check &
Choose
block.

If a sensor check results in *true,* the stack on the left is executed; otherwise, the stack on the right is executed.

• The Counter Sensor watcher, shown in Figure B-5, registers *true* only if the value of the counter is within the specified range at the moment the counter is checked. The available range is 1 to 32766.

Figure B-5:
Flip side of
Check &
Choose
Counter
block.

- The Light Sensor watcher registers *true* only if the current light value is within the specified range at the moment the light value is checked.

- The RCX Sensor watcher registers *true* only if the numeric value of the most recently received message is within the specified range at the moment the message is checked. The available range is from 1 to 255.

- The Rotation Sensor watcher registers *true* only if the current rotation counter is within the specified range at the moment the rotation count is checked.

- The Temperature Sensor watcher registers *true* only if the current temperature value is within the specified range at the moment the temperature is checked.

- The Timer Sensor watcher registers *true* only if the elapsed time in the timer is within the specified range at the moment the timer is checked. The available range is from 0.1 to 327.6 seconds.

- The Touch Sensor watcher registers *true* only if the sensor button is depressed at the moment the touch sensor is checked.

✔ **Counter:** This watcher (see Figure B-6) triggers and executes its stack whenever the counter moves into the specified range. After this watcher has triggered, the counter must move out of its range and enter it again for it to trigger again.

Figure B-6:
Counter
block.

To increment the counter, see **Add to Counter.** To set the value of the counter back to 0, see **Reset Counter.**

✔ **Light:** The Light Sensor watcher (see Figure B-7) triggers whenever the brightness of the detected light moves within a range. The sensor can be set to monitor the light sensor connected to one of the three ports labeled 1, 2, and 3.

Figure B-7:
Light Sensor
watcher.

There are two ranges, so this sensor controls two stacks. By default, the stack named *dark* triggers when the light moves into the range 0 to 50, and the stack named *bright* triggers when the light moves into the range 51 to 100. When your program first starts running, a sensor triggers immediately if the light is within its range. After a sensor has triggered, the light must move outside the range and back in again for it to trigger again.

The upper and lower values of each range can be set to any value from 0 to 100. To adjust the settings, the red and green colored sliders at the bottom can be adjusted on each end, as shown in Figure B-8. If the light value enters this range before a stack has completed execution, the stack immediately starts over.

Figure B-8:
Flip side of
Light Sensor
Window.

🖊 **My Commands:** You can use this block to construct your own commands. A command is constructed by inserting one or more blocks between the beginning and ending blocks of the My Commands pair of blocks. After you have created your custom command (shown in Figure B-9) and given it a name, it appears in the list of My Commands available to be inserted. You can insert your custom command into as many places as you wish, in as many stacks as you wish. Modifying your custom command modifies all occurrences of it in your program.

Figure B-9:
My
Commands
block.

🖊 **Off:** This command (see Figure B-10) immediately turns off one or more of the motors.

Figure B-10:
Off block.

You can select which of the motors labeled A, B, and C will be turned off by the command. You can select one, two, or all three motors. On the flip side of the block, an X by a letter indicates that the block is set to turn that motor off, as shown in Figure B-11.

Figure B-11:
Flip side of
Off block.

To turn a motor on, see *On.* To turn a motor on for a specific period of time, see *On For.* To set the direction of a motor, see *Set Direction* and *Reverse Direction.* To control the speed of a motor, see *Set Power.*

✔ **On:** This command (see Figure B-12) immediately turns on one or more of the motors.

Figure B-12:
On block.

You can select which of the motors labeled A, B, and C will be turned on by the command. You can select one, two, or all three motors. On the flip side of the block, an X next to a letter indicates that the block is set to turn that motor on, as shown in Figure B-13. To set the direction of a motor, see *Set Direction* and *Reverse Direction.*

Figure B-13:
Flip side of
On block.

To turn a motor off, see *Off.* To turn a motor on for a specific period of time, see *On For.* To control the speed of a motor, see *Set Power.*

✔ **On For:** This command (see Figure B-14) turns on one or more of the motors for a period of time.

Figure B-14:
On For
block.

You can specify which of the motors labeled A, B, and C will be turned on by the command. You can select one, two, or all three of the motors. The time is measured in seconds and can be any value from 0.1 (one tenth of a second) up to 327.6. On the flip side of the block, an X next to a letter indicates that the block is set to turn on that motor, as shown in Figure B-15. Also on the flip side, you can type in the number of seconds or use the + and – signs next to the time value to add or subtract 0.1 second to the time setting.

Figure B-15:
Flip side of
On For
block.

You can also specify that the length of time the motor is turned on is randomly selected when the motor is turned on. The random time is selected from within a range of times. To set up a random time, click on the picture of the die to the left of the window displaying the time. The word "random" appears below the time value, and the time value is displayed as a range from 0.1 to the current time setting. You can enter the upper limit from the keyboard, or use the + and – signs to adjust it (the lower limit is always 0.1 seconds).

To turn on a motor without a time limit, see **On.** To turn a motor off before the timer expires, see **Off.** To set the direction of a motor, see ***Set Direction*** and ***Reverse Direction.*** To control the speed of a motor, see ***Set Power.***

⮑ **RCX:** This watcher (see Figure B-16) triggers and executes its stack whenever a message is received from another RCX unit.

Figure B-16:
RCX
watcher.

The message is in the form of a number from 1 to 255. Setting the beginning and ending values specifies the range of message numbers that will cause the watcher to trigger. After a message has been received and this watcher has triggered, it is necessary to receive another message within its range for it to trigger again. Also, a new message can't be received by this RCX unit until the previously received message has been cleared.

To clear the previously received message, see *Reset Message.* To send a message to another RCX unit, see *Send Message.*

⮑ **Repeat:** This command (see Figure B-17) is made of two blocks that are capable of containing blocks between them.

Figure B-17:
Repeat
block.

A counter value can be set from 2 to 255 to specify the number of times the contained blocks are to be executed. Use the + and – signs to the right of the value to adjust the count, or enter the number directly from the keyboard. It's also possible to select the die to the left of the counter to specify a range of numbers. If a range is specified, each time the block is executed, the actual repeat count is randomly selected from a value within the specified range. (See Figure B-18.)

Figure B-18:
Flip side of
Repeat
block.

If a repeat loop is executing and the sensor watcher controlling its stack is triggered again, the loop stops immediately and execution begins at the top of the stack.

To repeat without a count, see *Repeat Forever.* To repeat depending on a sensor, see *Repeat While.*

✔ **Repeat Forever:** This command (see Figure B-19) is made of two blocks that are capable of containing blocks between them. The contained blocks are executed repeatedly until either the program stops or the sensor watcher controlling the stack is triggered again.

Figure B-19:
Repeat
Forever
command.

If a repeat loop is executing and the sensor watcher controlling its stack is triggered again, the loop stops immediately and execution begins at the top of the stack. (See Figure B-20.)

Figure B-20:
Both blocks
of the
Repeat
Forever
command.

To repeat for a specified number of times, see *Repeat.* To repeat depending on a sensor, see *Repeat While.*

✔ **Repeat While:** This command is made of two blocks that are capable of containing blocks between them. The contained blocks are executed repeatedly until either the program stops or the sensor watcher controlling the stack is triggered again.

• The Counter Sensor watcher registers *true* only if the value of the counter is within the specified range at the moment the counter is checked. The available range is 1 to 32766.

• The Light Sensor watcher registers *true* only if the current light value is within the specified range at the moment the light value is checked.

- The RCX Sensor watcher registers *true* only if the numeric value of the most recently received message is within the specified range at the moment the message is checked. The available range is from 1 to 255.

- The Rotation Sensor watcher registers *true* only if the current rotation counter is within the specified range at the moment the rotation count is checked.

- The Temperature Sensor watcher registers *true* only if the current temperature value is within the specified range at the moment the temperature is checked.

- The Timer Sensor watcher registers *true* only if the elapsed time in the timer is within the specified range at the moment the timer is checked. The available range is from 0.1 to 327.6 seconds.

- The Touch Sensor watcher registers *true* only if the sensor button is depressed at the moment the Touch Sensor is checked.

If a repeat loop is executing and the sensor watcher controlling its stack is triggered again, the loop stops immediately and execution begins at the top of the stack.

To repeat for some number of times, see **Repeat.** To repeat an unlimited number of times, see **Repeat Forever.**

✔ **Reset Counter:** This command (see Figure B-21) erases the current value stored in the counter and sets it back to 0. The counter is a built-in sensor that always contains a number. When a program first starts running, the counter is initialized to 0.

Figure B-21:
Reset
Counter
block.

To test the value of the counter, see **Counter.** To adjust the value stored in the counter, see **Add to Counter.**

✔ **Reset Message:** This command (see Figure B-22) erases the message, if any, that has been received from another RCX unit. The message is in the form of a number. A received message must be erased before another message can be received.

Figure B-22:
Reset
Message
block.

To send a message to another RCX unit, see ***Send to RCX.*** To detect the arrival of a message from another RCX unit, see ***RCX.***

✔ **Reset Rotation:** This command (see Figure B-23) resets one or more of the rotation counters to 0.

Figure B-23:
Reset
Rotation
block.

The rotation counter(s) to be reset is determined by an X placed next to the ports numbered 1, 2, and 3 on the flip side of the block, as shown in Figure B-24.

Figure B-24:
Flip side of
Reset
Rotation
Block.

To detect the rotational position, see ***Rotation.***

✔ **Reset Timer:** This command (see Figure B-25) resets the internal RCX timer to 0. The internal timer begins counting seconds, beginning at 0, whenever your program starts running.

Figure B-25:
Reset Timer
block.

To read information from the timer, see *Timer.*

✔ **Reverse Direction:** This command (see Figure B-26) immediately reverses the direction of one or more motors. You can select which of the motors labeled A, B, and C will be reversed by the command. You can select one, two, or all three motors.

Figure B-26:
Reverse
Direction
block.

On the flip side of the block, an X by a letter indicates that the block is set to reverse that motor, as shown in Figure B-27. A motor doesn't have to be currently running to have its direction reversed.

Figure B-27:
Flip side of
Reverse
Direction
block.

To specify the direction of a motor, see *Set Direction.* To start and stop motors, see *Off, On,* and *On For.* To control the speed of a motor, see *Set Power.*

✔ **Rotation:** The Rotation Sensor watcher (see Figure B-28) triggers whenever an axle rotates into a specified position.

Figure B-28:
Rotation
Sensor
watcher.

The watcher can be set to monitor the Rotation Sensor connected to one of the three ports labeled 1, 2, and 3. An internal rotation counter continuously monitors the location of the axle. Rotation in one direction counts up while rotation in the opposite direction counts down. Whenever the value of the counter enters the range you specified, the watcher triggers and executes the stack. For the stack to execute again, the value must leave the range and enter it again.

When your program first starts running, the rotation counter is set to 0. A complete circle is a count of 16. The maximum possible rotation value is 32766, and the minimum is –32767. The default range setting is 0 to 160. The upper and lower range can be set by entering the numbers from the keyboard. The slider at the bottom can be used to adjust the settings within a limited range of the current settings — see Figure B-29.

Figure B-29:
Flip side of the Rotation Sensor watcher.

To reset the rotation counter, see **Reset Rotation.**

✔ **Send to RCX:** This command (see Figure B-30) sends a message from this RCX block to another one. The message can be any number from 1 to 255.

Figure B-30:
Send to RCX block.

The default message number is 1. You can enter the number directly from the keyboard or adjust the number to be sent by using the + and – signs to the right of the number. Select the die to the left of the number to cause the transmission of a random number between 1 and the number you choose to be the upper limit. (See Figure B-31.)

Figure B-31:
Flip side of Send to RCX block.

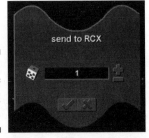

✔ **Set Direction:** This command (see Figure B-32) immediately sets the direction of one or more of the motors.

Figure B-32:
Set
Direction
block.

You can select which of the motors labeled A, B and C will have their direction set, and you can separately specify the direction setting of each one. On the flip side of the block, shown in Figure B-33, an X by a letter indicates that this block will set the direction of that motor. Below each X are two buttons: the top button specifies that the direction will be forward and the bottom button specifies a backward direction. When your program first starts running, all motors are set to run forward. A motor doesn't have to be currently running to have its direction set. Setting a motor to run in the direction it is already running has no effect.

Figure B-33:
Flip side of
Set
Direction
block.

To reverse the direction of a motor, see **_Reverse Direction._** To start and stop motors, see **_Off, On,_** and **_On For._** To control the speed of a motor, see **_Set Power._**

✔ **Set Power:** This command (see Figure B-34) controls the speed of a motor by setting the amount of power that's supplied to it.

Figure B-34:
Set Power
block.

You can select which of the motors labeled A, B, and C will have its speed set by the command. You can select one, two, or all three motors. On the flip side of the block, shown in Figure B-35, an X by a letter indicates that the block set the power for that motor. The settings for the power values range from 1 to 8, with 1 being the lowest. When your program first starts running, all motors are set to a power of 4.

Figure B-35:
Flip side of
Set Power
block.

To start and stop motors, see *On, On For,* and *Off.* To control the direction of a motor, see ***Set Direction*** and ***Reverse Direction.***

✔ **Temperature:** The Temperature Sensor watcher (see Figure B-36) triggers whenever the detected temperature moves within a range.

Figure B-36:
Temperature
Sensor
watcher.

The watcher can be set to monitor the Temperature Sensor connected to one of the three ports labeled 1, 2, and 3 — see Figure B-37. There are two temperature ranges, so this watcher controls two stacks. When your program first starts running, a sensor immediately triggers if the temperature is within its range. After a sensor has been triggered, the temperature must move outside the range and back in for it to trigger again.

Using the setup screen, the watcher can be configured for either Fahrenheit or Celsius. By default, the stack named *cold* triggers when the temperature moves into the range 32° to 77°F, or 0° to 25°C. The stack named *warm* triggers when the temperature moves into the range 78° to 122°F, or 26° to 50°C.

Figure B-37:
Flip side of
Temperature
Sensor
watcher.

The upper and lower values of each range can be set to any value from
–20° to 50°C or –4° to 122°F. To adjust the settings, the red and green colored sliders at the bottom can be adjusted on each end. If this happens
before a stack has completed execution, it immediately starts over.

✔ **Timer:** This watcher (see Figure B-38) triggers and executes its stack
whenever the program timer moves into the specified range.

Figure B-38:
Timer
watcher.

This timer starts at 0 when your program starts running and runs continuously. The time is specified in seconds and can range from a minimum of 0.1 to 327.6 (almost 6 minutes) — see Figure B-39. After this
watcher has triggered, the timer must move out of its range and enter it
again for it to trigger again.

Figure B-39:
Flip side of
Timer
watcher.

To set the value of the timer back to 0, see **_Reset Timer._**

✔ **Tone:** This command (see Figure B-40) causes the RCX to emit a tone.
Also see **_Beep._**

Figure B-40:
Tone block.

The frequency of the tone can be set to any value from 1 Hz to 20,000 Hz (cycles per second), as shown in Figure B-41. Very low and very high values will probably not be audible because the extreme settings are beyond the range of human hearing. The default setting is 2,000 Hz. The duration of the tone can be set as short as 0.1 seconds to 2.5 seconds.

Figure B-41:
Flip side of
Tone block.

✔ **Touch:** A Touch Sensor watcher (see Figure B-42) is triggered both by having its button pressed and released, so this watcher is capable of controlling two stacks.

Figure B-42:
Touch
Sensor
watcher.

This watcher can be set to respond to one of the three Touch Sensors labeled 1, 2, and 3 — see Figure B-43. Both stacks can be running at the same time if the press and release sequence happens quickly enough. If the Touch Sensor triggers a stack that's already running, the stack immediately quits execution and starts over again.

Figure B-43:
Flip side of
Touch
Sensor
watcher.

✔ **Wait:** This command (see Figure B-44) causes a stack to pause for the specified period of time. The pause only applies to the stack in which the block is inserted; the other stacks all continue to run. The time is measured in seconds and can be any value from 0.1 (one tenth of a second) up to 327.6.

Figure B-44:
Wait block.

On the flip side of the block, the number of seconds can be entered from the keyboard, or the + and – signs next to the time value can be used to add or subtract 0.1 second to the time setting. See Figure B-45.

Figure B-45:
Flip side of
Wait block.

You can specify that the length of time of the pause be randomly selected. The random time is selected from within a range of times. To set up a random time, click on the picture of the die to the left of the window displaying the time. The word "random" appears below the time value, and the time value is displayed as a range from 0.1 to the current time setting. You can enter the upper limit from the keyboard, or use the + and – signs to adjust it (the lower limit is always 0.1 seconds). This causes the actual time of each wait to vary and to be between 0.1 seconds and the amount of time you choose.

To pause a stack until an event occurs, see *Wait Until.*

✔ **Wait Until:** This controller pauses the execution of a stack until a sensor test result becomes *true*. This can be used with any of the sensors configured into your system.

- The Counter Sensor watcher registers *true* only if the value of the counter is within the specified range at the moment the counter is checked. The available range is 1 to 32766.

- The Light Sensor watcher registers *true* only if the current light value is within the specified range at the moment the light value is checked.

- The RCX Sensor watcher registers *true* only if the numeric value of the most recently received message is within the specified range at the moment the message is checked. The available range is from 1 to 255.

- The Rotation Sensor watcher registers *true* only if the current rotation counter is within the specified range at the moment the rotation count is checked.

- The Temperature Sensor watcher registers *true* only if the current temperature value is within the specified range at the moment the temperature is checked.

- The Timer Sensor watcher registers *true* only if the elapsed time in the timer is within the specified range at the moment the timer is checked. The available range is from 0.1 to 327.6 seconds.

- The Touch Sensor watcher registers *true* only if the sensor button is depressed at the moment the Touch Sensor is checked.

Appendix C

About the CD

● ●

*T*his CD-ROM contains the following color version of all the photos in this book, RCX sample programs, some programming languages that increase the capability of the RCX language, and a few other miscellaneous goodies. This appendix shares the details.

System Requirements

Make sure that your computer meets the minimum system requirements listed below. If your computer doesn't match up to most of these requirements, you may have problems using the contents of the CD.

- ✔ A PC with a Pentium 166 or faster processor.
- ✔ Microsoft Windows 95/98/ME.
- ✔ At least 32MB of total RAM installed on your computer.
- ✔ At least 150MB of hard drive space available to install all the software from this CD. (You need less space if you don't install every program.)
- ✔ A CD-ROM drive — double-speed (2x) or faster.
- ✔ A sound card for PCs.
- ✔ A monitor capable of displaying at least 256 colors or grayscale.

If you need more information on the basics, take a look at *PCs For Dummies,* 7th Edition, by Dan Gookin; *Windows 95 For Dummies,* 2nd Edition, by Andy Rathbone; or *Windows 98 For Dummies* by Andy Rathbone (all published by IDG Books Worldwide, Inc. — check out www.dummies.com).

If you're using a Mac under Windows emulation (see Chapter 12), you'll need to allow enough hard drive space for both the emulator program and the Windows requirements listed in this section. Follow the instructions for using the CD with Microsoft Windows.

Using the CD with Microsoft Windows

To install the items from the CD to your hard drive, follow these steps:

1. **Insert the CD into your computer's CD-ROM drive.**

2. **Open your browser.**

   If you don't have a browser, we've included Microsoft Internet Explorer and Netscape Communicator. They can be found in the Software folder on the CD.

3. **Click Start⇨Run.**

4. **In the dialog box that appears, type** D:\START.HTM.

   Replace *D* with the proper drive letter if your CD-ROM drive uses a different letter. (If you don't know the letter, see how your CD-ROM drive is listed under My Computer.)

5. **Read through the license agreement, nod your head, and if you want to use the CD, click the Accept button.**

   After you click Accept, you'll jump to the Main Menu which will display a file that'll walk you through the contents of the CD.

   To navigate within the interface, click on any topic of interest to take you to an explanation of the files on the CD and of how to use or install them.

6. **To install the software from the CD, click on the software name.**

   You'll see two options: the option to run or open the file from the current location or the option to save the file to your hard drive. If you choose to run or open the file from its current location, the installation procedure continues. After you're done with the interface, close your browser as usual.

   Some of the programs will launch a vbscript which then asks you for the letter of your CD-ROM drive. Input the letter of your drive and follow the instructions on your screen to install the software.

 In order to run some of the programs on the *LEGO MINDSTORMS For Dummies* CD-ROM, you may need to keep the CD inside your CD-ROM drive. This is a Good Thing. Otherwise, the installed program would have required you to install a very large chunk of the program to your hard drive, which may have kept you from installing other software.

What You'll Find

Here's a summary of the software on this CD arranged by category. If you use Windows, the CD interface helps you install software easily. (If you have no idea what I'm talking about when I say "CD interface," flip back a page or two to find the "Using the CD with Microsoft Windows" section.)

✔ **Color photos:** LEGO bricks are much easier to recognize in color than in black and white. For that reason, you can find all of the photos that you see in this book in color on the CD.

✔ **Robotics Invention System sample programs:** Think of these programs as a series of tutorials that go along with Chapters 9, 10, 11, and 12. You must run the installer to add these programs to your LEGO MIND-STORMS directories. After installation, each chapter will have its own user in the MINDSTORMS system.

✔ **Gordon's Brick Programmer (by Malcom S. Powell):** This freeware program is more powerful than RIS programming and allows access to powerful features of the RCX brick.

✔ **NQC (by Dave Baum):** NQC is an open source program that's based on the C programming language and allows you to write a program as a text file and run it through an NQC compiler to convert it into something that the RCX can understand.

✔ **PBForth (by Hempell Design Group):** PBForth is another freeware program that gives you much greater control over your RCX brick. PBForth allows your RCX brick to run the Forth programming language.

✔ **RCX Command Center:** Commercial product. RCX Command Center assists you in programming LEGO MINDSTORMS robots. It provides a higher-level interface to the RCX.

✔ **Miscellaneous other goodies:** You'll find the following helpful products on the CD:

- Jasc's Paintshop Pro: Evaluation version. A graphics program that you may want to use to view the color photos included on the CD.

- Microsoft Internet Explorer: Commercial verison. A popular Internet browser that you can use to download files from the Web (provided you have Web access through an Internet Service Provider) and to view the color photos on the CD.

- Netscape Communicator: Commercial version. Another popular Internet browser.

- LEGOMac.exe: Freeware version. A simple program that makes Windows emulators (for Macintosh) operate more smoothly with the LEGO MINDSTORMS CD.

If You Have Problems (Of the CD Kind)

We've tried our best to compile programs that work on most computers with the minimum system requirements. Alas, your computer may differ, and some programs may not work properly for some reason. The two likeliest problems are that you don't have enough memory (RAM) for the programs you want to use or you have other programs running that are affecting the installation or running of a program. If you get error messages such as Not enough memory or Setup cannot continue, try one or more of these methods and then try using the software again:

- ✔ **Turn off any anti-virus software that you have on your computer.** Installers sometimes mimic virus activity and may make your computer incorrectly believe that it is being infected by a virus.

- ✔ **Close all running programs.** The more programs you're running, the less memory is available to other programs. Installers also typically update files and programs; if you keep other programs running, installation may not work properly.

- ✔ **In Windows, close the CD interface and run demos or installations directly from Windows Explorer.** The interface itself can tie up system memory, or even conflict with certain kinds of interactive demos. Use Windows Explorer to browse the files on the CD and launch installers or demos.

- ✔ **Have your local computer store add more RAM to your computer.** This is, admittedly, a drastic and somewhat expensive step. However, if you have a Windows 95 PC or a Mac OS computer with a PowerPC chip, adding more memory can really help the speed of your computer and enable more programs to run at the same time.

If you still have trouble installing the items from the CD, please call the IDG Books Worldwide Customer Service phone number: 800-762-2974 (outside the U.S., call 317-572-3993).

Index

• *H* •

hat arm, InventorBot, 163, 165–168
head module
  InventorBot, 159–163
  R2-D2, 74–76
Help tool, 238
hoop module, Hoop-o-bot, 113, 115–118
Hoop-o-bot robot, 97
  ball thrower module, 105–113
  drive module, 98–104
  hoop module, 113, 115–118
  programming, 119–120
How's the Weather application, 290–291

• *I* •

indexes, Web sites, 312
infrared transmitter, 20, 204
insects, 332
inserting batteries, 123
installing
  CD, Windows, 356
  Robotics Invention System
    software, 205
  troubleshooting, 358
instructions, *Constructopedia* books,
  21–22
interchangeability, 13
interface
  programming, 178
  RCX, 335–336
  RCX, block categories, 336
  RCX, writing, 337–339, 341–346, 348–354
  RCX brick, 201
  Robotics Invention System,
    navigating, 220
  Scout, 181, 183–184

Internet
  LEGO MINDSTORMS Web ring, 313
  LEGO MINDSTORMS Web site, 311–312
  LEGO MINDSTORMS Web site,
    index, 312
  Machina Speculatrix Web site, 313
  RCX Internals Web site, 313
  Robot Arena Web site, 313
InventorBot robot, 143, 145
InventorBot robot, body module,
  145–151
InventorBot robot, hat arm, 163, 165–168
InventorBot robot, head module,
  159–163
InventorBot robot, slap arm,
  168, 170–172
InventorBot robot, standing base legs
  subassembly, 156–158
InventorBot robot, standing base
  module, 151–155
It's Alive, RoverBot application, 259–265

• *J* •

Jedi Knight Droid, 14

• *L* •

L-3GO Trainer Droid, 14
languages
  alternate programming, 295
  NQC (Not Quite C), 298–300, 357
  PBForth (Programmable Brick
    Forth), 301
lazy Susan piece, 49
left leg module, building R2-D2, 72

• S •

Notes

LEGO® MINDSTORMS™ For Dummies®

Cheat Sheet

LEGO MINDSTORMS Building Glossary

- **Axle:** Axles provide an axis around which wheels, gears, and pulleys can turn. You can also use axles to pin other parts together.

- **Beam:** Like a block, but without pegs on the top. We made up this name.

- **Block:** A block is a smaller-scaled version of a full-sized LEGO building block and features the unique peg system for interlocking blocks that's common to nearly all LEGO products. Some blocks have holes in them to accept axles and connector pegs.

- **Connecting wires:** These are two plates joined by a wire. You use the connecting wires to connect touch sensors or motors to the microprocessor brick.

- **Connector pegs:** Pieces that snap into holes in a beam, block, elbow, or other piece that connects larger pieces together. We made up this term.

- **Elbows, tees, cross fittings:** These pieces look like miniature pipe fittings and brackets — the pieces come in various angles and end combinations.

- **Gears:** The teeth around the circumference of a wheel-like piece are a dead give away that the piece is a gear. All the gears in a MINDSTORMS kit are designed to mesh with the other gears.

- **LEGO Lamp:** The LEGO Lamp is a small light bulb that you can add to your robot to provide general illumination or to serve as a visual alarm.

- **Light Sensor:** The Light Sensor contains an *electric eye* that can detect changes in light levels.

- **Micro Scout microprocessor brick:** The simplest of the three microprocessor bricks, the Micro Scout comes with the Droid Developer Kit.

- **Motors:** You use motors to make your robots move. Usually, the motor is connected to a series of gears or pulleys that transfer the motor's motion to where it's needed.

- **Plate:** A flat block that's one-third the height of regular blocks.

- **Pulleys and belts:** A pulley looks like a gear without teeth. Instead of teeth, it has a groove around the rim that accepts a miniature belt. Belts look like colored rubber bands. You can use a pair of pulleys connected with a belt to transfer output of a motor.

- **RCX microprocessor brick:** The most powerful and sophisticated microprocessor brick in the LEGO MINDSTORMS family, the RCX comes with the Robotics Invention System.

- **Rotation Sensor:** The Rotation Sensor block contains a small hub into which you can insert an axle, and it counts revolutions of the axle.

- **Scout microprocessor brick:** Offering more options than the Micro Scout, the Scout comes with the Robotics Discovery Set.

- **Temperature Sensor:** The Temperature Sensor can detect changes in temperature.

- **Top plate:** A flat plates with no pegs.

- **Touch Sensor:** The Touch Sensor sends a signal to the microprocessor when its button is depressed.

- **Wheels and tires:** Wheels are round with a hole through the middle, just like a life-size wheel. Tires have the donut-shape you expect of a tire and most tires are made of soft black plastic, although some of the smaller tires are gray.

LEGO® MINDSTORMS™ For Dummies®

Cheat Sheet

LEGO MINDSTORMS Programming Glossary

- **Block:** The smallest possible unit in a program. Each block serves a single purpose within a program stack. A program stack is composed of a collection of blocks.

- **Command:** A programming block that contains an instruction to be obeyed by the RCX.

- **Counter:** An internal device that keeps a count of any event and can be read by your program.

- **Download:** In the context of the RCX, this term refers to copying a program from your PC to the RCX using the IR link.

- **Inputs:** Any device, such as a Touch Sensor or Light Sensor, that sends data to the RCX or Scout.

- **IR (infrared):** The data link connecting your PC with the RCX unit. IR is also used by the remote control to send signals to the RCX, and by RCX to send signals to the Scout of the Robotics Discovery Set.

- **Messages:** Information that can be sent between two RCX units, an RCX and a Scout, or an RCX and the remote control.

- **My Commands:** Custom commands that you create and use in your programs. Also called *subroutines*.

- **Output:** A device, such as a motor or lamp, that can be controlled by the RCX or Scout.

- **Program:** A collection of one or more stacks that can be downloaded as a single unit from your PC into one of the five program slots of the RCX.

- **Program Vault:** The storage location on your PC that's used to save programs so that they can be retrieved for modification and/or downloading into the RCX.

- **RCX Code:** The main programming language, composed of blocks and stacks, of the Robotics Invention System.

- **Sensor:** A device that's internal or external to the RCX device. Sensors represent connections to physical sensors that detect light, touch, temperature, and other changes in the robot's environment.

- **Sensor Watcher:** A block that monitors the status of a sensor and executes a stack depending on that status.

- **Stack:** A sequence of blocks connected one after the other to make up part of a program.

- **Stack Controller:** A programming block or pair of blocks that may alter the direction of logic flow through a stack. This block can be looping, branching, or pausing.

- **Timer:** An internal stopwatch that keeps track of time and can be read by your program.

- **Trace:** A troubleshooting tool that allows you to visually see your program run.

For Dummies®: Bestselling Book Series for Beginners